TROEPIE

TROEPIE

FROM CALL-UP TO CAMPS

CAMERON BLAKE

Z ZEBRA PRESS

Published by Zebra Press
an imprint of Random House Struik (Pty) Ltd
Reg. No. 1966/003153/07
80 McKenzie Street, Cape Town, 8001
PO Box 1144, Cape Town, 8000 South Africa

www.zebrapress.co.za

First published 2009

1 3 5 7 9 10 8 6 4 2

Publication © Zebra Press 2009
Text © Cameron Blake 2009

Cover photograph courtesy of Jörg Wegner
Back cover photographs: Jaco van Zyl (1 & 3), Jörg Wegner (2) and Lionel van der Schyff (4 & 5)

PUBLISHER: Marlene Fryer
MANAGING EDITOR: Robert Plummer
EDITOR: Beth Housdon
COVER AND TEXT DESIGNER: Natascha Adendorff-Olivier
TYPESETTER: Monique van den Berg
PRODUCTION MANAGER: Valerie Kömmer

Set in Adobe Garamond 11 pt on 15.5 pt

Reproduction by Hirt & Carter (Cape) (Pty) Ltd
Printed and bound by CTP Book Printers, Duminy Street, Parow, 7500

ISBN 978 1 77022 051 5

*To Justus Ackermann
and all other troepies whose accounts
will never be told.*

Contents

Preface

'I don't know why you want to hear my story. What have I got to say that anyone wants to hear? The Special Forces okes – speak to them. I wasn't a Recce. I wasn't a Bat. I never even had contact. I never did anything special.'

'That doesn't matter,' I replied. 'Anything you have to say interests me.' I explained that I was not looking for war stories, but for any memories of his time in the military – no matter how seemingly insignificant.

'Why? There's nothing to say. It's over and done with. People don't want to talk about it.' Yet, when I asked whether he was glad to have done National Service, his immediate response was, 'Yes. I'm very glad. I'll shout it out as loud as possible – I'm proud!'

This book is a compilation of individual recollections of life as a conscript in the former South African Defence Force (SADF). The accounts of National Service collected here supply valuable insight into a largely unrecorded history. As one interviewee said, 'That flash in your head – that memory – is like a dream. Yet I know it was not. I saw it, I lived it, and I cannot forget, while others do. Let it not be forgotten. We were there and I want it to be remembered.'

I assist in The Africa Star, a small shop in Cape Town that sells coins, medals and surplus military items, some of which are SADF-related. The merchandise triggers memories in many customers; over the years I've listened to dozens of former National Servicemen recall their time in the South African military. My interest in the individual stories of ex-Servicemen dates back to my teenage years, when I came across a book of personal accounts of American Vietnam war veterans. I have long felt the need for a public record of our own men's experiences, and when JH Thompson's *An Unpopular War* was published in 2006, I was inspired to start documenting the stories of those who served in the SADF.

The first person I interviewed talked with such fervour and in such detail that I felt somewhat overwhelmed. Yet the energy with which he spoke and the ultimate success of the interview gave me the validation I needed to continue with the project. Within weeks I had collected several interviews from a variety of people: I interviewed strangers who walked unsuspectingly into the shop, customers I've known for years, friends and family members. Included in the book are the accounts of a city planner, a computer technician, a doctor, a jeweller, a lawyer, an operations manager, a professional musician, a property consultant and a traffic officer – an extraordinary assortment of people with a diverse range of opinions and experiences.

I focused exclusively on National Service, beginning most interviews with the question, 'Where and when did you klaar in?' From there, the recollections flowed. Some remembered only the good times, others remembered only the bad, but most of the interviewees were forthcoming with their experiences, whether positive or negative. It quickly became apparent that the level of the responses varied: there were those who had told their stories time and time again, their material polished and entertaining, and there were those whose stories were filled with fresh emotion and significance. In speaking about their past for the first time in years, these men were taken by surprise as old memories resurfaced. Every interview was unique: some interviewees spoke with passion and excitement, while others' words were soft, slow and deliberate. Some recalled minor incidents in incredible detail and others brushed fleetingly over major events. Some spoke for hours; others for no longer than five minutes. The past is skin deep, I realised. Feelings are strong, and only a question away.

On occasion, those who had consented to discuss their experiences with me were selective about which memories they chose to share and which they withheld. A few men refused to talk about their time as conscripts at all, reacting negatively when I approached them for interviews.

Many years ago I was at my brother-in-law's house for a braai. Late in the evening, while we were sitting around the fire, one of the men present recalled the time his section had hit contact. A bullet had narrowly missed his heart. He survived, but most of the men in the patrol did not. When

I began this book, he was one of the first people I intended to interview. Understanding how sensitive the subject is to him, I left a written proposal in his letter box that said he was welcome to phone me if he wished to talk. I didn't hear from him for two months, so I went to his house and asked him personally for an interview, explaining that his story was important and would not only be a valuable contribution to the book, but would be beneficial to those who had undergone similar experiences. He kindly told me that it was the wrong time; he was too busy. 'I'm sorry,' he said. 'For now I must say no.'

After a few months I approached him again, yet still he declined. 'I'm busy sorting out the farm. If you don't hear from me, please just forget about it.'

A psychologist in the SANDF recommended that I leave the matter alone, advising me to respect his decision not to discuss the past. 'Some men won't talk – can't talk – about such things. It's too deep. It's been buried. He wants to keep it that way. If he doesn't want to go back there, then don't dig it up.' At that, I let it be.

A while ago, a young woman who appeared to be in her early twenties entered the shop. She saw the notes resting on my desk and casually asked what they were. I told her that they were part of the record I was compiling of National Service. Since she seemed to be about the right age to have a father who had been a conscript, I expected her to respond with a knowing nod or an appropriate comment or question. Instead she asked, in all innocence, 'What's National Service?' I couldn't believe what I'd heard.

'You mean you don't know what conscription was? Surely you remember or have been told about it?' But she hadn't a clue.

'No … What's that?' It was at that moment that I knew that these narratives *must* be compiled and published. How could a young South African not twenty years younger than myself be completely oblivious to this component of her country's recent history? I was genuinely taken aback by her ignorance.

A week before I submitted my final manuscript for publication, another customer of The Africa Star, who looked to be in his early forties, noticed the manuscript on my desk and asked what it was. Having had the question put to me many times by this stage, I replied simply, 'It's a collection of personal accounts of National Service.'

He laughed patronisingly, 'What accounts? Weren't they all the same? What've they got to say, except to recount the times a corporal shouted at them to hardloop en die blaar oppie boom te kry and then that dis die verkeerde blaar and they must go and get *that* leaf?'

He suggested that I speak to the guys who had been on the Border or in Angola, adding that he supposed I couldn't relate their experiences because 'that's all political stuff'.

I replied carefully, telling him that some of the interviews *are* of course about the Border and Angola. This grabbed his attention. I then asked him when he had klaared in and, unsurprisingly perhaps, he said that he never had. 'I went overseas for six years, instead. I was supposed to go in, in the early eighties.' He went on to explain that neither he nor his parents had supported the National Service system, believing it to be 'nothing more than a tool to keep apartheid alive in order to suppress the blacks'.

I told him that if he genuinely felt that, then he was indeed fortunate to have had the money to go overseas. 'What about the poorer okes who grew up with nothing?' I asked. 'They didn't have the same options as you, even if their beliefs were the same.'

'What? What money?' he retaliated. 'All it cost my parents was a one-way plane ticket.' But, on pressing him, he admitted that his parents had had the contacts to pull a few strings and organise him a job and accommodation. For the majority of conscripts, alternatives like this were simply not available.

We chatted further and I explained the book in more detail. I noted how his initial dismissal of the project turned quickly into genuine interest. 'I can't understand why so many of my friends tell me it was the best two years of their lives that they would never want to do again,' he said, perplexed. 'Why is that?'

I looked at him, unable to reply in only a few sentences. 'For some,' I finally responded, 'the decades may have added a touch of nostalgia.'

The narratives in this book have been kept anonymous. The chapters are structured according to the general sequence of a conscript's progression within the SADF, from klaaring in and Basic Training to uitklaar and camps. Although the dates, events and places mentioned in the interviews have been verified, the narratives in this book are individual accounts rather than solemn testaments, and will naturally contain generalisations, misconceptions, discrepancies and perhaps even untruths. Some readers may, therefore, dispute or disagree with the descriptions of particular incidents or people, and some of the interviews may upset former personnel from certain units, who may object to the opinions expressed. It is not my intention to offend anyone or any of the units mentioned, disbanded or current, military or paramilitary. The accounts are subjective recollections; they are based on personal memories and beliefs. I have recounted them here as they were told to me.

The book's appendices ground the interviews in historical context. They include information about National Service, the Border Campaign, township patrols and other elements of military life.

Being a newcomer to the publishing world and hence unfamiliar with its norms, the length of my original manuscript was more than double that of a standard publication of this nature. There was thus no option but to halve it, and I was faced with the difficult task of deciding which material to omit.

Ultimately, it was a few of the longer narratives that were excluded, as well as a series of interviews with civilian women – mothers, wives, sisters and girlfriends – in which contemporary attitudes towards the past are explored. Also omitted was a chapter in which ex-Servicemen reveal how their military service in the seventies, eighties and early nineties – which often included active involvement in the Border Campaign and in the townships – affects them today.

It was a great pity to have to leave these contributions on the cutting-room floor, so to speak. Yet these testimonies will not be lost to the public: it is my hope that they will be released in a second book in the near future.

This book will resonate with former National Servicemen, who will identify with the experiences related here. But, for people like the man and the young woman I encountered in The Africa Star, these stories will shed light on a part of our history that, today, is seldom discussed and is improperly understood. Regardless of its politics, this enigmatic period of South Africa's complex and turbulent past deserves acknowledgement, if only for the deep and lasting impact it has had on the lives of generations of men and their families.

CAMERON BLAKE
May 2009

Acknowledgements

To my wife, Ilse, who listened to my ideas and doubts, time and time again, and who gave so much constant, tireless and patient reassurance.

To my little girl, Kate, who missed out on so many nights of bedtime stories, and who added her tiny, well-meant scribbles to my transcripts. Thank you both for being my foundation.

To my friend Eric, for your kindness and tolerance in allowing much of this venture to happen in your shop. Without it, this book would indeed have been far more difficult to achieve.

To Dennis, Eric, Frank, Kobus and others, whose positive attitudes and interest in the project kept me motivated.

To the whole team at Zebra Press, thank you for assisting me in turning this project into a reality. To Marlene Fryer: I will never forget the day you contacted me and gave me the green light. To Robert Plummer and Beth Housdon for gently guiding me through the editing process, and for knocking the rough edges off my manuscript and polishing it into its current shape, usually with a laugh. It was an enjoyable and positive experience. To Jaco Fouché and Nelani Pfaff for your work in translating and editing the Afrikaans version.

To JH Thompson, for the words in your book *An Unpopular War*: 'I hope there will be many more books on the experiences of South African soldiers, for there are thousands of stories that should be told, in print, not just among close friends.' I couldn't agree more. On that note, if my book inspires even a single individual to further record and publish any of the endless personal tales from that time, every minute of this project will have been worthwhile. I hope this book motivates others as JH Thompson's book motivated me.

And, most importantly, to the men and women I interviewed, even though the words of some do not appear in this publication. Thank you for your support, honesty and encouragement and for making me believe that what I was doing was both worthwhile and achievable. Without your collective past this book would not exist. I extend my gratitude and hope that your expectations have been met.

You are: Adrian, Agnes, Alistair, André, Andrew and Andrew, Andrew F, Anton, Barry, Brett, Colin, Dennis, Donovan, Frank, Fred, Gabriel, George, Glen, Grant, Greg, Henry, Ilse, Isobel, Jaco, James, Jasper, Johan, John and his brother, Karina, Kevin, Leonie, Lionel, Louis, Lourens, Mark and Mark, Marques, Matt, Naomi, Paul, Phillip, Quinton, Rob and Rob, Rory, Rudy, Steven, Thora, Waldo and Wayne – and a few who prefer to remain anonymous. Thank you all for your individual contributions; they are much appreciated.

CAMERON BLAKE
May 2009

Use kids to fight a war – if you're going to use anybody. They're the best. They're still learning. They can hump the hills. They can take it. And they don't take it personal.

Thank God for your eighteen-year-old. Politics is not why he's there, the whole right and wrong thing. — EXCERPT FROM *NAM*

Maybe it was great in Pofadder or Pretoria when you came down on pass. There I can imagine a troep with a short haircut and a tan walking into a bar – he was probably God, and got a bit of koekie. But in Cape Town the girls couldn't stand us. 'Army boys!' they'd snap, and stay well away.

We were back for such a short period of time, but it took forever to readjust and to find out that nobody was interested in your army stories. They couldn't care less what your corporal shouted at you or what you shot at or what the Border was like. They were too busy carrying on with their student lives at varsity.

We used to go to the Pig 'n Whistle, an old student watering hole near UCT. We'd talk to our friends and try to chat up the girls, and sometimes we'd start to speak about what we were doing. Nobody was interested. But the army was our life, what we'd been doing for so long, what we'd been doing to 'save' the country. 'Why aren't you guys interested?' we'd ask. We'd be ostracised for that. By the time you came to realise that nobody gave a damn, you were on a bloody Flossie going up north again. I felt almost angry with them, and found myself thinking, 'Thank God I'm back here in base.' In a way, you were actually safer there than you were amongst your best mates.

You were completely excluded – almost shunned. Nobody wanted to know. It's like nobody even cared.

BEFORE

As a schoolkid I knew that everyone had to do their National Service. Whether it was right or wrong, I didn't really give a damn. It was conscription. If it meant I had to go to the army, well then I'd go. It's just the way it was. We all had a sense of trepidation; didn't quite know what to expect. We were all eighteen or nineteen. What did we know about life? I just wanted to get it over with.

I felt excited about going to do National Service – although a bit scared – but I felt it was the paraat and patriotic thing to do.

It was 1976. I was one of the freaks who couldn't wait to get out of school to go to the army, which other guys were trying to avoid. Everybody was trying to think of ways to get out of it, but I couldn't wait. It wasn't even for the patriotic duty. I just wanted to be there. I even left school early, in Standard 8, to join. Maybe my childhood interest in military-collecting helped. I'd always seen the obstacle courses on TV and in the movies and I just wanted to go. Sure, I was proud of my country and happy to serve, but that wasn't my main reason for going.

The mid-seventies were when things started happening up on the Border. I never felt that I had to go in or do my duty. I was totally against it from the beginning. It was just my spirit; I'm against fighting. I didn't think it was right. Why couldn't we all sit around a table and talk about it? My parents disagreed. I grew up with a very conservative Afrikaans background and my parents were especially conservative. There were a lot of arguments in my house about me not wanting to go. My father was never in the military but he believed in it. Bang! That's it. I felt there were other ways to sort out disputes. I thought the whole thing was a waste of time.

I matriculated in '75 and had the opportunity to do my nine months' National Service in 1976, which ended up being two years by the time I went. So, in that sense, I regret it in some ways. A lot of guys in my school couldn't wait to get to the army. They liked fighting and that way of life. That's why I clashed with my father. He had the wrong attitude. His belief was that every Serviceman had to do Border duty. I said, 'Why must I go? What are we doing there? Going in and killing people? What's going to happen? Are we going to do this for the next twenty years? Somewhere along the line we'll have to stop.' He believed all the propaganda and was outraged. I bluntly refused to do my National Service while we were still in Angola.

I became a provincial athlete as a middle-distance runner. I was also studying my BSc, which I qualified for after four years, then studied medicine for another six before going to the army.

My mother was quite liberal. Somewhere the idea was planted in me that what the whiteys in South Africa were doing was wrong. In school I had an argument with somebody, who, by the way, is now living in Australia, who told me that 'not in a hundred years will blacks rule the country'. I argued that they would, and long before that, too. This was in the seventies; completely different times to now. It was unthinkable then. I had a strong guilt feeling during school.

At sixteen we had to fill in forms for ID books. That's when the army must've got us onto their records automatically. We didn't even know. I certainly don't remember anyone coming around and telling us to fill in forms to register for the army.

I matriculated in 1979. I was a non-conformist. I didn't do sports, but rode motocross bikes every afternoon instead. I was an Afrikaans kid in an English school, so I got all the usual taunts – Dutchman, rockspider, hairyback – all that crap.

The army was something I didn't want to do. I was forced into it. I could've been an objector, or run away, or done time in prison, or joined the police, but I was like the rest of the 30 000 guys a year. I thought, to hell with it. Let's go and get it over and done with. Rather two years done and finished than having to avoid detention and mess up my life.

I knew I'd have to go. There was no choice about it. I can't remember how my family felt. I don't even remember my mom or dad saying it was a bad idea or trying to get me out the country. I served, my brothers served, all my friends that I ever knew served – we all went in – but there were a few guys who left and studied overseas, usually in America, and mainly the Jewish guys.

I grew up with a mother only. I was *bang* to leave the old lady at home but I felt my service was the right thing to do, so that's what I did. I come from a very proud family. It's in me. It's in my blood. My dad's Scots and my mother's English, but I was born here. My dad came here in the fifties and taught people a trade in Jo'burg. They were pro–South African. They came here for the sunshine and the people. They didn't know what was going to happen, politically, twenty or thirty years down the line.

As a small boy it was put into me, 'This is your home now. Do what you have to do.' In 1972 we returned to the United Kingdom for a while, then my mom said that we were going back to South Africa. My brother, who's eight years older than me, said, 'Not a hope!' My mom said if that's what he wanted to do then it was fine, so that's what he did. I hated him because of it and his not wanting to do the army. I couldn't believe there was more for him there than here, but I was only nine years old. He was seventeen. I came back, finished matric in 1981 and went straight in.

In the early eighties I remember seeing death notices come up on the TV screen of all the SADF soldiers killed on the Border. Names were white on an orange background. This was the six o'clock English news. Michael de Morgan read on Mondays, Wednesdays and Fridays. Riaan Cruywagen had his turn on Tuesdays, Thursdays and Saturdays during the Afrikaans news. I looked at the names and thought, 'Oh well, I'll be fighting up there, later on, but I just hope I won't end up on the news like one of them.'

You're preconditioning yourself, even at such a young age. That's what we grew up with. I was thirteen.

The only thing I feared tremendously about going to the army was I really wished I wouldn't have to watch guys die, and kak like that, but I said to myself that it would give me a hell of a lot of training to do things, like camping, properly, and it would teach me how to survive. Boy Scouts, but more.

I didn't question National Service but I did question the system, like the big issue between black and white. I could never get my head around it. Coming from Botswana, this just wasn't an issue for me. I enjoyed black people. I enjoyed Afrikaners. That's the way I was brought up. Then suddenly, coming to this country, there was this black–white, left–right thing. I could never figure it out.

The college I went to had a history of its boys going off to war, with a full-on monument to those old boys who had died. Once a year we had a parade in their honour and it was all pretty serious. We also had cadet training once a week, where we met the boys from 6 SAI – National Servicemen – who helped in training us to drill, but not hardcore. It was more tongue-in-cheek. They were having their fun with the schoolboys and told us that when we got into the army on a parade ground in front of a sergeant major he was going to seriously donner us unless we could come to attention correctly. They were prepping us. We got the gist of it. We felt quite proud, really, learning how to be in a platoon and march on the parade ground.

Grahamstown was in the thick of it. I used to watch them, the army ous, in the Buffels. During prep at night we used to hear gunshots from the location. I thought, 'Well, my turn's next. When I'm conscripted I'll have to be on those trucks too, and when they tell me to open fire I don't have to hit the person that's shooting us.'

You're figuring it all out. I didn't want to have to kill anyone.

Every year my family and I took the N3 highway down to Durban for school holidays. This was in the early eighties and I was a laaitie. I'll never forget the soldiers in their brown uniforms, stable belts, flashes, berets and canvas balsaks. There they were, alone or in pairs, *gooiing duim*. There was a little outlet on the side of the road where they could hitch a ride. They stood under an officially erected signpost, which was a profile of a soldier within a castle-shaped star on a green background. They also wore a neon-orange 'Ride Safe – Ry Veilig' sash.

I always asked my folks to pick them up. I was fascinated and in awe of them. A real live soldier! As a twelve-year-old I really wanted to talk with them and find out what a gun was like, but my parents were very reluctant to stop. At that time an urban legend had it that a serial killer, posing as a National Serviceman, was getting a lift, tying people to a tree with barbed wire, raping the woman and then slitting the couple's throats. Come to think of it, maybe it was anti-apartheid propaganda and disinformation to help the 'struggle'. So on we drove as I watched them go by from the rear window. 'Somebody else will pick them up, boy,' my dad said. I felt so disappointed, almost ashamed.

The following year the awe vanished when my family and I were on holiday in Margate on the South Coast. I used to spend a lot of time in this little café playing arcade games. One day I was doing really well, breaking my record. Next to me were three Afrikaans guys, about eighteen years old, with short, cropped hair. I heard them talking about their korporaal and about the army, so I knew they were on leave. This, and because they were rowdy, made me feel somewhat intimidated. I wanted to leave because one of them kept bumping into me, but I had to continue breaking my record. I loved this particular video game. Then this oke decided I'd played for too long. He wanted to play, so he pushed me. Stubbornly, and stupidly, I stood my ground, as nervous as I was. Then he stripped his moer, grabbed me by the shirt, threw me to the ground and swore at me in this harsh and guttural Afrikaans accent. I didn't understand what he said except for 'fokken' this and 'fokken' that. The Indian café owner did nothing. He didn't want trouble. I got up and left. I was upset but what could I do?

I don't know if it was just because he was an arse or because he was angry from the army, but I'll never forget it. It left such a bad feeling about the army – and Afrikaners, as an English-speaking kid. For the next five years I feared it would be these types I'd have to encounter when my turn came. I was right.

In matric we received our first call-ups and were given our magsnommer. Mine was 85296150 BA. Then you knew that there was no escape. I was sixteen in 1985, in Standard 8, and the first two digits denoted the year you were first on the list. Twenty-three years later I can easily recall that number. No wonder – it had to be memorised.

A couple of years later, in matric, we were busy writing our final end-of-year exams. One popular guy, called Chris, had an older brother already in the army. He was really proud of him. We all were. Well, the guys were, anyway. Girls didn't really give a damn. We felt it was a pretty big thing to be in the army, so we all shared his pride.

During one of the last exams a teacher came into the hall, spoke to the teacher on duty, came over and quietly whispered something to Chris. He got up and left with the teacher. I happened to be looking up and saw this. I presumed he was in trouble again. He was that kind of guy. After about half an hour Chris came back, shaking and looking pale. I could plainly notice it. There was definitely something wrong. He looked upset. He sat down and began to cry. We all looked at him. The teacher in charge came over and allowed him to excuse himself without completing the exam.

It turned out that his brother had been killed on the Border. Where and how I don't know, because he wouldn't talk about it and I wasn't a close friend. I don't think *he* even knew. A couple of days later school was out forever, so I will never know what happened. I never saw him again.

Why he had to be informed during the exam, I can't understand. Couldn't they have waited for him to finish? I suppose it was because of the seriousness of the situation. Nobody wants to tell a person something like that. There *is* no correct time. I expect the headmaster informed him as soon as he himself found out.

I went to a commercial Afrikaans school in Springs, but it wasn't the usual Afrikaner school like you'd think. Some of us were PFP, anti-apartheid and free-thinking. I wasn't all patriotic about having to 'do my duty'. Not everybody bought into that. My friends and I were pacifists. They anti-brainwashed me. We refused even to do school cadets.

I felt, even then, the Africans should be in charge – no matter how good or bad they were. I refused to use the 'k-word'. It was normal for school-boys to use it in their daily language. Half the school wanted to beat up black guys just because they were black. I could never get the idea why a person's skin colour was such an issue. I studied things about Nelson Mandela and didn't conform to the NP crap. I was reading leftist Afrikaans papers and couldn't see anything remotely communist about him. Another thing I always asked myself was why they locked up Breyten Breytenbach. He was a poet! What damage could *he* do? I felt the system was trying to get to our minds and thoughts.

I wasn't looking forward to the army. The whole thing seemed strange. I didn't know I had an option to refuse my call-ups and go to jail instead, otherwise I would've.

You had to greet our English teacher with, 'Guten morgen, Herr L.' If you didn't write with a fountain pen he put a line right through your work and refused to mark it. This oke was befok in the head.

I was in a welfare school, so how true the following is I can't prove. His son had hit a double-cheeser. This wasn't in a vehicle. He was a mine-clearer. The top mine would be removed, detonating the bottom one. They found a piece of his son's watch which they sent back to him, as it was all they could find. It arrived by registered mail.

I find the watch part a bit much. We knew that his son had definitely hit a double-cheeser, but the story of the watch arriving in the post was perhaps just for the benefit of the schoolkids.

Yes, of course I shat myself in the expectancy of having to do National Service. You heard all these horrible stories of the inspections, the drilling, the screaming corporals, the kak food, the opfoks, the waking up at four in the morning, the PT courses, the route marches – and that's just Basics! You heard it via the grapevine from friends in school, from older family friends who were in, from their parents – almost everyone had something to say about it. The subject hardly ever arose, but, when it did, all I heard was negative stuff. There was absolutely nothing positive about going to the Defence Force, so of course I was crapping myself.

During your school years you'd be forgiven for not identifying with older guys who'd been to the army, whenever you stood around a braai listening to them talk. During my varsity years I'd still have to endure all the 'Remember when …' stories. You couldn't really participate in the conversation, but only ask questions and feel somewhat awed and clueless. One thing

I remember my older brother-in-law telling me was, 'Never be first, and never be last, but stay in the middle. That way you'll be unnoticed. And in there you don't want to be noticed. Also, play deaf. If you're in a group of guys, never turn around if you hear somebody calling. Ignore it. Let one of the others turn around.' His advice helped.

I knew a guy who didn't go to the army on religious grounds. This was in the early eighties. They were giving religious objectors a break, then. I think he was a Jehovah's Witness. He refused to take up arms.

In my department at work, the Roads Department, we had a big library. The librarian was doing his National Service there for R16 a month. The Defence Force had said that he had a choice between going to jail or doing his two years' National Service. They gave him the option of doing it in a government department, but on army pay. He had obviously trained as a librarian; you could see his heart was in the job.

There were ways of dealing with genuine objectors, then. Afterwards they became heavy-handed and simply chucked them in chookie.

I finished matric in 1983. At my school, no one was looking forward to National Service. Everyone was of that sort of ilk that no one wanted to go. I don't know if it was the liberal upbringing we had, but our parents were all against it. They were all worried that the wrong things would happen.

Going to the army was never an option – I was always going to go to university. So, in I went, and while I was there they kept sending call-up papers. In the beginning they were always to revolting places, like Mechanics Division in Bloem, mainly. I just thought, 'There's absolutely no way I'm going.' Not then, not ever. I just really didn't want to go. I thought I would completely hate all the authority, with some oke telling me what to do. I don't know, maybe it was just the way I grew up, but I was really and truly not going to do it.

I had two older brothers who went in before me. One went into the air force and became a PF for seven years. He's four years older than me and had been in the air force for three years before I became eligible. He never went on pilot training because he was too tall and too big. There was a certain height limit. He also had a fractured leg, which helped negate him – but he loved it. He was an ATC and did Jan Smuts Airport, Waterkloof Air Force Base and a long stint up on the Border. He saw a lot of planes leave for cross-border raids. ATC was in on it. They had to direct the pilots to where they were going and give all the signals and codes. He was also at Katima Mulilo.

My other brother finished varsity after five years and then went on an Officer's Course, because he had a degree, which gave me some relief because I knew I'd go that same path with my degree. He went to Waterkloof, in Voortrekkerhoogte, for Basic Training in the air force. It was a killer for him. He'd had the life of a long-haired, hippy student. You're twenty-three and suddenly you're in Basics.

Eventually I also got called up to the air force, so I knew what to expect. I couldn't think of anything worse – from okes standing in their uniforms to being treated like shit. I'd heard all the stories. I thought, 'Please, let this be over by the time I have to go.'

One of my close friends used to AWOL all the time and stay over at my place. At one stage he AWOLed for five months. He knew he couldn't keep evading them, and became tired of it, so he turned himself in. He was in huge trouble. He made out he'd cracked and was mad. They sent him to the psychiatric ward, Ward 22, 25 or 52 – I can't remember. After months of 'insanity' they let him go with a dishonourable discharge.

I was at varsity for five years. By the time I finished studying it was the end of 1988. Conscription was still alive and well, so I registered at UNISA to study further. You had to pass a certain number of courses in order to qualify for the next year and, in turn, avoid conscription. You couldn't just register and goof off. You had to write exams and pass. I did two subjects a year, which was the minimum. I didn't pass the first year, but the army let me off. I wrote to them and explained that I was trying again. I think because I'd been at Wits for five years and had my degree, they believed I wasn't really messing around. 'He must be serious. Must've had a blip.'

The next year I passed only one of the two subjects. Then I think they started getting suspicious. At the same time, though, they weren't so fanatical about getting me, as this was now the end of 1990. I stayed registered at UNISA for five years, until the end of 1993. The funny part of my story is that I kept my student card after registering. There were massive discounts to be had on all sorts of things with this card. Medical aid was R6 a month and at any golf club it was R5 to play – that's when I started playing golf – so it became financially viable to keep my student card for as long as possible. There was no age limit on it.

The last call-up paper I received was in 1992. I wrote my usual letter telling them that I was still registered at a university and still following my academic career. Finally, my conscription papers never came. It was over. When I found out that conscription had ended I was ecstatic, absolutely ecstatic. I was ecstatic that I'd managed to get away with avoiding that world.

You ask if I feel bad that I didn't go. Well, I don't know what to regret. I heard stories from other people. It was always things like Basics being terrible, being a real hassle. I saw all my friends and family go – a lot of guys. I just never, ever thought that it would be for me. I was happy that I missed it, and I still am.

I didn't do National Service because I joined the police. I'm still with them. Every year I'd get my call-up papers, but the police would notify the Defence Force that I was in their service. They'd provide proof. The police required your service for four years. If I'd left within the first three years, I would've had to have gone into the army from the beginning. By that stage, though, I was rooted in the police and wanted to stay there, anyway.

Before matric, I didn't know what I wanted to do – the police or National Service. I joined the police force when I left school. I was eighteen, and I wanted to be a policeman. My father was a policeman. He had done his military training – one year, then. After that he joined the police. In his time, Basic Training in the police was a year long. Mine was only six months.

In 1991 I got my call-up papers to klaar in at 8 SAI. My psychologist told me to go to 2 Mil, where I was officially exempted. They diagnosed me with periodic psychotic disorder. It's a neurological problem – something wrong with my brain. The doctors said I was eligible for the reserves, but that never came about. I was angry and destroyed all my papers.

I wanted to be PF. Both my great-grandfather and grandfather were career military men. My father and uncles were in the navy at the time. My father was a submariner, which meant that I could go on his strength. I wanted to be in the Medical Corps.

I went to a co-ed government high school in Jo'burg. We'd have mock 'terrorist-attack' drills. In case of such an event, we were to get down on the ground, crouch under our desks as cover and wait until the 'all clear'. I wondered what good that would do. What if it really happened? Then what? Would we look around nervously in the hope that no black men armed with AKs would enter the classroom and shoot wildly about, screaming, 'Viva ANC! Viva!' – or what?

I honestly used to believe something like that could, and would, happen. I didn't even have to go to the army to believe that. I was seriously under the impression that blacks were going to take over the country and kill all us whites and destroy the country for some evil purpose. My history teacher, who'd done his National Service in about the mid- to late seventies, tried to instil in us a liberal and open-minded approach to what was happening, to think for ourselves, and that the army was a lie. He was very cynical about it. As much as I admired him and thought he was cool with his long hair and his listening to Led Zeppelin, I felt he was wrong and only represented a small minority. I was brainwashed but prepared. I was ready to join the army to defend my country.

Twice a week we had Youth Preparedness lessons, which meant that we went down to the fields to do marching. We'd drill in our ties and blazers in a really half-hearted way. It was actually jol time. Got away from class and out into the sun. The teacher who drilled us was this really tough Portuguese sports coach who always laughed at our dismal performance and told us how much we were going to suffer when we got into the army unless we got it right. He joked about the times when he was in. His favourite line was what his corporal screamed at him: 'As 'n vlieg in jou neus kruip en in jou longe kak, BEWEEG JY NOG STEEDS NIE!' Oh, great. Great expectations.

The girls either had cooking or sewing classes, or joined us down on the field where they played softball. They ragged us by saying how us 'poor little boys' were going to have to go to the army when we finished matric. We, in retaliation, pulled their bra straps and stung their backs – hard.

After school I was accepted into art school at university for a four-year course, and knew I'd have my National Service deferred. Your National Service could be postponed until tertiary education was complete. Each year my call-up papers summoned me to places like Phalaborwa, Potchefstroom, Upington and Grahamstown – all as infantry. When my brother-in-law heard that I might be going to 6 SAI, Grahamstown, he *lagged* and told me I was going to kak off. He was there in the mid-eighties.

During varsity I didn't give a damn about going. Never thought about it. Lived for the moment. I was getting too stoned, too drunk, having too much sex and too much of a good time to worry about it. After graduating, my call-up for the 1992 July intake was approaching. It was only when I spoke to some of my friends who'd come back from the army, and I knew my time was coming, that I began to think, 'Oh shit. Time to start doing a bit of PT to get into shape.' But my friends said, 'Nah, you don't have to worry about that. You'll manage.'

At that stage the End Conscription Campaign was in full tilt. Some guys were not complying with call-ups and refused to go. Because there were so many, the army was overwhelmed and simply didn't have the resources or inclination to arrest them. Nobody really knew what was going on, but it was generally accepted that if you didn't go you'd be okay. The ECC said so, but the Defence Force said otherwise. They still threatened to prosecute the dodgers, no matter how long it took. I wasn't prepared to take the chance, and wanted a clean slate with my country.

As it happened, the well-known and brilliant political cartoonist – I won't say who, it's so obvious – was my neighbour. I bumped into him on the street and casually mentioned I was about to comply with my call-ups.

'You're mad!' he burst out. 'Open your eyes! Look around you! See what's happening! You'll be fighting for apartheid ... defending it!'

I understood where he was coming from, yet it was the first time anyone had made me seriously doubt my decision and the situation. He was in complete disagreement with my going, to the point of being angry, but I told him that I wanted to find out for myself what it was all about.

He thought I was silly. A fool. He was a leftist. A liberal. He did *not* want me to go, but I had to. I was curious and, besides, for my whole life – twenty-two years – I'd been mentally preparing myself. You grew up with it. To suddenly realise it was all for nothing just didn't work for me. It's like I owed it to myself.

S.A. WEERMAG — S.A. DEFENCE FORCE

Registrasiebeampte SAW
Registering Officer SADF
Privaatsak / Private Bag X281
Pretoria
0001

READ THESE INSTRUCTIONS CAREFULLY

[Conscript's address]   Magsnommer..................

                               Force Number...............

NOTIFICATION OF ALLOTMENT FOR NATIONAL SERVICE

NOTE: NO RE-ALLOTMENTS WILL BE MADE

1. In accordance with the provisions of the Defence Act, 1957, you have been allotted to:

2. UNIT: ....

3. DURATION OF SERVICE: ....

4. PLACE OF SERVICE: ....

5. If it is your intention to enrol at a university/college/technicon for the first time next year, and you have been allotted to the July intake you may proceed with any arrangements that are required of you for enrolling. You must, however, after you have actually enrolled, obtain a certificate from the university/college/technicon and forward it to the Secretary, Exemption Board, at the above address.
   On receipt of the certificate you will be granted postponement from military service until the following year. If you change your mind and decide to first render military service, your allotment will not be changed to the January intake.
   If you have been allotted to the January intake and you now prefer to first commence with your studies, you must immediately write to the Secretary, Exemption Board, whereafter your allotment will be altered to the July intake so as to enable you to make the necessary arrangements. If, however, you again change your mind, your new allotment will not be altered. If you are presently a student and you have been allotted to the January intake and it is your intention to continue with your studies next year you must write to the Secretary, Exemption Board, as soon as possible for a ruling concerning further postponement. If you are presently a student and you have been allotted to the July intake, then further

postponement of military service will only be considered
by the Exemption Board provided you have made satisfactory
progress with your studies since originally commencing
therewith. **You must therefore not take it for granted that
further postponement will be approved merely on the grounds
that you have enrolled at a university/college/technicon.**
Should you have any doubts on the matter, write to the
Secretary, Exemption Board. In the case of postgraduate
studies the same procedure will apply.

Note that when a student does not make satisfactory progress
in his studies e.g. where he has to repeat a year of study or
where he changes his direction of study or degree, deferment
of military service will not summarily be granted. Such
persons must not bind themselves for further studies or enrol
before finality thereof has been obtained from the Exemption
Board.

6. If you are an employee or will be taking up employment you
   must present this notice to your employer immediately and draw
   his attention to Section 4 of the Defence Act, 1957, which,
   for easy reference, is quoted on the reverse hereof.

7. All enquiries regarding your initial period of military
   service must be directed to the Registering Officer SADF,
   Private Bag X281, Pretoria, 0001.

8. Your final call-up instructions and the necessary rail warrant,
   where applicable, will be forwarded to you approximately 30
   days before commencement of the period of service.

9. If you intend enrolling in the SA Police, or Prison Services,
   your attestation in the relative force must be finalised
   before your reporting date. If not, you must adhere to all
   call-up instructions.

10. Persons may under no circumstances report to any unit of the
    SA Defence Force at will. Those who do this will be rerouted
    at their own expense either to their homes if they were
    allotted to another intake, or to the unit where they should
    have reported.

11. REMEMBER TO INFORM THE REGISTERING OFFICER SADF IMMEDIATELY OF
    ANY CHANGE IN YOUR ADDRESS. THIS WILL ENSURE THAT YOU RECEIVE
    YOUR FINAL CALL-UP INSTRUCTIONS. AT ALL TIMES QUOTE YOUR FORCE
    NUMBER, UNIT TO WHICH ALLOTTED AND PERIOD OF SERVICE.

Registering Officer SADF

REPUBLIC OF SOUTH AFRICA

SOUTH AFRICAN DEFENCE FORCE

INFORMATION FOR THE GUIDANCE OF SERVICEMEN
CALLED UP FOR MILITARY SERVICE

ADVISE YOUR EMPLOYER IMMEDIATELY

1. If you are already employed, you must present your call-up instructions to your employer immediately and draw his attention to the fact that he is, in terms of the Defence Act, 1957, compelled to afford his employees all reasonable facilities to render military service.

DEDUCTIONS

2. Take note that R10,00—R15,00 per month is deducted from your pay for haircuts, bioscope, etc.

CONTROLLING AUTHORITY

3. Until you report for service, you must communicate with the Registering Officer, SA Defence Force, Private Bag X281, Pretoria, 0001, in connection with anything concerning your military service.

CHANGE OF ADDRESS

4. Until you report for service, you must advise the Registering Officer, SADF, immediately of any change in your address. The Defence Act, 1957, provides that failure to do so is an offence which renders you liable to a fine of up to R200 or six months imprisonment.

EXEMPTION FROM OR POSTPONEMENT OF SERVICE

5. If you have valid reasons why you cannot report for service, a written application should immediately be submitted to the Secretary, Exemption Board, Private Bag X281, Pretoria, 0001. You must state your reasons clearly and attach any supporting documents or certificates. Unless and until you are notified of the result, you must report for service as directed.

SUPPLEMENTARY EXAMINATION

6. Military servicemen who are notified that they have to write supplementary examinations in one or more subjects in their final examinations, may for this purpose, apply to their commanding officer for —

a. in the case of three or more subjects, for deferment of military service until a later stage; or

b. in the case of two subjects, for leave of absence to rewrite the two subjects provided that the absence of military service is restricted to the absolute minimum. See brochure concerning military service.

POSTPONEMENT OF SERVICE — RETURN TO SCHOOL

7. Any person who has failed his examinations and who plans to attend school full-time for a further year must, if he has already commenced service, submit an application for postponement of service to his commanding officer. The commanding officer will forward the application to the Exemption Board for a decision. If such a person has not yet commenced his service he must not report for service and his application for postponement must be forwarded direct to the Secretary, Exemption Board, Private Bag X281, Pretoria, 0001, without delay.

USE OF PRIVATE TRANSPORT

8. No remuneration or liability in the event of injury, etc., will be paid or accepted i.r.o. the use of private transport to and from your place of service and no parking facilities for private vehicles are available at such places.

MEDICAL EXAMINATION

9. You will be subjected to a medical examination on reporting for service. If found to be unfit for service, you will be discharged and sent home. Ensure that you are in possession of a discharge certificate before leaving the camp.

Should you be of the opinion that you are medically unfit for military service, proof thereof should be submitted at your medical examination, to the medical examiner.

IDENTIFICATION DOCUMENTS

10. Security plays an important role in the South African Defence Force and the essential identification documents for members of the citizen force consist of a paybook which will be issued by the military authorities and your identification document, which must be in your possession when reporting for service.

If you are not yet in possession of an identification document and have already turned 18 you must, in accordance with the Population Registration Act, immediately apply therefore to the Registrar, Population Register, Private Bag X114, Pretoria, 0001.

ITEMS TO BE BROUGHT ALONG

11. a. A minimum of civilian clothing. You will be issued with a military uniform and you will not be allowed to wear civilian clothes until after completion of your period of service;

b. After you have received your complete issue of uniform, your civilian clothes must be returned to your home or parent's home at your own expense. No provision exists for the safe keeping thereof at the unit;

c. Personal necessities such as shaving kit, toothbrush, soap, a towel and underclothing;

d. Sport equipment for the types of sport in which you normally participate;

e. Any musical instrument which you can play, should you wish to bring it;

f. Bible and Hymn Book;

g. A certified copy of your marriage certificate (if married);

h. Your call-up instructions (Form DD 1303);

j. Your driver's licence;

k. Your identification document;

l. Certificate (or certified copy) of your highest educational qualifications; and

m. If you are professionally academically qualified a registration certificate (or a certified copy) issued by the relevant council.

N.B.— ENSURE THAT YOUR WILL IS IN ORDER BEFORE REPORTING FOR MILITARY SERVICE.

KLAARING IN

There I was, chewing gum, quietly freaking out. The bus was an arbitrary Smartie box of guys. We were Afrikaans, English, leftists, rightists. From all over the place. You were all on your own. Totally alone. You didn't know anyone from a bar of soap. It was a mixed-up, muddled mess.

The guy I was sitting next to is a complete blur. Didn't really chat to him much. I think he was younger than me and Afrikaans. I remember he was shitting himself and almost crapping in his pants. He'd just come out of a nice, comfy home. He had a girlfriend and showed me her photograph – his engeltjie that he loved very much – and a picture of his matric dance. He said he was very much into wearing the right clothes. The right haircut. The right look. In my view he was just verkramp.

A while into Basics I saw him in the san. I heard he'd cracked. He couldn't take it. He just couldn't take it.

In 1951 I was called up under the ballot system for three weeks' service. You were notified in the post by registered mail; a beige envelope with the big black letters 'OHMS'. It stated that you had been placed in the year's ballot. The next letter would say that it was most unfortunate that you had not been selected. They didn't really know what they were doing. At one stage I'd been issued with three call-ups to present myself, so off I went. You went in if your mates went in. You'd register at the police station and they'd send the documents off to Pretoria. They'd ask which regiment you wanted to join. We all chose the Highlanders because all the girls loved the skirt. Nobody wanted to go to the Duke's.

Then they said they'd put me on the reserve list – which I was on for five years. They were full up. The next letter I received said that I was no longer required to furnish the officer with any change of my residential address, and that I must sign in front of Konstabel So-and-so. I still have my signing-off papers.

Within the ballot system, if you were lucky, you got away with it. If you weren't, you'd get called up and that was that. Nine months, in my case, which was in 1964. The chaps before me had only three, then six, months. In '66 and '67 National Service was put up to ten months, and then in 1968 the ACF ballot system was abolished and changed to compulsory National Service. Service became mandatory for a full year until 1977. But the way I look at it is like this: In those days, you had the Russian threat. That was the big thing. Everything was about the 'Russian threat'. And the Cold War was at its height. Berlin was still a divided city in a divided country; the world was East against West. In the sixties we, of course, never went up north to the Border. Only when the MK boys started coming into play did they begin to jack up their system. They then found it necessary to increase the training.

Basics, even in 1964, took three months. You could ask for a delay if you were studying. They were very good about it. You could ask for a transfer, for instance, if you were assigned to the navy but couldn't swim. They would meet you on things like that and perhaps send you to a different unit. I was a driver in St John's Ambulance. Most of the ambulance drivers were sent to the Medics. We capitalised on any bit of training we could get, which suited me to the ground. We were posted to 2 Mil Hospital and we spent six months there.

I was called up and served for a year in 1971. At that stage your preferences regarding where you wanted to go were still given consideration. They heard what you had to say. I explained that my mother was a widow and needed me close to home, in Pretoria, which had a strong air force presence. The last place I wanted to go was Oudtshoorn as infantry.

I went to Cape Town Castle to report for service in July 1979. Got lost. Took the train from platform twenty-seven up to Pretoria, which was good fun. The guys got drunk. Had some good laughs. I didn't drink – I wasn't a drinker then. We were dressed in our civvies. The one oke, an Afrikaans guy, wore crimpelene pants. He lowered them, lifted up his legs, placed a lighter by his arse, lit it and farted. A big blue flame shot out and his tracksuit caught alight. I'll never forget it.

The guys got really drunk on the train. Mainly boere-boys from the surrounding districts. No one was shitting off. They were having a jol. Drunk as skunks. They didn't know what was going to hit them – or maybe they had brothers already inside and felt confident.

After the long train trip, we arrived at Jo'burg station. It took about two hours to get to Voortrekkerhoogte. They gave us the worst ride – the 'rofie' ride' – in a Bedford, where they slammed on brakes, went over all the bumps and accelerated fast. When we arrived it was dark. Hadn't been given lunch. Slept that night without having eaten supper, as well. Next morning we were given breakfast. Then they started sorting things out.

When I went to do my two years, in '80 and '81, a bunch of Jewish friends told me to go in as a Jew. They said I'd get an extra seven days' leave a year for Passover and eat better than the rest. So I decided to do it. I klaared in to Kimberley as a Jew. I arrived on the train and stepped off. They told all the Jewish guys to step to one side. I went and stood with some other guys, and that was it – a Jewish guy in a transport company. When I got there the rabbi looked at me. We chatted and he asked me to tell him more about my Jewish background. I said that my mom was Jewish so I had to take her religion as according to Jewish custom. This was a lie. My mom's NGK. I dropped one letter of my mom's maiden name which ended up rather like a Jewish-sounding name. The rabbi liked me.

I went in from January '83 as a medic, which I hadn't intended to be. I knew nothing about medicine. My call-up papers said to go to Klipdrift in Potch. When I arrived they asked what I was doing there because I was supposed to be in the navy at Saldanha. So I said, 'Okay, I'll go.' They told me I didn't have to – I could stay – and that's how I ended up in the Medics. They made the mix-up, not me. I don't know how they did it.

Went into the air force in January 1988. Klaared in at a deurgangs-kamp. There were too many people to accommodate and they didn't have lodgings for everyone. It was on a huge dirt field just outside of Pretoria. It was a base made up entirely from army tents. Tent City.

So you arrive at Nasrec. Mom and brothers giving you all the spirit. Mom's loaded all kinds of goodies, sweets and smokes in your bag. Made sure you've got all the correct stuff. Locks, iron, washing powder, boot polish, the special little civvies kit – all the prerequisites – plus dubbin. I wanted dubbin. You don't know what the hell is happening but you know you're going somewhere. Hold Mom's hand. All the girlfriends are loving and kissing their boyfriends. 'We'll be with you. We'll get through this.' Brothers say, 'Just be tough now, my china.'

The loudspeakers play the Vietnam song, '*Nuh-nuh-nuh-nineteen, nine-teen.*' Hey, this is cool. Bring it on. Then it's the long walk to the hangar. You get inside. You're told to sit in rows, in your specific groups, depending on the destination. Then they read out all the kak. 'Are you on medication? Drugs? Anything illegal you wish to declare? Knives? Porno?'

They confiscate alcohol. You're hoping you don't have some sort of drug stashed away somewhere that you've forgotten about. They're warning you to declare now or they'll kick your heads in. You fill in the forms. Give in your individual magsnommer. Depart.

During a pit stop on the way to Kimberley one oke decides, 'Bugger this. I'm gonna run to the bottle store.' He runs off. Gets his six-pack of beer and smuggles it onto the bus. Sits at the back and dops. About an hour down the line he needs a piss, but the trick is they aren't going to stop. They specifically don't stop. They know he's done this. They are punishing him for trying to beat the system. Now he really needs a piss. 'Please, sir. I need to go.'

'Jammer, boetie. Byt vas of pis in jou broek.'

Now he's absolutely desperate. He's bent over in discomfort, but the bus continues. It won't stop. He pees in the can. He is humiliated. Day one in the army.

The buses picked us up at Wingfield Military Base in Cape Town. Drove to Infantry School at Oudtshoorn. It was a long trip. They went about forty kilometres per hour up the hills. It was also a long day. We stood in the clothes we arrived in and had to open our bags while the MPs searched them. You had to have the absolute minimum with you. Anything else they took. They even took our bags away.

I'll never, ever forget klaaring in. It was at Nasrec, just outside of Jo'burg. My parents dropped me off. We sat on a concrete grandstand overlooking a soccer field. It was mid-morning. I wore civvy clothes and had my little bag with all the requirements: padlocks, a two-metre length of chain, brown boot polish, polish brushes, pens, envelopes, stamps, writing paper, washing powder, toiletries, a small amount of cash – basic things – and, of course, your call-up papers.

I was nervous. I checked out all the other guys, shitting themselves as much as me, and felt more at ease. Playing repeatedly over the speakers was a combination of Scottish bagpipe music followed by *langarm sokkie-sokkies*. I guess the rank had it all down to a tee in an attempt to give both the English and the Afrikaans guys something to identify with. Then a sergeant, very nicely, called for us to say our goodbyes and gather on the field. My heart was thumping and I felt apprehensive, yet excited. This was it! Hugs and kisses.

'Goodbye, Dad! Goodbye, Mom! Here we go! It's now or never. Let's see what it's all about.'

Suppressing the ache in my throat I headed to the field. Flight or fight, I felt. Did I turn now and retreat, which I could've, or did I keep on going? 'No!' I thought. 'This is it! Keep on going, man. Keep on going.'

This was a big moment in my life – in all our lives: from civvy to the unknown entrance into the army. A rite of passage. It was almost as if I was finally allowed access into a secret, mystical society and was now going to find out first-hand the answers to the questions I always had.

We lined up. The sergeant, again very nicely and almost big-brotherly, ordered us to approach the hall. This time, though, his voice was a lot sterner. The hall came closer and closer. I looked around and saw my parents in the distance, waving at me, but I didn't wave back. That hurt. I just smiled but was too far away for them to see.

Then came the song which they must've been dying to play, '*You're in the army now, whoa-woo-woe, you're in the army … Now!*' And then I thought, 'Oh, flip! What've I done?' But it was too late. We entered the huge hangar-like building, and the sliding doors slammed shut.

We were ordered to line up in rows and place our open bags in front of us as neatly as any self-respecting civilian could. We were silent. Nobody wanted to draw attention. Then some NCO shouted, 'As julle rowe wil gaan, kan julle, maar julle sal vandag nog in die DB wees want van nou af noem ons dit AWOL! As enige van julle dwelms of alkohol het, verklaar dit nou terwyl jy die kans het, want die honde gaan julle uitruik! Niks sal met julle gebeur as julle dit nou verklaar en erken nie. Nou!'

Wisely, perhaps, a few guys stood up and were quickly escorted out of sight, along with their bags. The corporals, with their impressive rifles and sniffer-dogs, walked slowly up and down the lines, giving us the skeef. I remember some chancers being bust. The MPs, with orange peaked caps, surrounded them and manhandled them away.

After the 'all clear' we were screamed at to exit the building and make our way outside to board the buses. I looked at the grandstands for my parents. They, and everyone else's, were long gone. The last time I'd felt so nervous and alone was as a thirteen-year-old boy, when I said goodbye to my folks on my first day of boarding school.

The journey took a couple of hours. We arrived at Voortrekkerhoogte and stepped off the bus onto a large, open gravel field and were then divided into our different units, which meant that you never again saw any of the other guys who'd been sitting with you on the bus. They went their way and you went yours. There were about thirty busloads. Corporals walked up and down the lines, looked at your call-up papers and told you in which area to go and wait.

Our group numbered about forty guys. A bus drove us over to Personnel Services. There was an old-fashioned cast-iron gate flanked by a guard post. We stood there, still wearing civvies, with our little bag of basic requirements. The corporal told us to place our opened bags on the ground and step away. From out of the guard post stepped this skinny, tall, gangly, nerdy-looking runt of a guy with frizzy red hair, and covered in big yellow chorbs and red blotches on his face. When he fell out of the ugly-tree he surely hit every single branch on the way down. I'll never forget the sight of him.

He approached us with his impressive-looking R4 slung across his wimpish chest. The corporal acknowledged him and, as was planned, I'm sure, just to welcome us to the army, they looked through our bags. I couldn't see the point as they'd already been thoroughly searched at Nasrec and we hadn't stopped en route. I could see this troep couldn't have given a damn what was in our bags, anyway. He was just doing what he was told.

July 1992 was the second-last compulsory National Service intake. What makes it interesting was the fact that everyone, from the *rofie* to the top brass, knew political change was unavoidable. The SADF was in its death throes and I was there witnessing it. It was a weird feeling. Everyone knew what was happening but nobody seemed to know what to do about it, or what to do with us, or why the hell we were even there! Voortrekkerhoogte, a huge place that used to accommodate thousands of troops, was empty. At Personnel Services Corps there were nothing but dozens and dozens of empty bungalows, once bursting with recruits. Only one bungalow was occupied, and by my intake. It was a ghost town and very, very lonely.

I thought to myself, 'Where the hell *is* everybody else?' Then it dawned on me that I was one of the very few poephols who'd complied with the call-up. Your buddies hadn't, and you realised – too late – that there was nothing you could do, and that there was no escape, because … *'You're in the army now, whoa-woo-woe.'*

So it was business as usual while the system collapsed in on itself. The manpower was no longer available. Dodgers never arrived for their service. The change was as clear as a sunny day. Historically, though, I'm glad to have been involved with that particular intake.

BASIC TRAINING

There were three drawbacks you could have when in the army: being tall ('Hey! Langmoer! Kom hier!'), wearing glasses ('Hey! Four-eyes! Kom hier!') and being English ('Hey! Soutpiel! Kom hier!').

The army wasn't like the navy, one month Afrikaans and the next month English. It was one month Afrikaans and the next eleven months in Afrikaans as well!

Being treated like shit when you went through Basics was par for the course. Everybody went through it. You can't say it was unique to you. It's the way things were done. Even old Magnus Malan went through it when he did his Basics. I didn't enjoy being treated like shit, but we all went through it, so what's the problem?

'Word wakker! Word wakker! Die dag word al hoe kakker!'

Orientation

This was when we got all our shots, received our kit, learnt how to do inspections and got assigned to our corporal and lieutenant. Learnt how to iron, wash our clothes and make our beds, and got accustomed to taking orders and waking up before the crack of dawn. All of this – or so they hoped.

The first week was a very nervous time for us *rofies*. You hadn't a clue what to expect. You'd heard all the stories from family and friends who'd gone before, but this – now – was *your* reality.

I was afraid of the older guys in the previous intake. I was unsure how they would treat us or what to do if the situation arose. Thankfully they were kept apart, but we still felt intimidated at mealtimes, when we were together. But they left us alone. I don't remember any serious incidents. You'd make the inevitable eye contact and quickly look down or glance away. None of us new intakes was going to be *wys* or do anything to get noticed. You just kept below the radar and blended in.

Went up to the bungalows and got placed in our different rooms. After that was uitreikings, which lasted for the next week, where we got given all our kit. *KM store toe*. One of the first things we got issued were kousrekke, which tucked your pants in underneath so you always looked neat and tidy. One Saturday night I made gyppo-*nate* in my overalls so, no matter how badly I ironed them, there'd always be a seam down the front. One guy was really good at sewing and showed us how.

Got our weapons, which we never fired for the first three months. Just did drills, drills, drills.

On our first night we slept inside a huge bungalow filled with rows of double-bunks. I was passing the time making sketches in a drawing pad I'd brought along. We were all complete strangers to one another and kept to ourselves. Only a few were boisterous and loud.

There was this one guy lying on his side, curled up on a top bunk, a couple of beds opposite mine. He hadn't been feeling well. The corporal said it was okay for him to rest. He'd been like that for about half an hour. Suddenly I heard a splash and looked up to see him puke out a stream of vomit. It looked like oatmeal porridge. This poor guy just couldn't stop. He tried to contain it but it just kept on coming. He lay heaving while the vomit ran over the mattress and down the side of the bed onto the bunk below. The oke lying underneath didn't move in time and got partly drenched.

The puker and I ended up becoming buddies during Basics. We were assigned to the same squad. Eddie and I formed a great friendship during those three months. He told me later that he'd felt ill the day he klaared in and it must've been a bug, combined with nerves. It wasn't due to anything it shouldn't have been, because he was a hardcore religious oke who didn't drink or smoke, let alone do drugs. His habits were the complete opposite of mine. He wasn't a Bible-basher, though, but was quiet and reserved about it. That's what I liked about him. He was a beacon of level-headed sanity for me throughout that time; I drew strength from his calmness. I still think of him and wonder what has become of him.

That first night passed. I'd struggled to fall asleep. We were woken by a shouting corporal at 4 a.m. and told to be ready and waiting for our first army breakfast – at 5 a.m. We marched to the mess hall as best we could, but we were clumsy and completely out of step. We hadn't a clue how to march as we were still essentially civilians. We hadn't even been there for twenty-four hours. I remember waiting in the long queue. It was still pitch-black, the stars were up and it was ice cold. I clearly recollect gazing at the moon, which was full and bright. It was all that connected me to the world outside. I thought, 'Is this what it's about? This is going to be quite tough – starting the day *so* early.' But it was also a matter of thinking, 'Well, you're in the army so obviously this is going to happen. Take it and accept it as it comes.' I was psyching myself.

Over the next couple of days our basic clothing items were issued. Overalls, boots, web belts, bush hats, shirts, pants, bush jackets, towels, underwear, shorts, takkies, balsak and so on. Did a lot of hanging around over that period. There was no real structure yet and guys were still in a civilian frame of mind.

There was this really paraat, nervous-as-hell, scared-to-death Afrikaans bloke called Willie. He was short and stocky with black hair and freckles and he was really overweight. He and I were ordered to the linen room to sort out the mess. The corporal said he'd return later. We did what we had to do and waited. There was a mountain of dirty linen in the corner. I couldn't resist the urge to jump on top of this soft pile of fabric. The linen was cool compared to the outside heat, and it had been a long twenty-four hours. I lay back, settled in and relaxed. 'Kom, Willie, rus 'n bietjie, boet. Park off.'

'Nee! Ons kan nie dit doen nie. Die korporaal sal ons vang. Ons sal in die moeilikheid beland. Ek kan nie.'

'Well, let's take turns. We'll keep a lookout for each other.'

'Nee, nee, ons moet staan.' He was becoming irritated. I didn't argue. It was pointless. I kindly asked if he could keep a lookout for the corporal. It was no fun with him. He was totally verkramp and serious. The corporal forgot about us. I fell asleep and after an hour Willie woke me up and we left. He wanted to stay because that's what the corporal had ordered. I reassured him that it would be better to return to the others. It was interesting to see how some guys really stressed out.

Later that day I was having a pee against the urinal. This huge Afrikaans guy walked in. He was really dik, but more overweight than muscular, and wore glasses. He was in his late twenties – the oldest out of all of us – and was married with kids. He'd studied first, like most of us there. He stood next to me, unbuttoned his pants and, while doing his business, let out this massive, unashamed, rasping fart. Then he said, 'Ja, boet, 'n pis sonder 'n poep is soos 'n plaas sonder 'n stoep!' and he looked at me and laughed. He didn't give a damn and felt no skaam.

The first couple of days were pretty slow. Nothing was too hardcore yet. They were basically easing us in, showing us the ropes. The corporals weren't so *hardegat* yet. The corporal assigned to us was one of the unusual ones and totally different from what I was expecting. He seemed a decent guy and didn't get into the whole thing too fast or too seriously in those first few days. He asked me something, I really can't remember what, and I answered him, thinking I was all paraat, 'Ja, meneer!'

'Ek's nie jou meneer nie, *roof*, ek's jou korporaal! Het jy my?'

'Ja, meneer!'

'Wat? Is jy dom, *roof*?'

'Nosir! Yessir! Nee, meneer! Korporaal!'

'Ek is nie ... jou ... fokken ... MENEER NIE! EK ... IS ... JOU ... KORPORAAAAL! HOOR JY MY, TROEP?'

'Ja, Korporaal.'

'SÊ DIT WEER!'

'Ja, Korporaal!'

'SÊ! ... DIT! ... WEER!'

'JA, KORPORAAL!' My head was spinning.

'SAL JY MY OOIT WEER MENEER NOEM, *ROOF*?'

'NEE, KORPORAAL! DANKIE, KORPORAAL!'

He drilled that into me very quickly and much to the benefit of my fellow *rofies*, who didn't want the same attention I'd just received. It was a gentle initiation and a necessary one. I realised I had to keep my head level and be on my toes. Things could turn pear-shaped very quickly, otherwise.

Klipdrift was a tented base, and we did the whole of Basics there. We didn't have bungalows but there was a mess hall and showers, which were both mobile. There was also a rehab place nearby. Even as medics we did the normal Infantry Basics for three months. In the beginning I thought it was really lousy, but I eased into it. It was fine. Luckily I grew up in the Western Transvaal so, even though I'm English, my Afrikaans was fine. Spoke it fluently. Didn't stick out like those Durban okes. It helped a lot.

On the second day our new corporal was marching a platoon of us around the place. In spite of the fact that most of us had high-school marching, we must have looked really awful and out of step. It was a winding march, left and right in between the bungalows, which were laid out in a grid formation. The corporal was tuning, 'Peloton … regs! Peloton … links!' depending on the turn. We were approaching a left but the call never came. Meanwhile a brick wall ahead of us was getting closer. Still the call never came. One oke piped up, 'Let's walk straight. See what the corporal does.' We went along with the joke. Lines of three, row after row, piled into the wall until the whole platoon was in a complete shambles.

It was a childish thing to do but it broke the tension. The corporal had been distracted, but when he saw what was happening he went along with the joke. We got away with it because it was early days and the corporal was a genuinely nice guy who didn't have a carrot shoved up his bum. There was also no one else around to witness what had happened. I think he didn't feel embarrassed and therefore didn't feel the need to scream obscenities in front of his fellow corporals.

We had our haircuts on about the second day. I had long hair before I went in so cut it quite short before klaaring in. I thought it wouldn't be so noticeable. Some guys had really gone mad and cut their hair extremely short, almost bald. Compared to them my hair was like Tina Turner's. We stood in line outside the barber in our baggy overalls and waited, chuckling and giggling like little girls, awaiting our turn. You didn't have to wait long because they were very quick, having had countless hours of experience, and this wasn't exactly a high-street job.

It was a small room with two chairs and mirrors on the wall. The two barbers inside weren't from the army, but were private individuals contracted for the day. They were also rough-and-ready types, a cigarette dangling from the lips, smudged tattoos on their forearms and, funnily enough, long and greasy hair. At least they wore white shirts. They sat you down on the chair with a gruff grunt. The electric shears buzzed in your ears and vibrated your scalp while they skimmed away your sides, back and top. They left a bit of length on the top, but it was bald above your ears. A real short-back-and-sides. They weren't exactly gentle and didn't give a damn. It was obvious in the way they pulled your hair and tugged your ears out the way of their blunted shears. A few guys got cuts. The hair made your overalls itch inside.

When we'd been processed like sheep we all looked at each other and laughed. We all looked the same. It was the first time my hair had been so short. It felt quite good, actually. Easy to wash and get dry. It pricked for a while, but that eventually went. It's no exaggeration to say that the pile of hair grew into a mound when swept into the corner. I'd never seen so much human hair before.

After arriving at Saldanha for the navy we had to fill in an evaluation form, but, by the time they got to our barracks, only Afrikaans forms were left. One of the questions was: Are you physically attracted to other men? So, of course, we all wrote 'no'. This one guy, from Natal, couldn't speak or understand Afrikaans. He said, 'Chaps, what must I fill in for that one?' We told him to put 'yes'.

He never forgave us because the psychologist kept singling him out and grilling him about having a boyfriend. The poor guy became more and more indignant, and explained that he hadn't understood the question and that we'd set him up. He even got a letter from his girlfriend and proudly showed it to the officers. Not even that convinced them.

I remember a guy getting screamed at by a corporal because he was crying. 'Moenie fokken huil nie! Jy's in die mag, jou bliksem! Moenie huil nie!' The guy got up and belted the corporal.

Then he got *kla'ed aan*. He was questioned as to why he'd hit the corporal. His reply was that he'd never worn boots before. He was so poor that receiving a pair of boots, even from the army, had moved him to tears.

When they supplied us with our boots, the brass eyelets for the laces were painted brown. Our corporals thought it looked lekker to have this paint off. They gave us steel wool and told us to strip it down, which took a couple of hours. There are eighteen small eyelets per boot, and two pairs of boots, which equals seventy-two eyelets. We Brassoed them – they had to shine like gold. I don't know if it was a standard army thing that everybody had to do. I've never found out.

You could spot the other boarding-school types. Guys who had the drill of prefect inspections, the routine, being away from home for long periods and following some sort of rigid discipline. You could see they had experience and practice with this. Inspections and being buggered around were nothing new. Their asses hadn't been wiped by their parents all those years. The army was new but the shitty situations, as may be encountered in boarding school, were not.

I was at boarding school for two years. The prefects would overturn your bed if there was one tiny crease or fold out of place. They'd strip it and throw your sheets, blankets, pillows and mattress all over the dormitory. Occasionally the bedding was thrown out the window, to land downstairs, or you'd have inspection and Prefect Prick would shout at you for virtually nothing. Then he'd storm off to his room and slam the door. Maybe he was missing Mummy and took it out on you or the harmless bed. Trash my bedside table as well, why don't you?

Getting to the army, nothing changed, but I wasn't a thirteen-year-old kid any more – I was twenty-two – and when I saw it happening all over again, I rolled my eyes, took a deep breath and thought, 'Here we go.'

The only difference was the intensity and seriousness of it. This wasn't school; this was the army, yet the childishness carried on regardless. It seemed so pointless to trash the dormitory. Boys don't change.

I sustained a knee injury playing rugby in high school. I'd been to the doctor about it. He said the knee cartilage was damaged but would heal over time. It was a problem, but not a serious one. Anyway, thanks to school rugby, I had a trashed knee.

The week before klaaring in I went to the civvy doctor and asked for a recheck, which he did, and he also gave me a letter explaining the medical terms: 'Chondromalacia of patella'. He advised against 'performing exercises which may aggravate the condition'. Naturally I was happy but also ashamed about this. I won't say I wasn't relieved, though.

During the medical check-ups I showed the medic the letter. With the roll of his eyes I knew he was thinking, 'Ja, sure, another *luigat*.' He took me out the line.

'Let's have a look,' he sighed. I got on the table and he examined my knee and foot, and, sure enough, the medic – not a National Serviceman, as he was a two-pip lieutenant – said, 'Ja, I agree. Your knee is damaged. I can feel it.' This was after lots of prodding and painful rolling of the kneecap, with me having a contorted facial expression. I eventually got sent over to a troepie who issued me with a little pink card – G3K3. This meant no hard drill, route marches or lifting of heavy objects. 'Geen strawwe dril, LO, roetemarse, hardloop,' it read.

This pink card was both a blessing and a curse. We had to wear it in a plastic bankie pinned above our left breast pocket for the entire duration of Basics. It made for easy spotting and constant taunts from the corporals and fellow troepies. It may well have been a bull's-eye to indicate, 'Korporaal, rondfok asseblief.'

Did my Basics at Upington, 8 SAI. It was summer and it was hot. I went through the medical inspection thinking, 'Great! A G3. Great stuff. Now I can go and sit in the shade and drink water while everybody's running around in the hot sun.'

That's the impression the medics had given me. I had flat feet and was really overweight. I thought they were going to give me a break. I was set up and ready to go for G3K3. I got to the end of the line celebrating, but there was this fat dude sitting there in civvies. 'What's your story?' he asked.

'G3K3,' I said, all excited.

'Nee wat, vetseun Engelsman. Jy kan lekker hardloop.'

He had this little pencil, and over where it said G3K3 he wrote G1K1. Just like that. This guy reckoned I could run in the sun. 'Lekker pret,' he laughed.

We'd only been there about a week. Some high-ranking officer – a major, I think – was addressing us, doing a lot of shouting, and pretty much explaining the whole propaganda thing. 'Are there any questions?' This one *rofie* put his hand up and asked, 'Sir, is there freedom of speech in the army?'

'Yes, of course there's freedom of speech. Sergeant, take that man outside and fuck him up!' It was tongue-in-cheek – a bit of a joke – but he was taken outside and given an opfok, anyway. Chased him around for a bit, with lots of obligatory shouting and gesticulating.

Telephone: 314-3074   TS Training Centre

Inquiries: 2 Lt J. H. Vorster   Private Bag X1030

                                        Voortrekkerhoogte

                                              0143

STATEMENT RE POLITICAL ACTIVITIES

I No........................   Rank...........................

Full names and surnames:...

Hereby confirms that I am conversant with the SADF Policy
regarding Political Activities by Members of the SADF and
undertake to comply therewith.

1. Political activities of members of the SA Defence Force.
   a.   Members of the SA Defence Force are at all times forbidden
       to participate in or promote any demonstrations or
       processions with party-political aims.
   b.   Under no circumstances may any member of the SA Defence
       Force attend such gatherings, wherever they may be held,
       in uniform. Members may however attend political meetings
       in civilian clothes.
   c.   Attendance of a political meeting by a member of the SA
       Defence Force does not include his active participation
       in the proceedings and the exercise of his right to vote
       involves the full extent of his permitted political
       rights.
   d.   No member of the SA Defence Force may be nominated or
       elected as member of the House of Assembly or House of
       Representatives or the Legislative Assembly of South-West
       Africa or prescribed public body.

Witness: ....   Signed: ....

Date: ....   Date: ....

Translated from a combination of English and Afrikaans in the original

Keuring

The dog handlers came around. The last thing I wanted to do was end up as Security, even though I liked dogs, but they were short of guys. It didn't matter to them whether you wanted to do it or not, they just sent you there anyway. Tough. They sent us to Hoedspruit for security training. Security was all about standing guard at gates and doing patrols with dogs.

In 1976 I was called up to the Air Force Gymnasium. The first week we were there we did a mini selection course for guys who wanted to become instructors. I volunteered for that straight away.

Then they came: the Dog Squad, Berede, the Paras and Recces, but mainly the Paras. They wanted guys. When they came a-looking, not a damn was I going! I didn't want to get in. Bugger that. But we all had to run the 2,4 and do all the other shit anyway. I could've made the keuring but I wasn't interested in the Bats. It was hard enough in 6 SAI. Did I really think I wanted something harder? 'Kom! Kom! Kom! Roer jou!' Ha! Not a hope, meneer. I felt I'd do the best I could but wasn't going to go *that* far! No way.

The usual guys came around for keuring. One thing I still regret very much today is that I didn't volunteer for Bats. The thing in your head was that you didn't volunteer for anything, but they also made it clear that to become an ops medic was more prestigious than being even a Bat. Only after Basics could you volunteer to do ops medics, or do bugger all and become an orderly in one of the military hospitals.

I wanted to become a Parabat because if I ever got to jump out of an aeroplane I'd find freedom and wouldn't have to pay for it – the government would. I knew I wanted to be a Bat way before klaaring in. All my friends at school said, 'Don't be ridiculous! Don't do it.' But that's exactly what I wanted to do. I really wanted to be a Parabat. I wanted to know what it was like to jump out of a Dakota or C-130, and the opportunity would only come once in my life. You don't get that opportunity again.

I also wanted to make something out of National Service. At the time I didn't even know the Parabats were an elite force. All I knew was that they jumped out of aircraft. I was clueless. 'It's very hardcore. It's very serious. It's very difficult. This is what Parabats are about,' they said. 'If you don't want to do it, you don't have to do it. If you really, *really* want to be a Parabat, you can, but first of all you have to pass the keuring.'

They told us there was a PT course of three days and two nights that had to be passed, and the only thing special about it was getting to the end. All they could do was hint to us and put a fear factor into the situation. They said the PT course was going to be our worst nightmare. 'You'll piss blood,' they said, and used all those types of expressions. If you passed every test along the way then you'd qualify to enter the hangar, which is like a Viking soldier allowed entry to the Great Hall. Valhalla. Unreachable. You had to go through hell to get there.

I wrote my name down. I was hearing all these war stories from the other troops about how the Bats brought back blood-coated axes and weapons. But they didn't know. It's like when the Reconnaissance got accused of breaking puppies' necks. What crap. What bull. 'You're mad to do the Bats,' they said. 'You'll go crazy! They'll turn you into a killer!'

I had a buddy. A soutie as well. He also wanted to do Bats. That's all he ever opted for. That's how we got to know each other. There were a few Dutchmen whose motivation was cherry. They knew that when they went home they'd get some serious cherry. They'd be *helde*. Arrive in your slangvel and you'd have all the porridge you wanted. It made the girls giggly. They got all squealish.

They said if we wanted to choose the Bats we'd have to pass three initial fitness tests and have an interview before being considered. We had to run a 2,4 kilometre in under twelve minutes. I hadn't run for three years and they wanted me to do this, then sixty-seven sit-ups in two minutes, followed by thirty push-ups? But we were given a week to train.

I ran the 2,4 in just under ten minutes. Came in at the front, but not first. Put everything into it. Gave it full gas. After recovering I remember drinking water, and it tasted like honey it was so good. Didn't pass the sit-ups but was close enough. Lots of guys hardly came close at all. Because I messed up on my sit-ups, I thought, 'Well that's over. No Bats.' But there was still the interview.

We were told to *tree aan* outside the interview room and undress to our undies. As I said, because I didn't properly pass the physical, I skiemed I wasn't going to make the selection. I realised I may have to lie in order to get in. I was checking the previous guys coming out and they'd failed. They had things like bilharzia, malaria and even tattoos. Married, or didn't belong to an established religion? You're out. Any criminal record, or record of alcohol or drug abuse? You're out. I'd been smoking a lot of zol for years. Bit of a hippy.

Then it was my turn. I walked in, stood to attention and strekked because I wasn't wearing a beret. I remember a sergeant major, a captain and a commandant sitting there. Head honchos. The interview room was painted red inside, with a big, growling cat painted on the wall. I was standing in my underpants, stiff as a board. They inspected my body. Checked for tattoos. They wanted to see if it was going to handle the stress it would be dealt. To see whether I was fit, whether I was strong enough. But I was a skinny little runt. They laughed at me. They seemed to think it was funny. 'Troep, hoekom wil jy 'n Parabat wees?'

'To achieve and accomplish something positive while in the army, Sa'majoor!' This was true.

'Drink jy?'

'Nee, Sa'majoor!'

'Twak, troep. Nou lieg jy vir ons! Natuurlik drink jy.'

'Ja, Kaptein. I do have the occasional beer, Kaptein.'

'En dwelms?'

'I beg your pardon, Sa'majoor?'

'Drugs. Do you use drugs?'

Then I had to lie. 'I experimented with marijuana in Standard 8, Sa'majoor.' Meanwhile my veins were saturated with it. Two weeks ago, just before klaaring in, I'd klonked a whole bankie. They asked if I could take a blood test.

'Ja, Kaptein.' I had nothing to lose. I really didn't think I'd be chosen. I was giving my spin. I didn't want to be hanging around Maintenance Division driving trucks and buggering around. I never got given the blood test, but they weren't stupid. They knew I was a little bit otherwise. They were going to change that. 'Reg so, troep. Jy kan maar gaan.'

'Dankie, Kommandant.' The interview was that simple.

About a week later we were sitting at ease on the parade ground. They were about to divide us into our various keurings. They called out the respective units and then the surnames. Then it came to Parabats. The guys got called one by one and lined up. I was sweating because I really didn't think my name would be called, but it came. I leapt up and went, 'Yeah!'

They kakked on me. 'Moenie jouself só wys nie, roof, jou bliksem!'

Out of about two hundred guys, only sixty-odd wanted to join the Bats and, of these, only fifteen made it. I *tree'd aan* and realised I was finally in the Parabats.

After school I klaared in from January 1989, to 2 SAI at Walvis Bay. When the Bats came around for keuring all the okes just went crazy. Everyone wanted to be out of that place. Anything would've been better, even the Bats – *anything* – to get out. Infantry, up there anyway, was kak. But I didn't go for it. It was too crowded. Too many people. Not many made it.

I had a choice of three things: Dog Unit, Anti-Aircraft or Catering. I thought Catering sounded the easiest, so I picked that and became a *kok*. I ended up running with gas bottles instead of a rifle. The idea was to wear the white uniform with brown boots, but I got out of that one, too.

Never completed the course. I said, 'Nooit, this is a lot of work cleaning the kitchen.' So I *gooied* the stress manoeuvre that I was freaked out from Basics, which worked quite nicely. That got me down to Cape Town.

It was odd. A lot of guys who were rebels at school, bad boys who didn't give a shit about rules – okes who beat the system – ended up in Intelligence. They couldn't believe it. I know. I met them again. They told me, 'We all beat the system. Why put us in Intelligence? And we were all getting Ds and Es in school.'

They may have had lower grades, but they weren't dumb. They just didn't conform. They thought of the system and tried to beat it, to beat the headmaster, and they did. They got away with it. Drinking at night. Smoking cigarettes behind the hall. Testing authority. Sex with the girls at the school over the road. Stuff like that.

As English-speaking National Servicemen we had no chance of really getting anywhere in the Defence Force. They came round to choose guys for Officer's School, and everything was in serious Afrikaans. I could hardly even speak Afrikaans at that stage. I had standard-grade matric Afrikaans. If your name was, say, Van der Westhuizen or Bezuidenhout, it was, 'Ja. Bakgat. Jy's oppie trok.' If it was, like, Baxter or Smith, then, 'Go run round a tree, soutie.'

DECLARATION

I, No. .... Rank ....

name ....

regiment ....

hereby certify that rifle/pistol No........... has been issued to
me, and that I have been warned—
   (a) to keep the rifle/pistol locked up when not in use;
   (b) to keep the magazine, bolt/slide locked up in separate
       places respectively from the weapon when not in use;

                    Date......................................

                    Signed by................................

                    Officer's signature......................

Telefoon/Telephone 24131   8 SA Infanterie Opleidingseenheid
Bylyn/Extension: 2000   8 SA Infantry Training Unit
Enquiries: Colonel J. Jooste   Privaatsak/Private Bag 5904
                                UPINGTON
                                8800
                                01 February 1990

Dear Recruit

1. Welcome to 8 South African Infantry Battalion. You will soon realise that it is a unit to be proud of.

2. Thank you for reporting for your National Service. Although it is expected of you, it is not taken for granted.

3. Our task is to train you as a soldier, a process requiring many adjustments and sacrifices, because there is no easy or instant method of turning out a soldier. You will have to acquire new skills and get to know yourself as well as your enemy.

4. With your co-operation and positive attitude we can carry out this important task without affecting your dignity. We believe in good communication, a healthy lifestyle and meaningful discipline.

5. You determine what your National Service will be like. I wish you the best with this specific phase of your life.

[Signed]
OFFICER COMMANDING 8 SOUTH AFRICAN INFANTRY BATTALION: COLONEL

Weeks 2-9

'Jy's nou in die army! Die army's jou ma, en ek is jou pa, en ons is nie getroud nie, so weet jy wat maak ek jou? Ek maak jou 'n fokken hoerkind!'

We wore our full browns only on Sundays because that's when we went to church.

I remember making a joke when they interviewed us after klaaring in. 'Are you prepared to die for your country?' they asked.

'No, I'll make sure the other guy dies for his country.' They weren't very impressed. What I should have said was, 'I'll make sure the *enemy* dies for his country.'

In 1964, Basics was fair but tough. Compared to what the Infantry blokes went through, ours was a dream. I initially went in as Cape Town High-landers Infantry, but then my papers came through and I completed Basics in the Medics at Voortrekkerhoogte. Still did the drilling, marching, mus-ketry and inspections.

Our Basic Training was only six weeks long. The navy GIs never chased you through the obstacle course and, because you weren't being chased, it became a pleasure. Yes, admittedly, this was in the late sixties, before things really got hot, but still, it made a hell of a difference. Only the guys that wanted to kick and scream got given shit.

The GIs were trained in England at Whale Island. Boned boots like you don't want to see. Spot on. Everything was so neat and correct. We used soap to get the *streepies* right – the creases in your shirts and pants. Soap the inside and iron. Sharp, like lathes. Lots of tricks. We had to embroider our name on our shirts and towels. They stamped them with a block of inked wood that had your surname on it. When the ink was dry you embroidered over it.

I left matric in 1974 and got called up in June 1975. I remember the day I got that long, brown manila envelope with a 3 SAI stamp on it: Potch.

I thought, 'Ag, no!' I'd so badly wanted to go to the navy or air force so, of course, I ended up in Potch for my Basics. All we did was spit-and-polish, drilling on the parade ground, inspections and basic shooting practice for three months. In my day we still used the R1 and did bayonet training.

All the Afrikaans ous were in the front of the bungalow, always cleaning, polishing, shining and sweeping. All the English okes were laid back, lying around at the other end. It was very much an English–Afrikaans thing – us and them – very much so. Then we'd have the buddy-buddy system and go through all the shit together. Trust me, when you got out of the army there was no difference between us. The guys that you detested when you started became your best buddies.

Then, in January 1976, I was sent back to Potch after becoming a corporal, and had twenty-two guys in the bungalow I was assigned to lead. When you got back, you knew how to shout. You'd get your first intake and you were now the korporaal. You were now God. You made them kak! I guess I was one of those poes corporals, but, then again, all corporals were poes corporals! It was part and parcel of it. At Infantry School we had a philosophy taught to us: Afkak is buggering somebody up, but he's getting exercise, so it's beneficial. Rondfok is just a mental thing. 'Must be up at 4 a.m. for a spit-and-polish and then have the korporaal chase me around for the morning.' I knew this and would just say, 'Fok jou, roof. I'm after you.'

To me, rondfok was the worst. Afkak you could at least run and be physical – even faint if it was too much. What could they do? But, as for rondfok, that was the worst part of the army.

There was a subcamp at Potch called Bloekombos. They really murdered those troops there. Those okes were so well disciplined. Their korporaals were gospel. You just didn't question them.

About this whole English–Afrikaans thing. Basics was the first time I became aware of this divide – that there were people who didn't think the same way that you thought, and who grew up differently to you. There was a cultural difference between the English-speaking and Afrikaans-speaking guys. At school we had some English-speaking guys but it was a dual-medium school and there were no problems. Then you arrived in the army and it was, 'Hey! Hairyback! Yes, you, crunchie.'

I thought, 'What the hell is this?' You're being called all sorts of names. That was an awakening. Then you'd retaliate with 'Voertsek, soutpiel!' We were still the same crowd in the sense that we all did the same job together. We actually became close friends.

Went straight in after school, in July 1975, to Bethlehem, Free State. I was 2 Genie. We'd done specialised training during Basics, doing landmines and claymore mines. Those were mean bastards. We were taught how to fuse and defuse them, along with basic booby-traps and how to make them. Stuff like that.

Finished our eleven weeks' Basics and got our first pass. Right after that we went up to South West without any secondary training. Training was more compressed in those days.

In Basics they used to bugger you around, but you became accustomed to it. You sorted out what you could or couldn't do. Inspections were bloody awful because, even after making your bed as properly as possible, they would always find something wrong. It was hard, but it was fair hardness. There was no unnecessary bull, and when you deserved credit you got it. I never saw anybody crack – but, bear in mind, this was still 1977.

When a guy caused shit we disciplined him ourselves. Sounds nasty, but when you had a chap who wouldn't shower, say, we used to take him into the shower with a wooden broom and that was it; he got showered. *We* disciplined. We *were* disciplined, but that was also because of school. At school we were disciplined, some of us by the cane, so when we came out we learnt that discipline just continued.

I wouldn't say I hated Basics, but they broke you down psychologically and made you feel you were nothing. 'We will build you up like we want to. You are a troep. You're nothing!'

Your corporal and lieutenant were the law. They were the first guys who gave you the roots of what it was all about, along with all the swearing and breaking you down. I remember the lieutenant shouting at the guys who wore glasses, 'Ek sal 'n draadkar van jou bril maak, rofie, as jy weer so skeef vir my kyk!'

I also remember a *rofie* hitting a corporal who'd come up to him while he was standing in line waiting for food. The corporal had pointed his finger straight in the guy's face. 'Stand still! Stop talking!' Suddenly – *bam!* – we saw the corporal do a backflip. The guy floored him – *pow!* Lights out. He lay there, not moving, on the tarmac in front of the hangar.

The *roof* was only given an opfok. Luckily the sergeant major had seen the whole thing and reprimanded the corporal for lifting his hand like that. It was an insult to point one's finger at another's face, especially millimetres away from the guy's nose. He should've kept an open-palmed hand. He paid for it.

Just before we arrived in 6 SAI the mess burnt down, so, in one of the old hangars, they had a veldkombuis with chairs stacked around it. We stood in rows in front of the hangar before the doors were opened and the chefs let us in. You stood with your varkpan being loaded with kak food.

I got through passing as a Jew because I'd grown up with a whole bunch of Jewish guys in the northern suburbs of Jo'burg and been to their bar mitzvahs. On some Friday nights I'd have supper at Shabbos with them, so

I had a fair idea of how the Jewish system worked. The whole time during Basics nobody cottoned on that I wasn't Jewish.

One day I went up to the rabbi and said, 'Listen. You've got in your mess these Afrikaans guys who are Seventh Day Adventists alongside the Jewish kosher guys, and now you're discriminating against these boys because they share the same Sabbath day and speak Afrikaans? And you keep on talking about discrimination against us Jewish people? I'm not eating in your mess any more, and I'm not coming back until you fix your own house first!'

He chased after me and pleaded with me to come back. My argument made some of the guys suspect that perhaps I wasn't Jewish. They didn't really believe me. They checked, right in the very beginning, to see if I was circumcised by having a look during shower time. The whole Jewish experience was crazy. Every Jewish guy in the camp was G3. They were always clerks or in the kitchens.

I was the tallest guy in the unit, so I became the marker. I was fitter than all the others. I used to enjoy it. I could get to the tree and back before everyone else but, being the marker, the okes would expect me to get to the sergeant first, and they'd all line up behind me. I was always under pressure because of this. Being tall, I stuck out, and the sergeant cottoned on to the fact that this 'Jewish' guy wasn't like the others – instead, he was physically active and fit. He liked that. I was well liked until I got bust smoking dope. The police came into the camp, took us out and locked us in a civilian prison. Five of us stayed there for three days and then were released with no charges except a suspended sentence and a ninety-rand fine or ninety days. The rabbi bailed me out.

We were supposed to drill the rofies for one week in English and one week in Afrikaans. But I'm Afrikaans, like the army, so it was always in Afrikaans. 'Moenie vir my loer nie, jou fokken troep! Ek suig jou oog uit en spoeg hom uit sodat jy self kan sien hoe 'n groot poes jy is!'

There's nothing more colourful than the Afrikaans way of swearing. Nothing. I mean, you watch the movie *Jarhead*. They do a great rendition of a sergeant major giving a marine an uitkak, but it's not nearly as descriptive and direct as the way only an Afrikaans guy can do it. It's almost as if the corporals were intentionally and specifically given lessons. It was almost like a competition.

They kept attacking your senses the whole time. They took everything away from you. Sleep deprivation. Breaking you down. Then slowly, slowly – after months of telling you you're the lowest of the lowest forms on earth – they brought you back up again. Shouted and screamed at you in all those wonderful Afrikaans words that I'd never heard before. Then slowly, 'Aah. Julle's bakgat. Julle kom reg.' Suddenly you felt a little bit *trots*. They built you up until by the end of Basics you were standing there saluting the State President and anybody else they wanted you to. It was very clever. It was bloody well done.

I arrived at 1 SAI in Bloemfontein for Basics in January 1982. All our instructors had been involved in Ops Daisy as drivers, so they were already kind of bossies. We were to find out just how bossies they were during those couple of months … but I won't go there.

It wasn't long after the commencement of Basics when we were shown this Ratel that got shot out and about six guys killed. It was standing in the transport park at the time, and would later be painted silver and paraded at Army HQ in Pretoria. It wasn't a pretty sight. It looked nothing like the pristine fighting vehicles we would train on in the future. At first glance it didn't even look like a Ratel. It was a rusted, black, burnt-out shell of its former self. Signs of where the four RPG-7s and two rifle grenades penetrated could be seen. The glass and steel armour had melted, and the heat of the subsequent explosions inside had actually made it bubble. No details about what had happened were given.

The PFs and instructors used it as a tool to warn us that we would end up like this if we weren't sharp, awake and, above all, paraat. They made out that the crew had been a useless bunch of conscripts who hadn't listened and got what they deserved. From then on most of us realised that this was no game – this was real; this could really happen – and a real sense of fear came over us.

I was in 6 SAI from July '82. Kak chow. Blind bloody haircuts. Went into bungalow T69. There were also names of places on the Border, places the guys had already been. One I remember was Eenhana, which I didn't know at the time. Later, though, when I got up north, I found out exactly what Eenhana was all about.

We had to fill up a coal urn to get hot water. It was cold at five o'clock in the morning! Freezing cold! We weren't allowed to close the windows at night. Had to leave them wide open. Your bed was right there. You froze. Weren't allowed to close them no matter what.

You just knew when the corporal walked in that he was going to naai you even though everything looked shipshape. You just knew it was shit-off time. It's hard to describe – I'm not Wilbur Smith. Other times we had to put our backs against the wall and bend down on our haunches with our arms outstretched. 'Draai hom! Draai hom!' Had to roll our rifles while singing 'Die Stem'. Then the corporal would yell, 'Liter water! Liter water! Nou!' You'd force down a litre of water and carry on turning. You kotched your guts out after a while.

They'd dress you in an orange overall. Call you a 'space-mannetjie'. You'd run from sunup to sundown in that orange overall and, wherever you went, whatever rank could tune you whatever he wanted. 'Sak! Do this! Do that! Kiss my boots!' and you just did it. You had to do it. I remember the stormbaan. The wall, the swings, the barbed wire. 'As ek die fluitjie blaas is jy af! As ek hom weer blaas is jy op!' Never stopped.

I loved drill. Couldn't get enough. Wasn't stoned then. I was stoned when I wanted to be stoned. When it came to doing things properly I did it. Wasn't a *slapgat* arse like those G3s! Pugh! Bandages and Merchurochrome! We used to mock those okes: 'Bee-ba-bee-ba! Here come the sirens!' The bliksemde Ambulance Brigade was looked at as being useless. They were treated with contempt.

Guys laugh at you when you tell them you were in a G3 squad – Light Duties, Ligte Vrugtes, lam-siek-en-dooies, the LSDs, or whatever the hell they referred to us as. We paid for it in other ways. We were the excuse for the corporals to mess the others around, which of course didn't make us popular with the troops. Ultimately, though, they understood our position. The guys knew we didn't have to do opfoks or PT, but we got plenty of rondfoks. The Light Duty squad was quite big – about twenty of us. We tended to stick together, but I was treated as an equal by the guys within my bungalow.

A favourite trick of the corporals was to order the Light Duties not to run – not even jog. We were only allowed to walk. But naturally we could run if we had to – we weren't complete cripples or retards! The trouble arose whenever the unit had to *tree aan*. There was only about one minute in which to do so, and if a single person wasn't ready in time, then the whole unit was given an opfok or serious bawling. The corporals made sure the Light Duties were standing more than a minute away from the *aantree* area. One of them would have us standing to attention, and when the order came to fall in we walked at extremely high speed to make it on time. The sight of twenty or so troepies doing this was funny, and the corporals took glee in it. Occasionally, when we knew we wouldn't make it, we broke into a jog – which is exactly what they wanted. They'd scream and shout and go berserk. 'Haai! Moenie fokken hardloop nie, jou fokken vuil hondekak!' We wouldn't make it in time and the whole unit would get a rondfok because of us 'lazy, good-for-nothing Ligte Vrugtes'.

This happened in the first few weeks of Basics until it suddenly stopped. Either the corporals became bored with it or the lieutenants put an end to it.

We had a week's smoking ban, but you could have a ciggie if you *tree'd aan* for the 'smoker's squad'. It was another way the corporals planned to have their fun. We stood to attention, then were ordered to stand in the 'present arms' position – right foot perpendicular to and behind your left heel. The corporal would shout the orders. 'Haal uit sigarette!' We'd try to be as unified as possible, as there was no proper drill for this. 'Monde toe!' But this was given in military command, so it sounded like, 'Monduuurh … toe!' Put smokes to mouths.

'Pakkieeees … in!' Packets back in pockets.

'Ligtuuuh … uit!' Lighters out.

'Sigarettuuuh … lig!' Light our smokes.

'Ligtuuuh … in!' Lighters back in pockets.

'Trek in!' Inhale.

'Uit!' Exhale.

'In.' You'd inhale and wait for the exhale order that wouldn't come. After maybe ten seconds, it was: 'Uit!' On it went. This all happened according to the speed of the corporal. You had to inhale and exhale at his whim, so your head started to spin, you felt dizzy and you began to think it wasn't such a good idea to have a smoke. It was like hyperventilating or holding your breath. If you didn't comply, the other corporals would kak you out, 'Jaai! Keep in time, keep in time!' Then we'd have to put our stompies in our pockets and bin them later.

Talk about childish pranks. The corporals loved it and, essentially, it was an unwinding time for everybody. The smokers got their smoke, the non-smokers got a laugh and it felt good to get your fix without being bust by lurking corporals – which would give them yet another excuse for a rondfok.

I klaared in at Infantry School in Oudtshoorn, but never got rank. I fell off JLs. Vasbyt, the route marches and all, was the beginning of the end. I asked for a transfer to Cape Town. It was denied. I couldn't focus on JLs much. My mom was going through a bad time. She was based at 2 Mil Hospital and in the Medics at the time. I wanted to be closer to home to look after her. I put in two verklarings which were totally denied. They said they were short of guys. My thanks for asking for a transfer was deployment to Grahamstown, even further away from home, and only two months into Basics. They transferred me and this other guy to 6 SAI. After Oudtshoorn, Grahamstown was a real eye-opener. All the downbeats were there, the guys who left school in Standard 8, kind of thing. There we came all paraat, brushing our boots with our tandeborsels. 'What the hell are you guys doing?' they laughed.

'We're from Infantry School. This is how it's done.' And everyone used to come around, check us out and just *lag*.

Our sa'majoor called me and my friend a pair of rejects to have left Infantry School. My friend had broken his leg during vasbyt so was automatically off JLs. One day my friend told him we were not rejects and to stop treating us as such. The sa'majoor later came over and apologised, in his state of being sober – which wasn't most of the time – and we were accepted after that.

I was often looked up to because I came from Infantry School and was older than the others, at twenty-two. These kids had either left in Standard 7 or Standard 8, or had just finished matric. The corporal in my group was a matriculant. They'd just finished Section Leading when I arrived. You had to listen to a kid giving commands, but there was some form of respect between the younger and the older guys.

Some nights we'd have competitions between the different bungalows as to which squad could strip their R4s the quickest. We'd pull our trommels away from the foot of the bed, sit on them alongside it and place the rifle on the bed. The corporal stood at the door, stopwatch in hand, switched off the lights and timed us. The bungalow fell into complete darkness. Then you fumbled around trying to disassemble the entire rifle. Firing-pin, barrel, spring, grips and so on. As soon as you were done you'd shout out a consecutive number, beginning from one and ending at thirteen, as there were only thirteen of us in the bungalow. At the shout of thirteen the corporal would stop the clock, turn on the lights and walk around inspecting the weapons. The next thing was to reassemble the rifle in the dark. We did this over and over again until we couldn't do it any quicker.

I wish I could remember the record, but, out of about twenty-five bungalows, we came second. Our corporal shouted and performed. He'd get so irritated because he wanted the record.

The blood-donor people came round needing blood. My girlfriend used to donate as often as she could, so I decided if I did it there'd be an invisible connection between us. Figured I could phone her later and say how proud I was. It would've been my first time. 'I'm tough. I'm in the army. This'll be a cinch.' The truth was we were heavily obliged by our sa'majoor to give blood.

I walked into the hall, took off my jersey and had tea and biscuits while waiting. When my turn came, the nurse asked me, very sweetly, 'Het jy al ooit bloed geskenk?' She had lovely lips.

'Nee, ek het nie, but my girlfriend does it often.' Beautiful eyes.

'Moenie bekommerd wees nie. Dit sal all right wees,' she assured me. I turned my head away – I couldn't stand needles. She stuck it in and I waited for the little bag to fill up. 'Hoe voel jy?'

'I'm fine,' I lied. I felt like puking up the tea and biscuits. Eventually it was over. She pulled out the needle and asked, 'Is jy reg om te gaan?' They needed the stretcher.

'Ja, I'm okay, thank you, Sister.' My head felt like it was floating and, as I stood up, I got this kick-ass head rush. I focused really hard to get to the exit, pretending that there was nothing wrong. I didn't want to make an arse of myself in front of all the guys. I tried to put on my jersey but couldn't. My arm went through the head-hole, my head was covered in stretched wool, my other arm went inside-out through the sleeve and I staggered away totally disorientated. I must've appeared to be drunk.

Someone helped me lie down on the floor, took off my boots and made me put my feet up on a chair. Everybody stared. So much for not making a doos out of myself. That was the first and last time I've given blood.

I didn't really enjoy Basics. I just endured it as best I could and didn't let it get to me. Did what I had to do without slacking off. I didn't want to get noticed, although it was hard not to. I'd just finished four years at art college and loathed any form of authority, even during high school. So I was like, 'What the hell is this all about?' I was an English-speaking artist with attitude. The corporals soon singled me out, like a pack of hyenas, quick-quick! They disliked me. 'Hierdie fokken soutie wat hom so slim hou.'

While screaming at you, as you're busy standing to attention, you were supposed to look over or under the corporal's eye-line. You weren't allowed to look into their eyes. I made that mistake, once, but a serious uitkak from my little kasern-korporaal made sure I never did it again. He was so short, the top of his beret was level with my chin. Although small, he had a rasping voice, and barked at me like a junkyard puppy dog until his voice went hoarse. All I remember was 'Hondkak!' and 'Ek sal jou piel uit jou pens ruk!' type of things. I went into a daze. Didn't understand the jibes and taunts because it was in this basic, gutter-talk, high-school Afrikaans slang. All his fellow instructors were lined up behind him, smirking and nodding their gleeful approval of their tiny companion doing so well – such a fine job – breaking down the *rofie*'s spirit.

I can't blame them. It was their job. It's what they'd been taught to do – to break down individuals like me – so I let them think they had succeeded. To survive in there you had to. You went into self-preservation mode. But I did one or two other minor things that pissed them off. I was one of the hard nuts to crack. They kept a close eye on me for the next few weeks, glaring at me with contempt for having *dared* look at one of them in the eye. Always with their corny, derogatory remarks. Real bully-boy types. Planks.

I knew that they weren't finished with me. I had become a personal issue to them. That time came right at the end of Basics. I was to get my own personal opfok by all the corporals and the sergeant in unison.

We did stupid things. 'Sien jy daardie boom?' All the new guys would say, 'Ja, Korporaal!'

'Well, why're you still standing here? Disappear!' They'd all wikkel off, run to the tree and run back.

'No! Not that one. The one on the horizon!' They'd run to it, run back, and they'd be panting and sweating.

'No. Not that one. THAT ONE!' So they'd run off and come back, and you'd say, 'No. Sorry. You went around the wrong way.' And off they'd go again. *Rondfok*. *Opfok* was just PT. *Rondfok* was just buggering the guys around. Two different things.

For inspection we'd stand clothes pegs under the mattress to level it out. The springs were so *pap* that they were shaped like a hammock, and the beds were trashed because they were so old and well used. Everyone was still expected to make a perfectly level, smooth bed. All National Servicemen did the clothes-peg trick out of sheer necessity, I'm sure, the mattresses always precariously balanced as a result of skilled dexterity.

We also put cardboard in our vests, T-shirts and shorts and stretched them tightly over it to make them look *lekker ordentlik*. You know how you find the same thing in clothing outlets? Well, ours were far better. We'd make any packaging look lousy in comparison. They were so straight you could set a spirit-level with them. Of course the corporals knew – they knew all the tricks – but I think they appreciated the effort. I believe that's what they were looking for. As long as everything was absolutely perfect, even if it was a form of gypping, they didn't freak out. It didn't faze them or get their piss in a froth. They just wanted to see the effort. If they didn't allow for peg support then I believe every troepie in the entire history of the SADF would never have passed a single inspection!

Our pillowcases had to be ironed into neat little criss-cross patterns. We couldn't gyppo by taking them off and not sleeping on them at night because our corporal would occasionally do surprise visits late in the evenings while we slept. If anybody was bust not sleeping with his head on the pillowcase we all got *kla'ed aan*. The only way to get around it was to turn the pillow over, which wasn't ideal, but which helped. The pattern would have to be reironed, but at least part of it was still there. If the surprise came you quickly turned the pillow over – if you woke up in time. I had a huge advantage by sleeping at the furthest end of the bungalow. I always had time to get away with it.

This particular corporal used to drive the Samil 50 around like a real childish wanker. We'd be crammed inside. It was totally overloaded. Guys would be standing nose to nose and bum to bum. If you were seated it was fine, but those left standing had nothing to grab onto when we shot around the corners or when the vehicle stopped. I'm surprised the canvas sail didn't burst open with the combined weight.

Once, we were coming back from church. The corporal was really hammering it. We were being knocked around and banged into each other. He braked, accelerated, braked, and so on. We heard him and the other corporal *lagging* away in the front. We shouted and complained, but nothing stopped him. Instead, the laughing got louder. I freaked out and shouted, 'STOP IT! For FUCK's sake!'

The Samil came to an abrupt halt, brakes squealing. The corporal, who had a bumfluff moustache, came around and screamed, 'WIE'T MY GEVLOEK?' His face was red. He was absolutely livid. Being English I didn't know what 'vloek' meant, so I didn't say anything. I assumed he was asking who'd sworn, but didn't want to take the rap for something I may not have done. Everyone kept silent. I noticed a few eyes looking at mine. He glared at everyone and, realising he wasn't going to get anybody to own up, called us all a bunch of 'hondekak!'

He pulled off with such force that some guys at the back almost fell out. The ride back was double as rough but we endured it well. Thankfully nobody split on me. Troepies: one. Corporals: nil.

The sergeant major was giving lectures in military law and etiquette – things about what we should or shouldn't do and could or couldn't do. It was so technical and boring. The purpose was to listen and take notes.

We'd have these talks in the hall after marching drills. The problem was we were so tired. The days were long. Getting up early, combined with mental and physical exertion and late nights, tended to numb the brain. You just wanted to fall asleep then and there. The sa'majoor droned on and on. My eyes would begin to close. They'd roll around in their sockets and lose focus. Everything blurred. I'd stare straight ahead and start to squint.

The guy's head in front of me would double up. I'd force my eyelids open. It was a constant, daily battle listening to this and trying our best to keep awake. Sometimes we'd have to nudge the guy sitting next to us back to reality.

The one time a troep had passed out and nobody had bothered to bump him awake. His chin was on his chest and he was snoring. The sa'majoor stopped his talk, called one of the corporals over and told him to get a bucket of water. The sa'majoor took it, walked down the row in between us, and poured the entire bucket over this troep. He woke with a jump and was bewildered for a few seconds. He was drenched. The sight made some guys hose themselves with laughter.

During these lectures I never paid attention. I daydreamt instead, and drew doodles on the back of the notes. I never concentrated at all on what was happening. I'd already decided I didn't want to become a lieutenant, and especially not a corporal, so what was the point? Was this school or the army? I didn't apply myself to the theory at all. I just wanted to stay an ordinary troepie.

I tried getting out of Basics before it even started getting too hectic. I didn't dig it. I knew I had to pull a move, so I said I was gay. I tuned them, 'Nooit, I'm homosexual. I've got to get out of here.' I did stupid things. I stood shaking while a female captain asked innocent questions about some ordinary, arbitrary stuff. I stared into the distance like I was totally freaked out.

They didn't buy any of it. Instead, I ended up with one of the worst corporals on the base. Korporaal D. His nickname was Satan. Korporaal 'Two-plus-three', in his little Beetle in Upington. He was probably going to be a corporal for the rest of his life, never to get any higher. Maybe he's still there. This oke was a bastard to the end. This was a prick amongst pricks. He was seen as a prick *by* pricks. King Prick.

He caught me lekker in an inspection. Right through Basics I'd been crooking him with my shorts. I already had my little inspection set up in my kas. Shirts, shorts, socks and all that. I'd taken a black civvy shirt and folded it up to look like shorts so that I'd never have to iron them. I stacked the real shorts up in the roof. I tucked a lot of stuff in the roof. This meant that my inspections were always ready. I had my spares, or back-ups, which looked how they were supposed to look. The shorts passed every inspection until the last one. Maybe he knew. Maybe he'd been playing the game all along. He pulled it out. Bust. Made all the other guys hold shell cartridges with straight arms. He said everyone could thank their friend over here, 'Vetseun Engelsman.' That was my pet name.

Right at the very end this oke became our china. Who would've thought? It's so predictable it's not even ironic – the guy you know you hate the most ends up being your buddy. In the end, when we got our two beers, he organised more for us, telling us all these funny stories. We were his best chinas all of a sudden, right at the end, after he'd buggered us up for months. Push-ups for letters and all that nonsense. I think he feared he'd get his head kicked in. He couldn't do anything to us any more. He couldn't punish us any further. We'd seen it all.

I was at a stage in life when I was tired of this. Seven years in boarding school. Getting messed around by the welfare places. Could never settle down. Always getting shunted around from one house to the next or one school to the next. I was just tired of it.

I went in from July 1982 during the winter, to Saldanha, which wasn't pleasant. Up at four thirty in the morning in the freezing cold and rain. Then we had to polish the decks, as they called them, which was actually the bungalow floor. The navy had this most perverse thing that even on land you had to call windows 'portholes', and crazy things like that. They'd get really upset if you didn't play along with those silly words. Then they'd come in for inspection. If there were any grains of dirt there'd be big trouble – shouting and screaming. Also, our one weekend leave was cancelled, which was pretty harsh. We'd been looking forward to it and they took it away in a second. I didn't enjoy that.

There were thirty of us in the bungalow. Eighteen were English. Our leading seaman – that's our corporal – was Afrikaans. He often gave commands using the wrong words, but we basically understood the gist of things. When he said things like 'The ship will drown' we knew he actually meant 'The ship will sink'. Because there were more English guys than Afrikaners he decided to hand out our written instructions in English, which I thought was pretty good of him.

I suppose wherever you went for Basics wasn't exactly pleasant, but I think we were better off in the navy than in the other forces.

I was supposed to go to Infantry but postponed my call-ups because I studied at college first. I went into Maintenance and ended up as a driver. My brother was a driver, as well, and was in three years before me.

In 1985 I did Basics at Kimberley, 1 Maintenance Unit. For me, Basics was difficult. They loved their punishment PT. Anything wrong and it was punishment PT. Running up and down hills, obstacle courses and crap. The corporals were full of nonsense. Out-pack inspections were a drag. Basics was tough but I used to try and keep a positive attitude about things. That's probably what got me through. I knew it would end, and I focused on that. There were one or two who cracked. A few guys AWOLed. Usual stuff.

The food? Fried eggs are supposed to have yellow yolks, right? Ours were blue. I don't know where the blue came from. From the pans? Reheating? Standing too long? Blue Peter? The whole egg was a grey, tasteless 'thing' and almost glowed.

The base was very quiet. It was Wednesday-afternoon sports day where most guys, even corporals, had sports pass. I made myself scarce. The remaining corporals were always on the prowl and ready to pounce. They'd always find some menial tasks for you to do if they saw you doing nothing. We knew they searched the empty bungalows for anyone hiding there, but occasionally we took the chance. I was tired and exhausted and needed to rest. But I couldn't sommer take a lekker dos on my bed. I snuck into my empty bungalow, slid on my belly along the floor – which was easy when it shone like a mirror – to keep out of sight from the windows, hid under my bed and passed out, but I was alert to danger. After a while I returned to my senses when I heard the door fly open and heavy footsteps slowly pacing down the aisle. I skrikked! Then a corporal's voice said, 'Is iemand hier?'

I skiemed, 'Bust! Here it comes.' I froze and kept kop. I didn't stand up but chanced it instead, because I'd get into trouble either way. There wouldn't be any lenience just because I'd given myself up, so I kept quiet. He got closer, but, as things go, he suddenly turned and left without coming all the way down. I knew I'd tested my luck and decided to leave as quickly as possible. It was a gut feeling. I waited a while, slid back along the floor to the door, got up, held my breath, opened the door and stepped outside. I walked away from my bungalow at double speed. I found out later that other guys had been bust and got a major *kla'ing aan*.

When we walked in to give inspection the kasernleier – the Bungalow Bill – would shout the attention. They would all stand for inspection. I'd walk slowly down the aisle. There was this fat oke from Springs who everybody knew was a lazy slob. I'd walk past him. He would think he'd passed. Then I'd slowly walk all the way back and stop at him. 'Maak oop jou trommel.' All I checked was just crap stuffed inside. Then it was 'Lêhouding af!' That was a favourite one. He had to stand to attention and fall flat on his face.

'Staan op! Doen dit weer!'

Do that a few times and see how sore you become. It kills you. The next morning the guy would have bruises all over his face. It was so funny. Our corporals did it to us and we returned the favour to the new intake. It worked like this: one oke failed inspection and everybody afkakked, not just the one guy. Then of course they'd bliksem him afterwards.

Para PT drills?! Every morning at inspection there was something wrong. It could then be a serious opfok or a general opfok, but there was always an opfok until you'd completed the task; until you'd reached the limit and simply couldn't go any further. You simply couldn't. Then a little bit of recovery time. And then they'd push you a little more. And then again. You walked around broken and could hardly move, you were so stiff, but it was to a humane level. In other words, you'd been pushed to the limit, but to a limit that you didn't even know existed. Your body is phenomenal in what it can do.

It was usually straight after lunch, when we'd eaten a lot of food, that we'd have some sort of opfok. We were called to the pakhuis where the parachutes were packed. The pakhuis ladies did that. It was a big building with a perimeter of about 400 metres. It was also about 200 metres uphill to get there. This particular PT was called the 'Pakhuis Blues'. We had to run around the building in ninety seconds. It was only when we'd all made it that they'd back off. Most made it the first time, but there were always a few who didn't. Only when everyone had stopped screaming at each other to get in on time, and had helped the stragglers instead, did the ninety-second system get resolved – usually after many times of circling the perimeter.

Hell, it was torture in the hot sun with a full belly! When we proved we could do it and bring in the last guys without half killing each other, the sergeant major's statement would be, 'Jy sien. Jy kan hom maak. En omdat jy dit aan my bewys het, kan jy dit weer doen.' So we did – until we'd got the message, which was that we had to work together as a single unit. And it didn't matter who we were, whether Afrikaans or English, from the Northern Transvaal or Natal, if we didn't work together as a unit and didn't resolve our issues quickly, we weren't going to make it into the Parabats. It was a very important lesson.

Once, during marching exercises, one of the corporals did a surprise in-spection of our boshoeds. Mine was sweat-stained on the inner forehead, which caused him to lose all self-control. He screamed some high-pitched 'hondkak' insults, nose to nose, and threw my boshoed on the ground, grinding it and stamping it under his boots. When he'd finished trampling the hat, he picked it up, jammed it over my head and slowly said, while puffing, 'Roof, *nou* moet jy hierdie ding was.'

He was absolutely right. At Voortrekkerhoogte the sand is red and fine, like talcum powder. I soaked and scrubbed that boshoed for half the day.

Another thing about our boshoeds was that we had to have V-shaped lines ironed into the front. Our corporals skiemed it checked cool, or maybe it was a Tiffie tradition, but it wasn't easy to iron in this tramline as the hat was made from thick cloth. I nibbled the lines in with my front teeth and added a bit of spit. Pinched it really hard to reinforce the lines. Some of the guys followed my example.

As *rofies* we polished our boots until they shone like mirrors. Every oke who hasn't been in the army or paramilitary can't believe boots can shine like that. Let's just say it took lots of polish, lots of time, lots of patience, lots of sun and lots of elbow grease. The girlfriend's old pair of stockings worked like magic. Time well spent every night, especially on a Sunday, the day off.

The fashion was to also have faded web belts. The corporals at TSC followed the trend that it looked lekker smart to do this to a brand new belt. They didn't want a new look. It had to appear old. We scrubbed these hard canvas belts for hours using washing powder and nailbrushes. Made them look sun-bleached.

I could take a lot of crap and do it laughing. There wasn't much in Basics I couldn't take. When they found an excuse to give you an opfok, it wasn't something degrading. The corporal and lieutenant were simply finding a legitimate excuse to make you tougher. That was their job, to make you tough to withstand a war situation. *Your* objective was to jump out of an aircraft and ultimately get your jump wings, but *their* objective was to turn you into a soldier and a survivor, not necessarily to train you to kill people.

By giving you an opfok they were doing two things. Firstly, they were turning you into a hard and tough soldier. If you were hard and tough and were going to go for it, they'd give you your wings. Secondly, the tougher, stronger and fitter you were, the more able you'd be to withstand the final

PT course. So any kind of an opfok was a little bit of a blessing – it could only make you stronger. It wasn't there to victimise or humiliate you. It was there to protect you, to turn you into a soldier, so that when the real shit hit the fan, you were tough enough to make it onto the other side. We had this drilled into us.

We had a Recce on the jump course. He was probably one of the sanest and most compassionate people there. He'd qualified the Recce course, which naturally meant that he didn't need to do our PT course. He just went directly on to jump training. All I will say about him is when you were right, you were right, and when you were wrong, you were on the other side of hell.

Went in from 1987 to the Medical Services at Klipdrift, Potchefstroom. I was twenty-eight years old already, because of studying medicine for the last ten years. I was treated well. Can't complain about it; it was fine. The colonel of Klipdrift also treated me well. I was quite a handyman. He sent a military vehicle over to fetch me. Gave me coffee. I got treated better than most of the officers. However, out of my whole platoon of thirty guys, twenty-eight of us were high-ranking provincial sportsmen. My corporal and lieutenant respected that.

Within the first six weeks I was allowed to drive out of the base in my own car, wearing civvies, for private training. Could leave at three o'clock every day and be back by seven in the evening. I was still participating as a provincial athlete and was therefore allowed to travel around the country accordingly. Gelukkig, but I worked hard for it.

Because there was an air force base near Voortrekkerhoogte, we used to watch the jets fly around. The Cheetahs took off in spectacular fashion once or twice a week. I think it was on Wednesday and Friday mornings at about 8 a.m. We'd be doing whatever it was we were doing, but, once we heard the thunder of the first aircraft, everyone would stop and gawk upwards, even if we were being drilled. The corporals also enjoyed the show.

They were beautiful aircraft to watch. About six would take off, shooting almost vertically into the sky, and follow one after the other. As they climbed, their afterburners would be fully engaged. They slipped through the air with a deafening, thunderous roar. It tickled your eardrums and shook the ground. They climbed straight up like missiles – shrinking to a speck in the sky within seconds – looped over, levelled out and disappeared. We'd stare up until they vanished. Then silence. It was a great spectacle to witness. Our own private air display, and free of charge. I'm sure civilians rarely, if ever, get to see that. Sure, at air shows they do, but not with as many aircraft all taking off within rapid succession, and not twice a week for three months.

Once, while on parade, there was a massive explosion. A cook had left a bush kitchen out in the sun without covering the gas tank with the flaps. The bottle was empty and, when he lit it, it blew. He was from the previous intake. He knew the drill to put the cover over it, which he didn't do.

The story was that his head got in the way. The bottle removed a piece of it and he died. That was the rumour, anyway. I never saw the head flying. I never saw the body. No evidence. But I felt the explosion. I heard it. It was the accepted thing that he lost his head. Who knows?

I went in straight after school, from January '89, to Upington 8 SAI. The first thing that annoyed me was the cutting of my hair. I'd never had such short hair. That was a big shock. We went in looking like individuals. When we came out of that machine we all looked the same.

From day one my mind was made up that I just didn't belong there or want to be there, so I made sure to let them know. They singled me out very quickly. I was a cheeky bastard, but nobody told me I had to submit. Nobody taught me that part.

On the second day I called somebody 'sir'. I hadn't been to cadets and was unaware of rank. He said, 'Do I look like a "sir" to you?'

'Sorry ma'am,' I replied. 'In that brown uniform it's very difficult to tell.'

He hit my shoulder with his rifle in such a way that I ultimately had to have an operation on it months later. He cracked the left collarbone and crushed the top rib – all for calling him a woman!

So I ended up in the LSD squad. I became a G3K4 thanks to the corporal. My left arm wasn't the same any more. The corporal was never reprimanded, let alone charged. They left him alone because I'd been insubordinate. Being stuck in the Light Duty squad was when all the trouble arose. The G1s could be kept busy, but the G3s are basically redundant to the army, so they just used us wherever they could. It was the perfect opportunity to screw up the system. You could think laterally as a G3. Nobody could really do anything to you after a while. You just flashed your card. The downside was that they attacked your humanity and sexuality. They called you a moffie, gay, faggot and queer, amongst other things, they pushed and kicked you around, and they told the other guys not to mingle with you.

A group of us became the 'trouble squad'. We refused to stand inspection. When we did, the standard wasn't high – our boots weren't well polished, we weren't cleanly shaven, our discipline wasn't good and we couldn't march. I was the only Afrikaner in that group. It was a big group and most were undereducated – not that I looked down on them. I spent a lot of time gyppoing. I became a master at gyppo. I was always the one telling my friends how to do it. The corporals resented me even more because I was Afrikaans and gyppoing. I should've got a medal for gyppoing but they didn't hand those out.

We ended up getting EDs – a lot of them. When we screwed up they gave us kitchen duty. Peeled potatoes. When that was finished we had to peel the onions, and when that was finished we'd peel more potatoes. Then we'd have to stand guard. It angered me how the kitchen staff, who were predominantly homosexual, got discriminated against and called names. The general verbal abuse they had to go through because of their sexual preference was utterly base. 'Die army's nie 'n plek vir moffies nie.'

Then at the end of Basics they transferred all the G3s out to Lohatlha in the Northern Cape. 'You're getting the hell out of 8 SAI! You're an embarrassment to this unit! We're a fighting, killing unit! We don't want you here!' But they never managed to break us during Basics.

As Light Duties we marched around during drill with the G1s but stopped after half an hour while they continued for another hour. Then we stood to attention. Every twenty minutes we could stand at ease for a while before being brought back to attention. Sure, we weren't drilling, but at least the G1s could move about.

Occasionally a corporal left his squadron and meandered over. We knew what to expect – a lecture on the sins of G3 – how lazy and utterly useless we were: 'Julle's almal hondekak!' Sad, sorry little tales of things like, while the manne were drilling like real soldiers, we *luigatte* were doing nothing by standing there under the sun. Always told in a sarcastic, patronising and sneering way.

The LSDs were put to use in other ways that the G1s didn't envy. We ultimately became qualified painters, bricklayers, renovators, sweepers and hygienic-services all in one. We henpecked various gravel parade grounds for stones and pebbles – thousands and thousands of them – and put them into plastic shopping-bags. The grounds were big, the size of rugby fields. I'm sure all the stones were spread out again for the next G3 squad from another unit to henpeck.

Other times we painted walls, fences and gates or made brick pathways shaped in wave-like curves. We'd dig the soil and lay the bricks. We also did a lot of sweeping. Swept the halls, the mess, the tarmac around the base, the canteen, the dirt paths – wherever a person could sweep, even if it didn't need a sweep at all.

The least favourite job was cleaning out the bogs. We often had kak-huisdiens. Scrubbed the basins, polished the mirrors, shined the taps, mopped the floors, and washed away the skid-marks and piss. All this with nailbrushes and rags. 'Alles lekker skoon, luigatte!'

'Ja, Korporaal!' Whatever, Korporaal.

It was asked who could draw. The Technical Services Corps needed an illustration of a buffalo, a symbol of strength, drawn onto a portable black-board for sports days and inter-unit events. I said I could do it. The corporals had never come across a real, living artist before and were completely amazed at the final result. They thought it was brilliant, especially the sergeant major. This blackboard was carried from place to place to be displayed, for any reason or excuse, to show off to the other units. It became something of a trophy to the corporals and the sa'majoor, and they were extremely proud of it. I couldn't understand what all the fuss was about. It was just a simple chalk sketch. It was a true likeness but, for me, as a trained artist, a mundane one. However, they revered it, along with the rest of the tiffies. If it was even slightly smudged I was summoned to return it to its former state. Only they and I were allowed to come near the board, and it was closely guarded. The other units couldn't wait to capture and deface it.

Maybe somewhere, long forgotten in the Tiffies base in Voortrekker-hoogte, lying under an old tarpaulin and tucked away behind a rusting kas, is a very smudged sketch of a fierce-eyed buffalo.

As soon as the corporals found out I could draw they cut me some slack, but only when their own needs were involved. They discovered I could do caricatures. My kasern-korporaal had seen the ones I did of the okes in my bungalow. Now *he* wanted one, so of course I obliged. He wanted to send it to his stukkie. He gave me this tiny little photo of him-self for me to use. He showed the drawing to the other corporals and they hooted with laughter.

Then they all wanted one to send to their noointjies at home, I guess to charm their *poppies* with their caricature of their funny, brave bokkie in *die mag*. Now I was their buddy. Now they eased off from giving me a hard time. Now they laughed and joked with me. I knew their game – it was so blatantly obvious – so I played along with them, but the last thing I felt like doing was drawing them in an amusing way. I really didn't find them funny. Why should I give them the satisfaction?

In the last few weeks of Basics I dragged and delayed my assurances about drawing them. I drew only one more, and it was for a corporal I actually respected. Bush phase came, which delayed it again. Then, before we knew it, Basics was over and I split VTH, along with those hondekak. Never saw them again.

As we're on the subject of corporal-bashing, I often used to think of slashing the tyres on their Baja Bug skedonkmobiles late at night, which they parked on base, but I never did. Spitefulness is a waste of time.

As corporals we'd get together and discuss how we were going to do things. But some were idiots. One made his rofie shave with a stone until he bled. 'Kry 'n klip. Skeer!' That's stupidity. Sheer stupidity. It didn't serve any purpose.

Occasionally we'd take turns to march the platoon around while the corporal followed behind. When I took command I'd shout, 'Platoon! Forward, march!' Then, instead of 'links, regs, links', I'd say 'licks, arse, licks'! I was ripping off the corporals, who each had their own unique calls. Some would go 'Oep! Oep! Oep-ah, oep!' As long as the guttural pronunciations were placed at the correct time and in the right rhythm, all was understood and you could call whatever you pleased. I ragged the corporals, who I felt always sucked up to the senior ranks. They never caught on to what I was doing and the English guys would have a laugh. The Dutchmen didn't get it. As soon as we approached any higher NCOs or officers I'd change my calls to the standard 'links, regs, links'.

It was in the army that I first saw radically different views to my own. There was this young, right-wing Afrikaans guy built like a brick shithouse. The oke was like an animal. You could comb the hair out of his body and make rope from it. Flat-footed, outback plaasjapie who hated blacks. He said he'd give me an example of why he hated them.

On his dad's farm they had built a compound for all the black farm workers. Everybody was supplied with electricity, a room, a showering area and ablution facilities. He said he didn't understand why they knocked down the walls and made fires on the floor of the rooms. They ultimately destroyed the compound, but he had his explanation for it: they were kaffirs.

Basics wasn't just about the running around, the jaagings and the standing inspections. It wasn't only physical. There was a lot of theory to be learnt, as well. I personally never took that side of it seriously, though.

There were also a lot of 'sign on the dotted line' forms to be filled in.

When you did so you became the property of the SADF and, subsequently, the property of the government. The government was the National Party – they ruled the SADF – and the NP *was* apartheid. But you had to sign forms stating you wouldn't participate in any political activity while in uniform, sign forms acknowledging security and military law, sign forms for this and sign forms for that. You just signed anything they handed to you. You basically signed your soul away without really understanding why, and you simply didn't give a damn, really. You did what you were told to, and that was that. You filled them in and hoped for the best, just to get through the system, but when they had your personal details on file there was no escape.

You had to fill in a lengthy questionnaire about who you were, what you were, where you'd been, where you came from, what your interests were, what your family background was, where you'd lived, and so on. They got to know everything about you. Even asked about your drug or alcohol habits. I didn't have the slightest ambition to become a corporal or an officer, so I told the truth about my drug habits during varsity.

By the time I arrived in Basics I wasn't really smoking zol or using acid any more. By then I enjoyed dopping, so the two beers they gave us per day in bush phase tasted exceptionally good. My friends didn't want theirs – very Dutch Reformed, you see – and gave them to me. A few of those every night when you're dry and fit tended to have the right effect. Couldn't wait for our first pass so I could sommer get vrot!

Food in the Bats: from day one that was our big privilege. We got good food – really good food – and a lot of it. All your food groups. Everything. It wasn't slop. It was the one timeout, the one sanctuary you could have in the Bats, eating a good meal. It was the one time they all backed off. For an hour no one gave you trouble. All you had to do was eat, and as much as you wanted. Rank-holders had plates and we had our varkpanne. We got fed well – steaks, pork chops, veggies, potatoes, lots of gravy, loads of rice, canned fruit, fresh fruit and lots of pudding. If you needed to fill up it was always tons of bread with lots of jam. You came out of the mess hall well fed. However, straight after lunch was an opfok and you threw it all up.

On our base at Tiffies there were some PF wives who helped us and themselves by selling delicious, home-made vetkoeks. Big, oily, doughy mince, pea and carrot vetkoeks. The food was so kak on base that these were such a kiff treat. The problem was that the wives never made enough, so it was always a mad scramble to get in line. The corporals would usually buy two or three at a time, as they had first dibs. The line became almost violent. There was little order. The corporals kept some sort of control, but they hardly exerted themselves. I think they enjoyed seeing us squabbling and salivating at the same time.

We were going on an inter-unit sports day at one of the other bases, so we went to get our packed lunches. Each consisted of a banana, an apple and an orange. On a zinc table was a mountain of these packs. I stood there, gawking at this sight, but I was also checking to see if there were any that weren't vrot. A staff stood next to them making sure we took only one pack each. He said to me, rather pissed off, 'Vat hom net, troep. Hulle's almal diesel'de, jong!' He was right. They *were* all the same. The bananas were black, the tiny apples had cuts and bruises in them and the oranges were so shrivelled and hard you could use them as cricket balls. Pigs would be given better fruit. But it was still food, I suppose. There were no sandwiches because boerie rolls and burgers would be on sale at the other base. We took the packs, anyway. Who were we to complain?

For mealtimes we'd all *tree aan* beforehand then fall out and form a queue. First come, first served. There was a random choosing by the corporals as to who would skep op. It was usually about six guys. A couple for meat, a couple for veggies, one for gravy and one for pudding. Nobody ever wanted to be an opskepper – it was a double blow. Firstly, you ate after everyone else – if there was any left – so you dished up in such a way to at least keep some aside. But the corporals knew that and made sure you dished up evenly. Secondly, by eating last, you'd have to eat fast. We'd have to *tree aan* by a certain time after meals. There'd also be a queue to clean up. It wasn't lekker fresh hot soapy water. At first it was, so the quicker you were finished your meal and in line, the better, because then it was easy to get your stuff clean. After dozens and dozens of guys cleaning their stuff in this water, it became a thick, slimy, stinking, cold brown soup. You could see all the colours of the rainbow on the water's oily surface. There was no time to refill the tub with fresh water.

We made sure our varkpanne and pikstelle shone like mirrors. The powers that be were totally paranoid about food poisoning. There couldn't be so much as a pinhead-sized mark on your utensils. If there was they'd make a huge thing of it. *Kla'ed* you *aan*, screamed in your face about what a dirty, filthy *vuilgat* you were. So you made sure they were clean. Simple.

Once, during a meal, I checked out my buddy's cauliflower piled high on his plate. I had given him mine because I couldn't stand the stuff, and he really enjoyed it. I was looking at it and feeling glad that I wasn't eating that slop. Then I saw something move. I looked closer. I was face to face with it while my china was tucking in. I saw tiny worms crawling around. They must've been hidden deep inside the cauliflower. 'Nooit! Check your cauliflower!' I said.

The oke went white. All the guys at the table had the same thing. Other tables, too. That night the *koks* had hell to pay from the RSM, who basically 'owned' the base. He, unofficially, was the highest authority there, like most RSMs.

Another time my fussiness saved me was when it was mutton ribs for dinner. Remember, this wasn't restaurant quality. I had never had this meal before, so I thought, 'Well, here I am, let's give it a try.' I didn't want to look bad, so I let the opskepper splat it onto my varkpan. It was grey, slimy, and smelt bad, but I had a taste, as the others seemed to be enjoying it. I didn't, so I gave it to my cauliflower buddy, Eddie. He also enjoyed his mutton – or maybe he just wasn't fussy – and devoured it.

The following day the whole base had gippo guts – all but a few out of hundreds. There were serious blowouts. The toilets were always occupied and the base stank. Okes were allowed to excuse themselves during drill, theory lessons, *tree aans*, or whatever, no questions asked. They would literally be unbuttoning their overalls while running to the shithouse, web belt in hand. It was comical. This lasted for about two days, in which time we G3s were kept very, very busy. Kakhuisdiens.

In '89 I went to Parabats, but halfway through Basics. Before that I was in the Infantry in Walvis Bay, *trapping* through the flippin' desert. I'd had enough of the desert. I thought, 'Nooit, I can't take this.' Then, funnily enough, a Samil pulled up. Parabats got out and told us they were looking for more volunteers. They didn't say why, but, as it later transpired, it was to look after the border area in the Northern Transvaal. I was the first oke to jump in.

When we arrived back at the base they asked us the weirdest questions I've ever been asked. Two funny questions I remember were 'Do you have an older brother?' and 'Do you have tattoos?' I think the first was to make sure that, if you died, there was someone to support the family, or something like that. If you didn't have an older brother or had a tattoo, then forget it, you weren't going. That was it. I don't know why. I didn't ask and they didn't tell. Only six of us met those requirements. I never got any rundown about having a matric or belonging to a religious group.

A Hercules flew us to Bloemfontein. When we arrived there was a cock-up with our arrival dates. They weren't ready for us, so we had the day off and did very little.

Because we'd done half our Basics in Walvis as infantry, and the same intake as us had started from the beginning as Parabats, we weren't well accepted and were treated as outcasts. The second night after our arrival the corporals made all kinds of derogatory remarks before shocking us on our hands with cattle-prods. Then we had to run in this dark hangar, where the parachutes were packed, as fast as we could. There were tight, horizontal cords from the 'chutes. We had no idea they were there. The wires caught us in the chest and landed us flat on our backs. We were then told to crawl down holes in the ground. It was pitch-black. Some guys were waiting down there and punched our faces. We weren't expecting it and couldn't see a thing.

The corporals would often amble into the bungalow and sit down. We knew what was coming. We'd make them coffee, eat biscuits and talk about ordinary things. Then we'd get it right afterwards. They'd say they were going to now moer us. The whole group would stand on our trommels and they'd give us a couple of klaps on the stomach, just for fun, which was a common thing. I think it was a tradition. They were trying to make us tougher. Sometimes we'd be hit with the wooden handle of an entrenching tool. They'd unscrew it and whack you. Vasbyt! Ja, whatever. They'd go round in circles from bed to bed and each take a turn. Sometimes we'd put our helmets on and they whacked them with the sticks, too. They were really aggressive. If they didn't like you they'd do a good job. Then they'd leave.

Right from the very start we were taught how to be aggressive. They made us fight against each other with boxing gloves. They wanted us to be aggressive. They felt we were one rung below the Pathfinders. Recces, Pathfinders, Parachute Battalion and then the rest. They were supposed to make us violent, and it worked. Hell, we used to klap each other!

It didn't help that you were also English. Not at all. There was always a definite line between Afrikaans and English. Everything was spoken and taught in Afrikaans. We were like, 'Oh, shit! What did he say? What did that mean?'

I'll tell you something. If you want to watch a black man turn white, then throw him out of an aeroplane. He's 32 Battalion – he's seen it all. But he has never been on an aircraft. He hasn't understood the concept of flight. He's never looked out of the door at 2 500 feet, the parade ground below, and had to jump! It's scary enough for us – even *we're* shitting. It doesn't matter who you are – you shit yourself at first. You're doing something against your body's instinctive way of survival. You have to fight against it in order to leave that door. Your body is saying, 'This is death. At 2 500 feet you will die if you jump.' But your mind says, 'It's fine, you've got a parachute on.'

Hangar training isn't anything like the day you first jump out of a bird.

Something very strange happened to me towards the end of Basics. I was told to report at the main gate in my Number Nines, which was another term for the ordinary army browns, as opposed to the large, gardeners' overalls we wore in Basics.

I wasn't told why to report and didn't ask, yet I was curious. An unmarked white Corolla with military number plates pulled up. A plainclothes man got out. He was in his late twenties and had short, blond hair, a slight mullet and a trimmed moustache. He wore a white short-sleeved shirt, a black tie and black pants. 'Klim in. Agtersitplek.'

We drove in silence out of Voortrekkerhoogte. 'Excuse me, sir, where are we going?'

'Jy sal uitvind.' End of conversation. He didn't let on about anything and didn't talk. I was apprehensive but kept calm. No need to panic just yet. I was racking my brain trying to think what I'd done wrong. Then we arrived at this sparse, rocky area in the veld. I remember this long, three-storey building with a koppie behind it, sort of in the middle of nowhere.

He escorted me up a flight of stairs and along a corridor, and pointed me towards a small room. Three other troepies from other units were already there, seated at a round table. None of us knew why we were there. We remained quiet and just sat staring at one another. In front of us were paper and drawing materials. I noticed a large mirror on the wall. Then an officer, I can't remember the rank, walked in. We strekked him. He greeted us and told us to design a logo depicting the common unity of the different military units. I immediately relaxed because I was a trained graphic designer. This was a cinch for me. We were given a glass of juice to drink.

I finished before the others. Their designs looked rather amateurish. I stared at my picture and wondered how long we'd have to sit there. That was the last thing I could recall before arriving back at base. A buddy asked where I'd been. He said I'd been gone most of the day. 'What? No way! I've only been gone about an hour or so,' I said. I thought little of it at the time, and soon forgot about it.

It was years later, out of the blue, I remembered the incident. I told my wife and joked that they'd experimented on us after drugging us. The juice! Then it dawned on me – what if they really *had* done something? I thought about it and I recall scattered memories of strange lights and voices. Maybe I'm living in the twilight zone, but it gets to me because I don't actually know if something happened or not. It's quite a scary thought. Perhaps I'm being delusional. I now think it was Military Intelligence seeing if they could put me to use after reading my questionnaire, in which I stated my drug-induced times as a university graduate – someone who 'thought outside the box'. I never got to find out, as I was transferred away immediately after Basics.

There were two things, apart from determination, that gave me the will to endure Basics. One was the thought of my girlfriend and knowing I would see her again. I also knew Basics was only temporary and would pass. One had to project one's mind into the future and believe it. The other was the English band Strawbs. I listened to them on my Walkman after 'lights out' at 10 p.m. It was one of the day's best moments. Lay on my bed in the dark bungalow. The base was quiet. The combination of thoughts of my girl-friend while listening to Strawbs put me in a completely different place, far removed from the current reality. I was often shaken awake by Eddie, because the music on my headphones was still playing well after I was snoring. I'd switch it off, turn on my side and drift away in a second, contented.

They were a huge help in staying focused. If it weren't for them I would've had little else to concentrate on. The majority of guys, I believe, all had to have an exterior frame of mind to pull them through. Some had God or the Bible – quite a lot were nuts about Jesus – while for others thoughts of their parents or home or whatever blew their hair back. I had my girlfriend – now my wife – and Strawbs. I still have the cassettes and the Walkman. You can bury me with them.

It wasn't in my nature to want to give rondfoks and opfoks. It was the culture. I didn't feel good about it, but I didn't feel bad, either. It made me feel like a good instructor. My guys were tough and they had discipline. I could see it when we ended up on the Border. When I later ended up in sickbay they all took the time to visit and say hello.

With hindsight it was good for infantry troops, because if you order some-one to do something and he's under pressure and he's scared, his training kicks in. 'If the corporal says I must do it, then I must do it!' So the training defi-nitely served a purpose in battle conditions.

Bush Phase

I know this is a bit of arbitrary information, but one of the many things I remember they taught us was how to scan the field of view in front of you: to move your eyes from right to left as opposed to from left to right. The reason behind it was that when you read you always use your eyes in the left-to-right direction, which means if you scanned the horizon that way your eyes would naturally move faster, and you could therefore miss any important detail. By scanning in the opposite direction, your eyes would move slower and you'd be more likely to pick up anything relevant, which could save your life. At night you'd use peripheral vision, the outer edge of sight, to detect an object. It was far more effective than direct focus.

We left Voortrekkerhoogte in a convoy of about twelve Samil 50s, en route to Walmannstal, in the Hammanskraal area north of Pretoria. We wore our full combat gear, with our unloaded R4s tucked between our knees. Believe it or not, I ended up being one of the last four troepies sitting by the tailgate, on the very last Samil.

The convoy trundled slowly along in the left-hand lane of the N1 North as civilian cars passed by on the right. I couldn't help but feel a sense of pride as most people smiled and waved at us, some gooiing the *min-dae* sign. I remember, as a kid in the early eighties, seeing these same nutria convoys with the same-looking troepies, grins on their faces. Now I was one of them, along with the same silly grin on *my* face. I then knew what they must have felt like all those years before. Would I be silly to say I had goosebumps?

The highlight of the journey, which took only a couple of hours, was when a really attractive young blonde passenger – the driver, who slowed down alongside us, probably her boyfriend – raised her top and flashed us her boobs, the most gorgeous, ripe, firm pair, while laughing all the way. I say a gorgeous pair, but then, it *had* been almost three months since I'd seen my last pair, just before klaaring in. We all laughed and cheered. For those of us who saw it, it was the most rewarding feeling and boosted our spirits immensely! It's truly amazing what a flash of flesh can do to a troep!

Eventually we arrived. It was a huge military compound – nothing but flat terrain covered in dry veld and red dust. It was a good feeling being 'officially' allowed into an area that was out of bounds to civilians.

Then I saw a sight I've never forgotten. Behind barbed-wire fences were hundreds of neatly parked vehicles: Elands, Buffels and other transports, row upon row of them, stretching over the horizon. They were all covered in fine red dust. To me it was incredible, all this hardware lying dormant – and such a huge amount of it.

Later, it seemed even more stupefying when, during opskep times, there were no serving utensils to dish our food with. Here the army could spend millions on vehicles and the logistics that they entailed, yet it couldn't find a way to organise these basic utensils. I found it so ironic.

The barbers on base were sergeants and staffs. We had our hair recut for bush phase.

The guys, long before us, used to have full uitpak inspection on Badkop Hill, out in the veld. Took their staalkas, bed – everything – as an oppie, until one guy got a haemorrhage when something fell over on his head. Then they stopped it.

My ous had a bos-op, which, luckily, I wasn't part of. The lieut said we had to run up to the tower and back in under a minute. I shunted. Those left had the bos-oppie. Sit, lê, staan, run. Half an hour. They were covered in dust when they finished; their overalls were red. They were stuffed.

We saw the mechanised infantry doing their exercises. At night they'd fire the 0.50 Brownings mounted on their vehicles at 1 000-foot flares. Checked tracers arcing up. It was like *Star Wars*. One guy fired from there, one from here, and others from elsewhere, all firing at the flare.

The place was enormous. It was hectares and hectares of training ground, down in a valley. We did a sweep operation. Alpha, Bravo, Charlie, Delta. All the companies made one long line, but you had to see your buddy next to you, so we were about five metres apart. We swept the entire area. Took us the whole day. We marked all the dowwerds with toilet paper.

We were camped out in De Brug eating rat packs, digging trenches, sleeping in trenches, doing bush-phase things. We were now going to do helicopter drills. I was really excited and looking forward to it. Helicopters were going to arrive and we'd do drills on how to enter and exit Oryxes, Pumas and Alouettes. We didn't know what was going to happen. I couldn't wait – it was a big day – but the helicopters were late. We were told to go back to the trenches and wait until called to *tree aan*.

I found a really nice, sunny spot. I was all laid back; life was good. I fell asleep – lights out. I came round with my name being called. I awoke from this groggy stupor. I was sun-goofed. Deranged. Then I saw that the company had already *tree'd aan*! I came running out the bush, and the whole company, including the captain and sergeant major, was waiting for me. The sergeant major asked if I'd been smoking dagga, because I looked so goofed. Of course I hadn't, but I knew an opfok was coming. I was told to get a sandsak and wear it on my shoulders. We then had to run about four klicks to the helicopters. Helmet, rifle, ammo, full kit and me with my sandbag. So, en route, my buddies made a small hole in the bag. The sand trickled out as we ran, lightening the load.

We did the drills in and out of the helicopters. There was no flying, which I was very grateful for, because I didn't want to ruin that experience with this goddamn sandbag. That would make a very kiff occasion a very lousy occasion. Everyone was watching us. Climb in, climb out, climb in, climb out – all with the darned sandbag spilling dirt all over the helicopter. The crew told my lieutenant that they didn't want that dirt in there and asked why I should have the sandbag on my back, anyway.

Only then did the lieutenant notice the hole. And that's when I was bust. He then wanted to punish me. He also wanted to show off to the fly-guys about how incredible we Parabats were – that we could do a hundred push-ups and another bloody hundred push-ups. He said that we were tough, and that we knew what it was all about, and he decided to use me to illustrate this. Everybody was watching. Flight lieutenants, pilots, the rest of the guys – everyone. I felt I just didn't deserve an opfok at that particular time.

'Sak!' he shouted. I got down and did a set of fifty push-ups, with the sandbag still on my back. 'Gee my nog vyftig!' I did another fifty and was exhausted. I was really straining. It took every ounce of strength I had, and I thought he'd stop. Then he said, 'Nog vyftig!' I managed to do a few more before my arms buckled. I had reached failure. I just could not do another push-up.

'More! I want twenty-five more!' He pressed my arse into the ground with his boot. He was humiliating me in front of all these people. The fly-guys didn't like what they were seeing. I didn't deserve to be humiliated. No one deserves that.

It was at that stage that I'd had enough. I focused on the lieutenant's nose and was going to move very rapidly forward, jump up on my left leg because he was tall, and belt the living crap out of his schnoz. I would've smashed it. I was at the point of legitimately clocking him, but striking an officer would mean DB, off the course and RTU. I rushed up and nearly clocked him. I yelled in his face, 'FUCK OFF!'

He didn't know it was coming and realised at that stage he'd pushed me too far. You can only get pushed so far. You can be tolerant and take as much flak as you can, but there's a point where that's it. If I feel humiliated in front of a lot of people, I'll fight, I'll struggle, I'll kill. But you know what? I didn't blame him. I still don't blame him. He liked me very much. We got along well. Good guy. I liked him, but this particular time everything went blurry. According to the specific profile of the scenario, I had cracked. I had actually cracked – and it was legitimate. I had told an officer to fuck off, in front of everyone, and I wanted to kill him.

This one dude was being opfokked. He was one of the nerds – but a decent guy. He wore glasses, was frail and thin, and always kept to himself. The corporals had been picking on him the whole day. He finally lost his cool and charged the one corporal, klapping him with his R4. He went completely berserk, but was no match for the corporal. They both flew into a thorn bush and started brawling in a cloud of dust. The nerd and the stocky, *woes* corporal were going at it.

He was quickly pulled off. They screamed abuse at him, all the while pushing him around and terrorising him. He had tears streaming down his face and was convulsing with sobs, but the corporals didn't let up. They frogmarched him away and detained him for the night, but he was never officially brought up on charges.

For the following two days, right at the end of bush phase, the corporals became stricter than normal. They had to assert their authority over us once again. They felt they'd become too soft – let their guard down – and now this had happened. And they made his time a misery. He had to report with full kit every hour. Half rations. No sitting. No talking. They bullied and henpecked him constantly. You could see this guy was suffering inside. I felt so sorry for him, but you had to stay well clear as he was attracting all the wrong attention. Nobody went close. He was shunned.

The greatest part of my training was shooting at things, blowing them up – just having fun. This was conventional weapons training with the mortar. The whole paraatheid of working with weapons was great. I practised to become a mortarist during our conventional bush-phase training in Grahamstown but, having just been posted from Infantry School, had almost completed my full weapons training. When I arrived at 6 SAI, these guys had only just started. I had done all this training already, and more, so when I got there I just went on with it. The whole route march – everything – again. You fired all the weapons and then decided what you wanted to become – an LMG gunner or a mortarist, or stay a troepie-doepie.

Before bush phase we'd been a few times to the shooting range, where I scored around the 90-per cent mark – a high mark and well above the average. This earned five of us a day's pass, as promised by the sergeant major to anyone achieving this. The corporals took note of who we were.

For some unknown reason I nicknamed the R4 I'd been issued for bush phase 'Blondie'. At first I intended to name it after my girlfriend, but decided against it as it didn't seem appropriate. One day I lost my temper, stormed into my section's tent and threw Blondie hard onto the ground – an absolute no-no and a cardinal sin in the army. I was extremely lucky not to have been seen by any corporal, as this was 'damage to state property' and would've resulted in a charge. After cooling down I picked up the rifle and observed the damage to the forward sight – which is about the circumference of today's one-rand coin – now completely bent out of shape. Panicking, I did my utmost to repair it, yet it didn't look the same.

A few days later we went for practice out to the local range. The corporals were watching the five of us with expectant interest. Obviously my score was completely kak, this time well below even the lousiest score there. The sergeant checked Blondie and came to the conclusion that she was indeed damaged, and that I must've been issued with her in that condition. It was inconceivable to them that I may have damaged it. It was only the guys in my section who knew the truth. I had to persuade my Bungalow Bill, a real butt-creeper, to keep his mouth shut. He had it in for me from day one, as I was the only English oke in our section and a bit of a non-conformist, which he hated. This ou was so paraat. Anyway, he agreed. I think he was wise enough this far into Basics to know that the whole section would've been rondfokked if he had split on me.

One of the biggest nightmares we had was blisters. Walking, PT, marching and running – everything – was done with your boots on, so you simply got them. You got blisters all over your feet. You popped those and had them looked at and treated. The medic was constantly treating them. Then you'd get blisters underneath those blisters. Blisters upon blisters upon blisters. So you'd end up with holes in your feet. Raw feet. This needed a lot of Mercurochrome. You could go on Ligte Vrugte because of this, but then you were off the Bats. 'Go to another base,' they'd say. The Light Duty option would get you labelled and they'd make sure you fell off the course somehow.

Only serious cases went on Light Duty. If there was an oke who chose to be there because of something like shin splints, he was immediately a wuss. He could go ahead and suffer his shin splints. Shin splints were nothing. They were sore, but it wasn't like he could stop doing what he was doing, or *had* to stop. He could move on. Moving on would do the splints good, anyway. As soon as you became a Ligte Vrugte you became 'enemy number one'. You had to have a serious reason to go – like you'd broken your knee in four places and it had pins holding it together. That was okay. That was all right.

This actually happened. One oke completed his course but didn't get his wings in the end. On the very last day of the course, the test that you did involved falling from the olifant. It was a big structure, made from poles, with a rope that hung down. You were supposed to hook your legs around this rope and slide down, using a special technique to hold it between your feet, with your boots as the clamp. Some guys couldn't get this technique right and just dropped straight down like a bomb – *vwodoof!* The problem was that okes had been in the mud, crawling underneath the wire, so all the ropes were slippery. If you hadn't grasped the technique, there was no way you could stop yourself from falling. And this oke fell, but he fell inside the olifant, where there's this log right in the way, and he smashed his knee into fragments. We couldn't believe it. On his very last test. He had plates and bolts put into his leg, so they didn't pass him. He never got his wings. He didn't make it. That's the way it went. He was a bloody good oke, a real farmboy who always helped me look after my truck.

Hey, check this out! This is one of my notes I wrote for standing guard during bush phase:

General instructions:
Under no circumstances does guard (a) leave guard area (b) change his uniform (c) use alcohol or drugs (d) receive any gifts (e) listen to radio, Walkman or TV (f) lay down his rifle (g) lengthen duty or leave post without being relieved (h) change or swop duties (i) eat, drink or smoke

(j) sit, lean against anything or sleep (k) converse, except as part of duties (l) have any reading or writing materials.

Ja, right!

There was an area of land where we'd be instructed to sleep. We were shown how to dig our trenches, about a foot deep, and then place our bivvies over them. Two guys buddied off together and slept underneath. It wasn't easy digging ground that was as hard as cement, but we managed. The idea was, because the bivvies were at ground level in an open and exposed area, you were hidden. The enemy wouldn't see you immediately. Army bivvies were dark brown, and we disguised them by laying branches and bushes over the top.

On the first night two okes decided to pitch their shelter next to an old tree stump. We fell asleep within seconds after another long and tiring day. You're dead-tired – dead to the world – completely passed out, in spite of being uncomfortable. When we woke up, before sunrise, these guys were covered in ticks, the one who'd slept next to the stump more than the other. He had dozens on him. He stood in his jocks with this revolted, shocked look on his face. He knew he was in trouble. So did the sergeant. They quickly took him away for treatment. He didn't return to bush phase but I'm sure he was fine.

Eddie had taken his tiny radio. He wasn't allowed to have it out in the bush, away from camp, but he'd sneaked it in. During the night he and I were shacked up together in our shallow trench, covered with our bivvies.

It was quite late and the guys were all sleeping. The corporals were never really around at that time. Eddie tuned the radio, very softly, and within seconds on came 'Hotel California' by the Eagles. This was, and always has been, one of my favourites. At that moment it reminded me of home.

Eddie explained to me afterwards that the song's all about addiction to drugs and alcohol. I couldn't believe it – coming from a conservative Afrikaans guy. How did *he* know? Whenever I hear it I always think of him and parking off in our old army sleeping bags, poking our heads out from under the bivvies, staring at the stars and talking about nothing. I have fond memories of that surreal, yet good, situation.

We'd had a long day of PT and opfoks and were really tired. It had gone on the whole day and into the evening. Our blisters were killing us and we were *gatvol*. We were told that we could go to our bivouacs and sleep.

We must have had our heads down for less than an hour before they *tree'd* us *aan* again. We were all nicely lined up. Then they told us to return to our bivouacs, restock our battle jackets, get water, get rifles and come back. We were then informed that they were going to divide us into sections to go on a night march.

It had started to rain and was cold. They gave us a map and ordered us out. There were about eight checkpoints we had to pass before coming back for a few hours' sleep. Of course, we all wanted to get this over and done with. I ended up with a section where there wasn't a blue bean's worth of intelligence as to how to use a compass. The only reason our section leader was chosen was because he wore glasses, therefore he *must've* been intelligent.

Off we went. We couldn't see the ground ahead of us. We were walking with blisters through the bush at night and in the pouring rain. The highveld bush grows in clumps of grass, so your ankle twists and rolls over them. It added a nice, burning edge to your blisters – it was really painful – and the only way you could stop the pain was by walking. Walking and walking and walking. As soon as you stopped, the pain came back. You walked it numb. Your brain had to turn off the pain. That's how sore it was.

So we got to our first checkpoint. We were damn sure this was the place, but there was no one to greet us. No one to sign our piece of paper. We must've seriously got our bearings wrong. We were lost, we were beyond exhaustion and we could hardly even talk. We didn't know what to do because we were sure that this was the correct bearing.

I gathered everyone together and we huddled down. I had an idea. 'Section Leader, this is what we do. Where's the map?' He handed it to me. 'What we do is drop it into this puddle of water and make it unreadable, all muddied.'

'Ja? Then what? D'you know how to get us back?'

'Ja, I can. This is what we'll tune the captain. We'll go back, ask for a new map, ask to start again and see what he says, okay? If he gives us a new map we'll carry on going. It has to be like that.'

The section leader thought about it over biscuits. 'Okay, let's try it, but it's a real gamble.'

We trundled back to base, explained the situation to the captain and asked for another map. He stared at us for a long while. We became fidgety. 'No.' he said. 'It's pointless. You'll only get back in the early morning. In that case rather get some sleep. You're let off this march.' We tried not to express our excitement and felt a bit guilty as we climbed into our bags. We fell asleep but were suddenly *tree'd aan*. We thought, 'Oops. The plan didn't wash over the captain's head so well. We're in for it now.'

Instead, he told us that we were indeed the weakest group, that we'd messed up badly and that he hoped we'd learn from it. He also said how tired he was, that he was off to sleep, and that he would like us to sit by the fire and tick off all the sections as they came in. 'Take it in turns. One hour at a time.'

It was belting with rain, but there was a big fire under the captain's boma, with bivouacs all around it, and there was coffee. On my watch, in came the first bedraggled okes. I was cosy and warm, with a smoke and a hot, steaming cup of coffee. It was so cruel.

We came clean with the others, though. When they found out they thought it was pretty clever. We'd used our nodules, our intelligence. I got a feeling that that was what the captain was actually looking for – that we'd beaten the system.

Most of us lost a lot of weight during Basics. By the time bush phase arrived we were used to having less food than one was accustomed to in civvy street. In bush phase they gave us two meals a day: brunch at 10:30 and what I called 'sunch' – lunch-cum-supper – at 16:30. They usually consisted of rice, a piece of brown bread, a piece of meat, an egg and fruit. The portions were extremely small, however. We used our dixies. I just told the opskepper to load my main meal and dessert into only the one. Saved on washing. Even though the portions were minimal, we were learning to appreciate and value food as a luxury and a necessity, and not just sommer take it for granted. Your fussiness, if you had any, quickly vanished. But by this stage your stomach had shrunk, your body was leaner and fitter and your mind was becoming more in tune with the bush. You were now basically ready for what they'd been preparing you for all that time – to be a tougher, stronger person, both physically and mentally: to be a soldier. I say this with hindsight, though. At the time, all you're skieming is, 'Why must I put up with this, and for *what*?'

I desperately needed a dump. The problem was I knew that we'd be *tree'd aan* for dinner in less than five minutes. There was no choice but to *tree aan* in time, obviously, otherwise you'd be in deep trouble. But I *had* to go. I had a quick decision to make. I thought I could hold out. A minute later there was just no way I could keep the loaf in. Decision made. I grabbed my bog roll and wikkelled off into the bush, simultaneously unbuttoning my overalls and unclipping my web belt. The turtle was poking its head. I was frantic. It was coming – forget digging a hole! I squatted, and out it popped – relief – but because I'd crapped in such desperation, I landed some turd on part of my overall, which I hadn't had enough time to move from my between my legs.

'*Tree aan*!' they shouted. One minute left. A couple of quick wipes, flicked the drol away, wiped my overalls, covered my evidence as best I could and yet again wikkelled off to the formation area. Made it within seconds. Of course I smelled suspicious, but we all stank, so nobody noticed – I hope. I was itchy down there for a while, but in those situations you grin and bear it.

We were in De Brug. It was early morning and freezing cold. It was hell. Hell's a cold place. I was sharing a cigarette with this Afrikaans guy.

'Do you believe in heaven?' he asked.

'Ja. I do believe in heaven.'

'Do you believe in heaven on earth?'

'Well, ja, there can be. I believe there is.' My cigarette was tasting good.

'Goed so. Nou praat ons. Nou verstaan ons mekaar. I'll describe to you what heaven is. For me, back home on the plaas, when you wake up in the morning, it's ice, ice cold. Your father wants you to milk the cows. You run barefoot outside to where the cows are. Then, what you look for is a big cowpat – a fresh one, warm and steaming – and then you stand in it. Hot feet on a cold morning, on the plaas met jou pa. That, for me, is heaven on earth.'

We'd had a rough day. We were casually cleaning our rifles. Someone had a Sparletta and smokes. Camels – real Camels, with the word *Camel* in brown. Relaxation time. Could catch up on inspection. Could spend time polishing our rifles. Almost like a sewing club. It was late afternoon and there was a cool breeze. No corporals or lieutenants were screaming at us. It was so relaxed – thinking of home, sharing a bottle of Sparletta, bouncing smokes, laughing. Must've been a Sunday.

One oke in my section asked the sergeant if he could have a cigarette. We were only allowed to smoke in a designated area and only at certain times. He took a chance in asking because we weren't in the right place and it wasn't the right time. 'Ja, oukei, haal hom uit. Maar dan moet jy hom nou klaar rook. Onder 'n minuut.'

'Dankie Sersant.' He hot-rodded his cigarette. Luckily for him it was a Camel, which is dry and loosely packed, so it burnt quickly. He managed to do what the sergeant ordered. It was nice, sitting there as a small group watching this guy hot-rod his *gwaai*, with the sun setting and a relaxed sergeant – at that time – all just chilling. It was a good moment. Then the sarge tuned him, 'For your reward you can have another one.' He was allowed to smoke it at his own leisure. Such insignificant, anecdotal things stick in your memory.

Another time, my squad was with this same sergeant and we were sitting admiring the stars. He pointed up, turned to one of the guys and asked, 'Wat sien jy daar?' I think he expected an obvious reply of 'stars and space', but this troepie was shrewd and quite religious, like he knew the sarge was, and replied in a stadig, emphasised, Dutch Reformed way, 'Sersant, ek sien God, Sersant.'

He knew he'd scored points. A very calculated reply, whether he really believed his answer or not. The sergeant nodded his head, deeply impressed. 'Ja, jy het hom, reg oppie kop.'

We sat in silence, listening to the crickets and distant chatter. The incident got me thinking …

A few days later the sergeant had a go at me. It was right at the end of bush phase, literally within the last half hour, just as we were leaving the training area. It all began when we were loading the Samil 100 with everyone's backpacks. As a G3 I'd been assigned to look after my squad's R4s, which meant that I had thirteen bootlaces tied to my wrist. I felt like I was about to take them for a walk. We were trained never to lose sight of our rifles. They had to become a part of us, always, constantly and forever. They were a physical extension of one's self. This rule was strictly enforced and we never forgot it, because they were tied to us all the time. You shat, ate and slept with them tied to you.

I was minding my own business, keeping clear of potential trouble, because the corporals were now seriously *woes* and looking for any reason or excuse to shout and scream. I thought I was safe. Then along it came, and out of the blue, in the form of this one particular corporal – one of three – who'd had it in for me right from the first week of Basics. This prick sauntered up and asked, 'Is jou sak oppie trok?'

'Nee, Korporaal!'

'Gee my jou pikstel.' His grootsak was already packed away and now he was hungry. I gave the leashes to another oke for him to look after and got my pikstel out my pack. Just before handing it to him I quickly wiped it on my bush jacket to dust it off, out of 'respect', in spite of the fact it was spotless.

'Hulle's vuil! Hoekom is jou fokken pikstel vuil, jou vuilgat?' I wanted him to go away.

'Korporaal, hulle is nie vuil nie, Korporaal! Ek wou net die stof vir Korporaal afvee, Korporaal.'

This wasn't good enough and he ordered me to follow him. He marched me over to the sergeant sitting in the Samil, who listened to his version, and then dumped on me for being a dirty dog. I tried to explain, but it was pointless. I knew trouble was coming. I felt that now was the time, their last excuse, to give someone a great big drukking-over. He became even louder and more in my face. I grimaced. 'Why is yous smiling? Does yous thinks it funny, *roof*?'

'Nee, Sersant!' I stared straight ahead, waiting for the inevitable.

'En hoekom is jy G3?' he asked as he read my pink card pinned to my pocket. 'Ah! Yous can'ts uses your knees. Well, you can uses your arms. Op jou rug, *roof*. NOU! Sandsak bo jou kop!'

By now this had attracted the attention of everyone around, including all the corporals, about ten of them. I noticed my corporal there, as well. I became aware of them surrounding me, chuckling with delighted, gleeful looks on their faces, like a pack of human hyenas. To them, Sersant was *die man*, jong! This was the same sergeant who'd been cracking jokes with my squad the night before. I hadn't given him any reason for this. I was confused.

After a while my one arm began to lower. 'Is hy swaar? Gee hom nog 'n sak.' My arms were burning.

'Ek kan nie, Sersant.'

'Kom, jou fokken soutie!'

My arms were giving in. 'Sersant. Asseblief … fok.' Then he lost it. Uitkak time.

'Wat? Vloek jy my? Moenie vir my FOKKEN VLOEK NIE, JOU FOKKEN HONDEKAK!' It reached that stage where I zoned out. Time shifted. I felt angry, frustrated and humiliated. Primal. Intense. Clenched teeth. I'm ashamed to admit that I was crying. Tears simply rolled out of my eyes. More laughter.

'Kyk. Soutie huil. Hy fokken huil!' Hysterics. They kicked sand in my face. I noticed all the other okes take a wide berth, but they had to continue packing the Samil. I'll never forget the looks on their faces. They didn't find the situation amusing.

This went on for about twenty minutes. Eventually the sergeant put an end to it. Their small minds had been satisfied. But they'd broken me, right at the very end, minutes before we were to return to base and within days of Basics ending. They didn't crack me, though; they broke me. Big difference. That final degradation and humiliation, right then, was too much. It would've been different any other time and I would've been okay, but not then.

I was told to leave amidst grinning, smirking faces. I sat behind a truck, away from the others, and gathered my senses. My head was swimming. The guys left me alone for a while. Sure, I'd had previous uitkaks, rondfoks and opfoks – we all had – but that time just did it for me. Just as I thought I was finished with all that bull, they klapped me with that one last surprise, and all together. Them against one. Flipping cowards. It sounds like nothing but, at the time, when you're there and experiencing it, it's different. Why get an opfok-cum-rondfok for nothing more than wiping your pikstel, which wasn't even dirty, and they knew it? How did it equate? It made no sense whatsoever. It had nothing to do with military training.

The call came to move out. We climbed into the Samils and at long last headed out of Walmannstal. The Samil benches were so close together that one's knees virtually touched the opposite guy's groin. Legs would be intertwined like the teeth of a zip. Within minutes most guys were sleeping helmet to helmet, or helmet resting on top of their blitsbreker. I looked at the training areas pass by, took a mental snapshot, closed my eyes and was asleep before the convoy even hit the highway back to Voortrekkerhoogte.

The Last Week

Bush phase finally finished. We'd returned to base the day before. I was told to *tree aan* outside my bungalow. A certain corporal had been ordered to locate me. He stood me to attention and informed me that I was to be transferred out of base the very next day – the day before the big *uittreeparade*, which would be followed by our first pass in three months. I couldn't believe it. What good news! I had tried for close on ten weeks to achieve getting down to Cape Town after Basics. You could try your hardest to get posted to your hometown, but almost always to no avail. The Welsyns Offisiere were masters at detecting bulldust – they could smell the faintest whiff from beneath your shiny boots. They were trained Permanent Force psychologists and had heard and seen it all before. They were trained to look you in the eye, listen to your bull and say, 'Seker. Kom volgende week weer,' all the while thinking, 'Vertel my nog 'n storie.'

So you'd return the following week, state your case and they'd say, 'Kom weer, volgende week' and so on. By the third week most *rofies* had given up trying. By then they had been weeded out and only the most persistent or genuine cases remained determined. Only by the fourth week would they start to listen to what you had to say. You had to build a case and prove your situation with extreme persistence – and without faltering or changing your reasons. Ultimately you had to be prepared in advance. I had a female first lieutenant. She was so sweet and caring. After a few more interviews, and having looked into my situation and acknowledging its validity, she placed me on the Critical Transfer list to return to Cape Town.

Unfortunately the particular corporal who'd been told to relay the news still resented me after all this time, for reasons known only to him. Yet he had always remained in the shadows and we'd never really crossed paths. Knowing I was out of there in less than twenty-four hours, he had to seize his opportunity to do something.

He'd been drilling for the parade and had his R4 with him, slung across his chest by its strap. After some derogatory remarks about how I thought I must be so hondkak smart to have wangled a transfer, it came. *Bam!* He struck me hard in the face with his rifle, from my forehead, over the nose and to the cheekbone. I'm not sure whether he actually meant to do that, or to simply give me a fright and misjudged his distance, but for a second I was stunned and staggered backwards. My immediate thought was to deck him, but I maintained my composure. I couldn't lose control and destroy everything I'd worked for.

He snorted. We made eye contact which, in Tiffies, for our corporals, anyway, was a no-no. But he did nothing. No uitkak. Nothing. He knew he had crossed the line. There were witnesses, and this could have had serious repercussions for him. There was nothing more he could do. 'Dankie, Korporaal,' I smiled. I was dismissed and we parted ways.

The incident left me cautious. I lay low not wanting any trouble, yet expecting it. None arose. I checked in my rifle, handed my bedding and equipment back to stores, packed my balsak, said goodbye to Eddie and the guys, had the captain officially sign my release forms and the corporal on gate duty clear my passbook, and I walked out of the gate. I got into my brother-in-law's car and kissed Voortrekkerhoogte goodbye. I never looked back. However, I'm a nostalgic person. Strangely enough I would enjoy walking around that place today. It would bring back so many bittersweet memories.

People will say I perhaps deserved the smack, that I must've done something for the corporals to have it in for me, and that I was a rebel. Yes, I was, yet I never intentionally meant to antagonise them. In short, they couldn't accept the fact that I had kept some of my individuality. They knew they hadn't completely conformed me – and a few others – into sheep. They took it as a personal failure. I know that they had a job to do, but let me see one or two certain corporals again and I'd walk across to the opposite pavement because I wouldn't want to tell them what I think of them. Others were decent and fair, and I respected them. Those are the leaders you'd do almost anything for. You earn respect. You don't command it.

It was quite funny. The guy's standing there, you're kakking him out, and you can just check he wants to moer you, but he can't. Then you bump into him later in life, on civvy street, and it's different. He's like, 'Hey! Korporaal! Howzit going?' No hard feelings.

Seeing my family again was almost shocking. It was very surreal when you came out of Basics and saw them again for the first time, because they were another world away. You'd been thinking about them for the last three months, and they obviously had no clue at all what you'd been through.

After three months we got our first pass. Went back home for a few days. Freedom, for a while. It took a lot of willpower and discipline to return, but you knew it had to be done. Besides, after being through Basics, it seemed almost like a new adventure awaited. It felt like the worst was over.

SECOND-PHASE TRAINING

In Infantry we were out on the shooting range virtually every day, banging away at the hundred-metre mark, the two-hundred, the three-hundred and so on, with full mags. Also trained on the usual support weapons: mortars, RPGs and snotneuse. I must say we only fired one RPG each, and once only, but the R4 we shot the whole day. We fired off hundreds of rounds during training.

After Basics I did a three-month driving course. Stayed at Kimberley, 1 Maintenance Unit, mainly learning how to drive trucks and how it differed from driving a car. We were in the trucks almost every day. Various Samils and Kwêvoëls, but not Buffels, which weren't in our camp. Cleaned the trucks often, which wasn't too hard, because we sprayed them down with waterhoses.

Klaared into 8 SAI at Upington in 1984. Did Basics there for about two months and then was sent to Infantry School. They put me on a Corporal's Course and I didn't want to do it. I wanted to be a lieut. I'd seen what corporals were all about. The army just had this policy that if they wanted you to be a corporal, then that was it. End of story. They refused to put me on Officer's Course, so I told them to send me back, and they did. RTUed me back to Upington.

After finishing Basics as a medic we went to Technical Services School and did vehicle training. What they thought training as a medic was, was quite strange, but never mind. We picked up most of our training in hospital. Real medic stuff. A medic private was known as an orderly, and you could stomp around the wards in your army boots and puttees.

In the late sixties we had a six-week course. I failed because my foot got buggered up, so I went to the san barracks, which was like a holiday camp. I remained there for six weeks then went back to Gunnery course. From Gunnery we went to the ships. I was on *Jan van Riebeeck* – South Africa's first aircraft carrier. It had two helicopters perched on the back. There we were, standing on deck, not knowing anything. 'Who wants to be a messman?' I didn't even know what a messman was. Nobody was volunteering for anything. 'Who needs to be a messman?' We stood still. Then it was, 'You. You. You.' I ended up being the chief petty officers' messman. It turned out to be a damned good thing.

I was an artillery bombardier back in the early seventies. Our overalls were a light sand colour, not nutria as they were later on. We used to fire our Bofors or 35-mms on Strandfontein beach out over False Bay. A battery had six sections and each section had its Bofors and about ten guys. We towed them down on the old Bedfords, which we learnt to drive. All of us had to learn how to drive. Our jeeps were green, short-wheel-based Land Rovers.

The target was a red drogue towed hundreds of metres behind an old Dak. I recall the one, Zulu Zebra, with its yellow and black vertical stripes. There was no chance of us hitting the aircraft. The tattered drogue would be pulled in before landing.

We also went out to St Lucia, north of Durban, a swampy area where the Cactus surface-to-air missiles were tested. We had radar set up with a range of about sixty miles to keep unwanted aircraft out of the area for their obvious safety. I was inside the radar system. The guys liked getting inside because it was air-conditioned.

One day we had put up palm fronds as a windbreaker next to the radar but the wind blew them down. I was putting them back up again and looked to where I was about to place my hand, and there, literally a centimetre away, was a green mamba. If he'd bitten me I would've been dead. There was no serum around. I used up one of my nine lives. The rest of the guys caught it and chopped it into pieces with a panga then burned it on the braai. You just did *not* want a mamba hanging around.

I became an instructor after Basics and then did a six-week course in military law at Diensvaks Skool. Services School trained the MPs at Voortrekker-hoogte where they gave Officer's Courses and lectures. That's where I had my first and last zol – in Services School. They gave us *boom* to smoke. We sat there in uniform, smoking *boom* in the lecture hall, took a couple of puffs and passed it on. How could you know what it looked like, smelt like or felt like if you didn't smoke it yourself? I can therefore say I officially smoked zol in the Defence Force.

Towards the end of my Basics, in September '75, the specialised units came around. The Recces, the Bats and Infantry School. I wanted to get some rank and decided to go to Infantry School in Oudtshoorn. Because they were pushing to get leadership figures out, I did a crash course there for three months. Ended up as a two-stripe instructor. I knew I was set to become a corporal because of my eighteen-month service. Only guys who'd signed on for a full two years could become a lieutenant, or a corporal, depending on their personalities. Usually the hard-ass guys became corporals.

The first part was drilling and more spit-and-polish bullshit, and how to instruct and drill troops. There wasn't a course or manuals on how to shout and scream at new intakes. You learnt it. Oh brother, you learnt it. It rubbed off on you. You picked it up from your instructors. You had to. You were threatened all the time by an RTU if you didn't make it. Not that many wanted to be, or got, RTUed. There was too much shame. It was something we looked down on. Came back with your tail between your legs. So, when drilling your own platoon mates, they'd try to make it as hard as possible for you. If you weren't loud and didn't use the army slang, you'd get RTUed.

Then we trained in counterinsurgency and conventional warfare. We had a go on all types of weapons – Brens, AKs and the PPSh. We shot from the R1 to the G-3. That part was amazing, but at times it was sheer hell. I know people always say their training was the toughest, especially the Bats, and of course the Recces, but apart from them Infantry School was really crap. Halfway through the course the sergeant major, who was well known throughout the army and had a massive voice, a thick moustache and was short and thin, stood on the parade ground one morning and shouted, 'Corporal! Turn up the speed!'

I thought, 'I'm not gonna make it. Please, no more. That's it! I've had it.' I've got photos of guys lying flat on their faces after passing out with sandbags tied to their backs. But after all the shit, you *did* make it through. We got rank and, I'm telling you, I felt so proud to have passed and survived all the rondfoks and opfoks.

Just before training ended, the situation in Angola worsened. On the parade ground they read out names of guys who were going up. The word had already spread that we were going into Angola. We were all praying, 'Please, not my name, because I've just got rank and now the lekker life's going to start when I get back to base.'

Did my secondary in 1976 at Bloemfontein in the Armour – 1 SSB. We learnt basics, like map-reading and stuff, and trained in Elands for six months, but it wasn't all just stick a 90-mm in the barrel and off it would go. You'd have to know how to aim it, where to aim it and so on. The driver generally looked after the vehicle and the maintenance. The tiffies used to help if you had a major problem, but the driver knew how to fix it if things went wrong. He knew what he had to do.

The first six months of my National Service after Basics was just training. Real specialist training. It was a tough unit, the 250 Air Defence Unit, almost a Special Forces unit. Everybody used to say that the air force was a nice and easy sort of vibe, but the 250 was a heavy unit to bear in terms of physical training and discipline, even in 1977.

In our unit there were very specific duties. There was the guy in charge, who'd have a certain rank or level of command, and I was the guy sitting there basically flying the missiles. It was an optical guidance system, very much like these computer games the kids play today. It had a little joystick to guide the missile visually, between you and the target, and you'd hope that the two would connect at some stage! That was the Tigercat system. And there was the French-designed surface-to-air missile system – the Crotale, or Cactus, as the Defence Force called it – which was a good system for its time, but it had a lot of deficiencies in the sense that it wasn't really suited to our terrain. It had electric motors driving the wheels, with a diesel generator giving the power. The idea was that these things had to be transported to wherever it was they were supposed to be, and in the last couple of kilometres you'd position it up and get it there on its own power. We drove it down to St Lucia in Natal and fired a few missiles into the swamps. The system itself was pretty spectacular. It would lock onto a target and then automatically go through various sequences before firing. About two seconds after launching, it would go through the sound barrier. It could chase a Mirage from behind and catch up with it. It was sad to me that each missile cost about R200 000, whereas a house was about R30 000 in those days.

In St Lucia the commandant had a Land Rover that he used to take down to the beach to go fishing with his buddies. He used to park it on a rocky slope. The one night they decided to camp over. When they awoke the next morning the vehicle was missing. He sent his one troepie, his skivvy, back to the base to have someone pick them up. When he arrived it was, 'Wie die fok ... Watter fokken bliksem het my fokken Landy gesteel?' We said it wasn't us. An Alouette was sent out and they discovered that the Landy had been sucked into the sea. It had rolled forward with the tide. It was hoisted out of the water. This thing was history – completely water-logged and salted. It was taken to Voortrekkerhoogte. When I was on camps, even years later, I would still see this old Land Rover in the far corner of the scrapyard, sitting there, rusting away.

We learnt to drive on those old Land Rovers. It was a bloody hard vehicle to learn to drive when you were eighteen. The steering wheel had a three-quarter play and you practically had to stand on the brake pedal. My one buddy reversed and made a big dent in it. 'Structural damage,' they said. They made this poor troepie pay four months' salary – about R18 a month – towards the dent, while the commandant didn't have to fork out a single cent for a complete write-off.

The PF guys just didn't seem to treat things that seriously back then. Everything was all a big joke. Got pissed, had a laugh, took the speed-boat out, went fishing and braaied. Everything was great. The National Serviceman was there not because he necessarily wanted to be there. He kakked off.

In October 1977, we left St Lucia early to attend the commandant's funeral. The helicopter he was in had crashed near Ermelo while returning from Pretoria. Three of them were inside. The commandant was burnt to a crisp, one guy was badly burnt and the third walked away unscathed. At a later stage I remember flying with the survivor who'd been burnt. He was then a flight sergeant and his face was scarred from the fire. He loved the army life. If that had happened to me in the bloody army I would've said, 'Screw this! I'm outta here!'

Klaared in from 1981 and was based at Potch, 14 Field Artillery. I was called straight into Artillery. My first option was to go to the navy, because I enjoyed swimming and the water, but it never happened. My dream was to fly choppers, but that was out from the beginning.

Basics was the normal Infantry stuff for three months. Second phase lasted for another six months. Some of the guys who trained us were ex-Rhodesian, like my major and staff sergeant. First we trained on the 25-pounders. They weren't used up on the Border, but for practice only. The army used to guard those old brass shells like gold. We had to collect and return every single one, as they were reusable. Then it was on to a bigger gun – the 5.5-inch. Both artillery pieces were from the Second World War. Vintage, but obviously upgraded. It was enjoyable. In Artillery you had a Number One, Two and Three. Number Three was the guy on sights. You had up to five guys on a 5.5. It could fire to about twenty-five klicks. The guns were very well looked after. We did weekly maintenances, monthly maintenances and six-month maintenances.

After 5.5s we went on to the new multiple-rocket launchers called the Valkiri. They copied those 122-mm Katyushas – Stalin Orrels – captured in Angola. Twenty-four units were mounted on the back of Unimogs, a vehicle that originated in Germany, with a left-hand drive. It weighed over six tons. The rockets had a minimum range of about seven kilometres and a maximum of about twenty. They later upgraded the system to forty-eight rockets, mounted on a Samil 50.

They chose a few guys, and that's what we specialised in. It was a big change going from artillery to rocket launchers because it was pretty new. There were a few mishaps, a few shorts. Guys would be driving along and rockets would go through their cabs but wouldn't detonate. This happened in the early phases. Nobody was killed, but they had to sort these problems out. There were two contact points. You'd load the rockets into tubes. If you drove around all over the place they'd connect and launch. The rockets would only prime themselves once they had trajectory. When that happened a sonar pulse would rebound off the earth. As it came down and reached a certain height above the ground – a few metres or more – it would explode.

I drove the Mog and was the Number One, the overall bombardier in charge of the vehicle. I was a two-striper. In the Artillery they're referred to as full bombardiers. We took full responsibility for our vehicles. On a rocket launcher there were only two of us. Number Two manned and operated the sights. The system was all hydraulics. When we got to the Border all the ordnance we needed was readily available. The missiles would be signed out at the armoury. As a Number One this was my responsibility. Everything was registered.

Artillery was different from Infantry. It was obviously more technical. We were always learning about things. In Infantry you'd just follow. In Artillery you were so thoroughly drilled you could eventually do things in your sleep. That's how drilled we were.

After Basics, at Bloem 1 SAI, I did JLs at Oudtshoorn. In Basics there were 3 400 guys in the intake, of which 1 200 opted to do the Officer's Course at Oudtshoorn. Within two weeks we were down to 800. In the end 178 got rank, of which twenty-one were English. Of those only three became instructors. I was one of them. I was too loud-mouthed to be a lieut. Had too much shit to say. Ended up being one of those corporals that had to drill okes, and had no problems doing so.

Then I specialised in mortars, back at Bloemfontein 1 SAI, with mechanised infantry. 1 SAI was very difficult. We didn't want to go back, because Oudtshoorn was like a holiday camp in comparison. In Bloem you ran everywhere, but in Oudtshoorn you marched. There was no real running or afkaks. After 5 p.m. they left you alone, whereas in Bloem you rolled and PTed all night.

In their second year the previous corporals at 1 SAI klaared out and we took over. I was lucky – I didn't get given new intakes. Instead I got senior troops who had done one year already. Still drilled and messed the ous up and chased them around. You had corporals with a real *hardegat* attitude, who said, 'We went through this shit so now we're going to take it out on these *rofies*. Payback time.'

Some okes died unnecessarily during training. Stupid things. An oke in the Bats took a mortar out of De Brug and hid it in the bungalow. It went off in the kas. Someone bumped it – I don't know what the story was – but it blew. We heard this *KWAH!* Three Parabats killed.

We were big enemies with the Bats. It was green beret versus purple beret. If you got a purple it was worth R50 plus a weekend's pass. We were at some sports parade. My mate had his beret on 'Eddie Murphy style'. Some oke put his hand on his head to turn the beret around. My bud just checked purple, literally and figuratively. He was a first dan in karate. He swung round and hit this oke in the throat. The guy just dropped.

'O fok! 'n Majoor!' We grabbed his beret and were gone. Double bonus!

After Bloem we went to Middelburg. We were the first company to go to 4 SAI to convert them to mechanised infantry. We were there for about a month busy training new intake. As corporals on duty we had to look after them and chase them around if necessary. Then we went to South West.

In 1982, the Ratel was the latest state-of-the-art SADF weaponry and God's gift to the infantry. 1 SAI was one of the first units to be equipped with them. We trained for a full year on them, including Basics. 1 SAI had its own instructors to train junior officers and NCOs. Specialist training was provided for drivers, gunners and general infantry troops on the various weaponry and, of course, training was given in how to operate with the vehicle in different battle situations at Platoon, Company and Battalion level. Almost six months of training went into that alone. By then you were operating at full-fighting-company strength. We weren't just normal infantry, but mechanised infantry, who would later go to the Border to be stationed at 61 Mech Battalion Group at Omuthiya, about forty-five klicks north-west of Tsumeb.

After Basics I volunteered to become an ops medic. Then we did another nine to twelve weeks' training, doing mostly medical stuff. I went to Baragwanath Hospital and spent many weeks in the casualty wards. Some of the other okes went to other black hospitals where they didn't mind them practising on people. We got used to blood and piss and shit – literally. It accustomed us. It took a bit of time to physically stomach the gore. People's guts were hanging out. It smelled horrible. They were moaning and complaining, but you got used to it.

I thought it was very interesting. I really enjoyed the medical part of it. Learnt how to stitch people up. It seemed a lot more humane and worthwhile. Instead of killing people, you're trying to keep them alive. This was more the constructive, and not destructive, part of being in the army.

We were almost killed during a mock battle operation at De Brug. A mortarist got it wrong. We were doing fire and movement while training with live ammo for Operation Pegasus, to get all the coordination correct. There were helicopters and jets and carpet-bombings. We were supposed to jump out of Flossies, land, get ourselves together, march to the battleground, and commence.

We were up on the hills and hadn't advanced yet. The first jet came in and carpet-bombed the area, then pulled up into the sky. The place thundered. Tore a hole out of the sky. Then the other pilot shot in from the other side and bombed the place. If you see carpet-bombing in the movies, it doesn't compare. In reality, when they strike, the ground shakes. It goes *bwoom-bwoom-bwoom-bwoom!* It's like a wall of fire. Then two gunships pulverised the zone with Brownings. When they'd finished their job the mortarists had their turn, and once they'd started, the fire and movement commenced.

As the infantry we were doing buddy-cover and moving in on the target. It's a quick process, and when it's time to go, the mortarists get aligned and mortar the hell out of the target ahead while we move in. They were behind us and shooting over our heads. The Number One's procedure was to slam his mortar tube into the ground. It had a knob on the top which set it from safe to arm. He clicked it and aimed according to where the projectile was to go by adjusting to the correct degree. He had his buddy, a Number Two, who carried the mortar shells. His responsibility was to arm the shell and drop it inside the mortar. This was happening quickly. There was no wanking around.

So what this mortarist did was slam it to the ground as should be done, but he was on a pluk where he had to obey commands, and was too hasty. At the last second he decided to readjust the pipe and he lifted it up – the split second the armed shell was dropped into the tube. *Gedoof!* Off it went. This meant that the projectile was going straight up, and not over our heads, which also meant it was going to come straight down on top of us. But a mortar travels quite a way up in the sky, so they'd already radioed the sergeant commanding the fire and movement that it was coming down on us, somewhere in the general area.

He was ahead and to the side and frantically motioned for us to lie down. He was waving. I think he was also waving goodbye to us, thinking, 'I'm sorry, but lie down anyway. When this thing hits, don't worry. We have an ambulance on standby for those of you who may survive it, but it's best to lie down, anyway. The shrapnel should go over your heads but if it lands on top of you, well, we'll just have to write letters to your moms.'

We were saying, 'What? We're in the middle of fire and movement going through trenches here! What've we got to do now?' We were confused but followed his command. We dived and lay flat. Then we heard it coming. It whistled, louder and louder, and then went silent. It landed four metres in front of my buddy doing buddy-cover ahead of me. I was covering him at the time, which meant that it landed about eight metres from me – but that's quite a distance, really. If it had gone off he would've probably only suffered concussion, but a mortar shell is not a funny thing. It has a coiled spring inside, divided into segments, with hard little pieces of shrapnel that go everywhere.

This thing, luckily, was a dowwerd so it didn't explode. After an exercise there were usually quite a few of them all over the place that could explode at any time. If you came across one you were supposed to mark it with toilet paper – white gold – and they had a sort of bomb squad who cleared them.

Nothing happened to the Number One. He was in shock. He got punished enough by freaking out. These things happened. This was training. This was why we trained, so things like that didn't, or shouldn't, happen in battle. Nobody was ready to blame the oke; it was just a mistake. You weren't really allowed to make mistakes, but they didn't do anything to him. He obviously got the message.

Me and my buddy also shot an RPG. The ones we used in practice were caches seized from Angola. We were the only ones to hit the target out of twelve guys in our section. The target was a bunch of drums representing a tank. We hit it square-on. All the others missed. And we were the souties, too. It was a tongue-in-cheek thing, but did we rip them off for the rest of the week!

In a cinema they have incredibly loud speakers that attempt to represent a war situation, but if they played the actual sound it would bugger up their system and probably the entire movie house itself! Listening to that is not like standing next to a fired RPG at all. It's the equivalent of standing next to an exploding stick of dynamite. That's how loud it is. It's moerse loud. You mess in your pants just because of the sound.

For security training we basically learnt to get to know dogs, train them and work with them. We learnt about weapons. Trained on R4s, Berettas and shotguns. That was about it. I liked dogs, which is why I eventually went for it, but, with hindsight, I would rather have just been an RP standing at a gate as opposed to a dog handler. That wasn't so nice.

I eventually landed up at Langebaan Air Force Base for the rest of my National Service. I volunteered for the Border but the closest they'd send me as a handler was Grootfontein. Never got there. That would've been far more interesting than staying in Cape Town doing nothing.

I remember a funny incident during grenade practice. For safety we all hid in a little concrete-and-brick bunker behind the practice area, which was a large, empty patch of open land. The bunker had tiny spyholes in the bricks to observe whatever happened. The chances of shrapnel hitting you were slim.

You were supposed to squeeze the grenade's lever, pull the pin out and, once you'd let go, the timer was primed. The next oke, about to throw his grenade, was shitting himself. He was shaking. I was watching this through the peephole. The corporal handed him the grenade and was very gently calming him down. 'It's okay,' he said. 'Just lean back and lob it over your shoulder. No problem.'

This oke pulled the pin and gooied it, but fumbled, and it landed just over the low protective wall. The corporal yanked the ou to the ground. Everybody did the same, and there was this *whoomph*, and a dust cloud threw dirt everywhere. Once the dust and excitement had settled, the corporal said, 'That is an example of how *not* to throw a grenade!' Occasionally there'd be dowwerds. What they then did was shoot them to get them to go off.

In Grahamstown our training was squeezed into three months with stuff they gave the other guys a period of six months, or even a year, to do when it was two years' National Service. I think the training we got was good. It was professional. You knew what you had to do and when you had to do it. There was a bit of politics in it, as well. They took us into a hall and showed us a video. Some guy from Intelligence showed us two versions of the same thing. 'This is what you see on TV.' And you saw these troepies opening fire on a group of marchers, but it had been edited. Then they showed the unedited version and you saw the troepies getting fired upon first, and opening up to retaliate.

'Just be *aware* of those types of things,' they said.

We started on COIN-urban and COIN-rural to prepare for townships and what we might be up against. There was a little township just outside of Grahamstown. Some of us went there to do a bit of training and to get used to a township set-up before being deployed to Natal. Once there, our home base became the navy base in Durban.

GENERAL SERVICE

There were three guys you made friends with: the medics, because they had access to all sorts of substances — except Voltaren injections, which you got for free; the chefs, because they had access to steaks (the army was full of steaks, believe it or not; you just had to have a tin of condensed milk — that was worth a couple of steaks); and the MPs, because they patrolled the gates. It was a very corrupt system — you could bribe anybody with the right things. For two cans of condensed milk I'd get a day pass. Just went to the guy and said I wanted to get through the gate. 'No, you can't without a pass.'

'Well, then, here's a can of condensed milk.' And out you went.

My duty as a chief petty officers' messman was the best job in the base —
when you were in port, that is. You had no other duties when you were in
harbour except to look after the chief petty officers' mess. There were only
four of them, and they buggered off every afternoon. In the morning, when
they returned, they wanted chow. And tea, they wanted tea. At lunchtime
they wanted chow again. So I used to set this lot up when their bellies were
full. 'Hey, Chief. How about a pass?'

'But of course, son.' Just like that. I had a pass nearly every single night
because I never asked the same chief each time. As long as you were back in
by midnight, the rank couldn't touch you. Of course, being in harbour, an
able seaman second class sleeps on the ship in his mickey – his hammock.
At night you'd dig it up from amongst the others, unlash it, put the spread-
ers in and jump on. When awake you rolled it up, lashed it and turfed it
in the corner. It had your name on it. But when I came back at night I just
kipped at the mess. I had a bed there. Lekker.

Because I worked for *them* I didn't have all this other nonsense, but
when you got to sea you kakked yourself. Then I had to look after these
guys twenty-four hours a day and still had other duties to do. The gunnery
ratings are the guys who also do the watches, which we did up on the
bridge for four hours, two guys at a time. The engineering guys had their
own watches down in the engine rooms.

We went up the South West coast chasing Russians and who knows
what all. We came back and had another six weeks before klaaring out.
They wouldn't let us go before then, but if you had wheels you could go
anywhere, do anything. Remember, a lot of guys in those days – the late
sixties – were in their twenties before they ever saw wheels. Today, as an
eighteen-year-old, if he hasn't got wheels under his arse he's nothing. Life's
changed a lot.

I had two weeks left before I was to be posted out to one of the other
bases. I decided to do a Security Instructor's Course, which filled the time
nicely for me. They posted me to Waterkloof Air Force Base in Pretoria. I
tried to get down to Ysterplaat in Cape Town. I'd heard there was a guy

there from Pretoria who wanted to get back. He was a security instructor so, luckily, because of the course, we swopped. So, for the rest of my time in Cape Town I was a security instructor.

There were eight of us. We taught basic security awareness courses, but there was nothing fancy about it. It was a time when you had the Big Red Bear, which we were all so worried about in those days. This meant looking after the camp. We patrolled the perimeter, checked lights, gates and fences. In those days we didn't have high walls around the place. All access control, including the dog handlers, fell under us.

After getting PF privileges, due to becoming an instructor, I decided to sign on for an extra year. I was enjoying myself at the time. I wanted to go to the Border but I never had the opportunity. As an instructor they kept you back at base. I thought the more trained you were, the better your chances of getting to the Border, but it didn't work that way. They'd given you the training and wanted you to put that to use training others, so it backfired on me.

Then I had a severe accident the month before I was supposed to klaar out. It occurred on a weekend pass. I was riding my motorbike on the way to visit my girlfriend. A car came from nowhere out of a side street and drove straight into me. My leg was nearly chopped off. Ten centimetres of bone – the width of the bumper – were completely gone. Needless to say, my military career was over.

It was common to smoke dope up on the Border. Everyone smoked, especially when on ops in Angola. Came back out, got caught smoking dope again, for the second time, and they put me in DB in Grootfontein before sending me to Klipdrift, just outside of Potchefstroom. By then I'd got rank. I was a lance jack, but they never stripped me of it.

Klipdrift was also a drug and alcohol rehab station. We had clinical psychologists monitoring us. The camp consisted of tents in a fenced-off area patrolled with dogs. I wasn't a hardcore druggie. Wasn't spiking Wellconal or anything like that. Just smoked dope, like most others. But the army took it seriously. 'Going to make an example of you, Corporal!

We'll teach you!' But what they'd forgotten is that they'd put me in rehab camp as a lance jack from the Border with about six months to go. Then all these new young troepies who'd come in and whinged about their drug problems were put in there with us. *We* taught them how to be army guys. We drilled them, gave them opfoks and PT. There was a strict hierarchy.

We managed to AWOL all the time to go to Potch to score more dope. Often we'd lock the 'doggies' out of the camp by putting our own chain and lock on the gate so that they couldn't get in. They had to get bolt-cutters to sort us out. We'd stone their dogs into a corner and then hop over the fences. The camp was L-shaped, so if some of us kept the one dog cornered, the others could jump. The boys went off to Potch and had a jol. The 'doggies' could hear the dogs barking, but they never came out. They didn't give a damn about them. They'd sit in their little huts, watching TV. They took us on once, but we destroyed their two little prefab asbestos houses with rocks. We locked them out and stoned their office. The place looked like a sieve after we'd finished. It was quite hardcore.

Growing all around the area were mielies. So, during the day, while we worked in the farmers' fields we'd find malpitte. Chowed them twice. Went off my head. I was told afterwards what had happened. Picked stuff out from thin air, grabbed things. One of my chinas swallowed his false teeth. We searched for days and couldn't find them. Nobody knew he'd actually *swallowed* them. He used to talk all retarded without them. There were a whole lot of ous who ended up in 1 Mil Hospital. One ou even tried to rape a sergeant major's wife who was a nurse there. It got really ugly.

Then I got taken out of rehab. On the way to the train station the taxi driver sold me dope. Got on the train, got goofed and went back up to the Border. On the way I was bust again and told that when I got to Windhoek they were going to arrest me. Just before we arrived I jumped the train and caught a truck out to Grootfontein, where I carried on as normal and finished my army service. Did no extra days.

After Basics finished, in early '82, they sorted ous out according to our education and fitness levels. They'd called up too many guys for my intake – about four thousand of us. I did a couple of courses during second phase and ended up as section leader – a two-liner. Got a small section of guys. We were stationed at Queenstown, just a little bit outside of Grahamstown, and we were about 150 guys. Stayed in the hangars. The African population in Queenstown was causing shit. We were sent there for the rondfok but also to keep an eye on them. Cars were getting stoned on that piece of road leading to Port Elizabeth. It was very, very dangerous. We were told not to hike that road. Whenever we left Queenstown we'd go on Samils to PE or East London airports when they needed to fly us to the Border. One section went up while another came back.

I bought zol in Cape Town when I used to come home from the Border. It was unreal. I would load it into my pocket and get it into camp at 6 SAI. Went to the civvy airport and walked straight through the line. Who'd search me then? I was property of the government! I just walked straight through; nobody worried me. It was so simple.

I knew of okes carrying balsaks of the stuff. I'm not lying. It's no bull. I've got a mate who did it. He took every bit of his gear and threw it away. Gear you could replace; you had friends. If a guy worked in the store he could get it all for you if you gave him a nice incentive. And it was new issue! My bud did it again but got caught. He had to do an extra six months, and that was it – but six months in Queenstown camp doing guard duty was to me far worse than doing Border duty. It was blind for him because he got no pay, no danger pay, no extras – no nothing. I never got stoned during Basics. I couldn't and I felt scared, obviously. But later you could get away with it. 6 SAI was so big and there were so many ous. It was a bit dodgy, but most times you didn't give a shit. You just did it.

I was pretty good with my fists – knocked a good couple of ous' front teeth out whenever I had the chance – so I did a lot of boxing in the army as a sport. I enjoyed it. There was this one guy from the Transvaal, a rooikop ou. We were good buddies but in the beginning we didn't like each other at all. I found out that he boxed for the Transvaal, so I said, 'Let's go for it and see what happens.' It was a draw. I was fit then.

After finishing Basics at Saldanha they transferred me to Simon's Town, where I remained based the whole time, until July 1984. Stayed at a place called Waterfall Barracks. Had our own rooms – sorry, cabins. Very nice. No complaints about that. Different navy personnel were coming and going all the time. Nobody knew who was supposed to be there permanently. Since it was a shifting crowd, inspections didn't happen much. We were left to our own devices, which was super.

Because I'd been classified G3K4 NP, due to a collapsed left lung, I was put on a course for stores. I don't know what the NP stood for. I thought it meant National Party. Then they decided I could do clerical work in one of the offices instead, stamping papers and documents. A particular commodore used to come in occasionally, although he wasn't based at Naval Logistics Command. He asked for certain files and notes, which I then photocopied for him. Whatever documents he wanted, I did. He was the boss. Then he was locked up. The MPs took him away. He was arrested as a Russian spy! His wife, too! All hell broke loose when they found out. There was a big inquiry. They asked all of us what we'd done for the commodore. 'I copied files for him,' I said. 'Any file he asked for. He was the boss.'

They asked me what school I went to. After I told them, they said, 'Ah! The commodore went there as well!' Then they saw I went to the one in Cape Town. Luckily he went to the one in Pretoria.

'Religion?' they asked.

'Catholic.'

'Ah! The commodore is a Catholic too!' I wasn't going to say anything more, otherwise I felt I'd convict myself. But, fortunately, that's where the similarities between us ended.

If he'd been doing it because he believed in the communist cause I would've had a little more respect for him, because at least, then, he'd done it for ideological reasons. But apparently it was purely for the money. The Russians were paying him. That's real political prostitution, doing it just for the cash. The navy had become suspicious of how a person on a commodore's pay could live so extravagantly. That's what tipped the whole thing. He was sent to jail for life but was released under the new system.

In the Parabats I was a machine-gunner. Did about fifteen jumps in total. Carried my pack plus the machine gun. Humped those around for a few days during operational exercises. We'd jump out of the plane, into the bush, and then walk for the day and then the whole night straight. Practising for ops there'd be lots of shooting but no action.

We went to the border, but not the one you think. Nope, our border was Beit Bridge, near Zimbabwe, in the former Northern Transvaal. We also patrolled the borders of Mozambique and Botswana. We camped with the locals. Terrorists were known to be in those areas, but were inactive. They wore plain clothes and blended in. It was rumoured that they were right in amongst the local population. We didn't know who was who, so we'd beat a few around in an attempt to get information. But nothing came of it. Just got given a whole lot of shit from them, that's all.

I didn't know where we were, half the time. The problem was you just got dumped somewhere. You were chucked out of a plane and there you went. On one phase we walked for three days on end. We didn't know where the hell we were. No road signs, no nothing – not even a tarred road. The corporal had a map but none of us knew what was going on. 'Take your shit and walk!' We had blood blisters all over our feet. Could hardly walk. People were crying. I couldn't believe it – grown guys out there crying. Couldn't take it. I honestly cannot remember how we were picked up. All I know is we got chucked out of a plane with all our stuff and started walking as soon as we hit the ground. No one told us what we were doing or where we were going or what it was for.

My back is still buggered from those packs and machine guns. We weighed the pack: sixty kilograms, excluding machine gun. Ammo, food, water. You're basically taking your little caravan with you. If you didn't have enough water, don't think someone else is going to give you some. Before leaving for patrols you broke down the machine gun, which also went into your pack. Everything went into that pack. It had to be a certain weight, but as a machine-gunner they took the extra weight into consideration. Everything was attached to a rope that dangled below you. When you landed, the gun was taken out, reassembled and then you walked. We did three of those patrols. I've still got a bullet I found that had fallen to the ground. It's all bent out of shape.

The last stretch at Beit Bridge lasted about three months. We did bugger all. It was like a holiday, but there was nothing to do. Complete boredom. There was no base. We stayed out in the bush, camped, ate rations and hung out, watching for something, for three solid months. Probably the worst part was the sheer boredom. Nothing ever happened. It was the worst. Did a lot of suntanning. In the end we were having gym classes. It even got to the point where we became skilled at making our own silencers.

Once, we ate a dassie. They're really hard to catch – they're quick. We didn't shoot them but chased them around the place. The area was covered in rocks and they'd scamper down the little burrows, but we managed to catch one. It was a group effort. We coordinated it. It was clubbed on the head, strung up and then braaied. It obviously tasted very gamey, and it was really tough and stringy – but interesting. You got tired of eating the kak out of those little rat boxes.

We swam in a dry riverbed that still had little pools of water. Crocs were in the area. Some croc prints we found were bigger than a man's. They must've been huge crocs. We spotted some that were about four to five metres long. So it was basically doing gym, suntanning, chasing dassies, eating rat packs, hanging with the crocs and talking about women. No lights, no music, no civilisation, no nothing.

6 SAI had long bungalows. There was a passage with rooms on either side. Four guys per room. The bungalows were really lekker compared to Oudtshoorn. The last room was the TV and relaxation room. Some rooms even had table tennis. There was always a video on Friday nights, which was controlled by a central command.

We marched at the Grahamstown Festival. Our company did a colour parade for it. Our sergeant major used to suip a moerse lot. We called him 'Sad Sack' because he had a big boep that hung over his belt. He also had a double chin and straight little legs. He was a dop-en-chop oke all the way.

After transferring to Youngsfield I reported to the RSM, who said, 'Okay, you're a tiffy. I'm putting you in the workshops'. I explained that I was a qualified graphic designer and knew nothing at all about vehicles. 'Sa'majoor, I was only made a tiffy because of the shortage of troops, Sa'majoor.'

'In that case, report to the sa'majoor at the media department. They need someone.'

The media department consisted of a humorous and good-natured sa'majoor, a civvy secretary whom we called 'Mevrou', and two laid-back civvy assistants: the technician and the casual worker. Apart from signing out audio-visual equipment, such as video machines, film projectors, speakers and overhead projectors, my main function was to photocopy and bind the many thousands of various training manuals. Military personnel came from all over the Cape to Youngsfield for various theoretical courses.

Media had a huge, monstrous, thoroughbred, kick-ass, mother of a photocopier. It could pump out about 120 pages a minute. I'd put in the master copy, some of which were hundreds of pages long, and hit the button. The machine could only process a certain number of pages at a time, so it was necessary to assemble the dozens of collated segments to make complete copies. It helped to pay attention to this procedure, otherwise it became confusing and could go pear-shaped. To make matters worse, the machine occasionally overheated and packed up. Nothing a good kick couldn't cure. *Beskadiging van staatseiendom.* The copies were then stapled, spiral-bound or glued together. Sometimes the captains or majors needed copies of highly restricted documents made. They stood next to me the entire time to make sure I didn't keep a copy for myself, to 'spread' around.

Sometimes Mevrou, the assistants and I played cards or watched TV or videos. Other times the technician snoozed on his chair while the casual slept on the piles of shredded paper, but out of sight, when the sa'majoor was away. Occasionally even I nodded off. We also had a ping-pong table. The captain and major would take time to challenge one another. I'd play against them, too.

People treated the media department as a relaxed place, which it was. The rank didn't give attitude if they wanted the job done. Give us a smile, hand over the documents and the copies would be finished in double-quick time, neatly bound and covered, with time to spare. Give us the standard army crap and it was, 'Well, sorry Sersant, the machine's busy. Ek doen die majoor se kopieë.' Or, 'Jammer, Luitenant, die masjien is gebreek.' This happened fairly regularly and, when a kick didn't fix it, civvy technicians from the manufacturers were called in.

Being in media was a mundane yet responsible job, and I applied myself and enjoyed it. This meant that the commandant was happy. If he was happy then the major was happy, and in turn the captain was happy, and so it trickled down to my sa'majoor, who was happy. If he was happy, I was happy. Happy Families. I made sure things ran smoothly and didn't bugger around. I think too many media department troepies had goofed off in the past and taken advantage of their good luck in ending up there. It was the best place, personally, for me to have landed. I felt extremely grateful because I could still be artistically creative, albeit in a restricted way. I illustrated various training manuals and designed posters for local events on base, as well as for the military exhibition at the annual Goodwood Show. The captain also asked me to do a caricature sketch of the colonel, the Youngsfield officer commanding, for his birthday.

They were going to frame the sketch and present it to the colonel. I pulled no punches and went in for the kill. The whole point of a caricature is to accentuate and overemphasise a person's features. I made him a Caesar. He had an oversized laurel wreath around his head, which rested on his big, floppy ears. The colonel had large ears. Everybody knew it. They were hard not to notice. It was rumoured that he had false teeth. I gave him a wide grin and gave the teeth a shiny flash. His glasses were like windscreens. I gave him a tiny little body, standing proudly in a Roman centurion's armour. He held an Ordnance Services Corps banner. It was a great rendition and much of the rank had a major laugh, especially my sergeant major, who had a Standard 7 education. The captain liked it too, but became apprehensive because it was he who had to present it.

The next day I was summoned to the colonel's office – a place where troops didn't want to go. I waited outside thinking I was in trouble and that maybe I shouldn't have poked fun at him. I felt like a naughty schoolboy waiting to see the headmaster and knowing that I'm going to get caned six, which only happened four times in my school career. The secretary told me to go inside. I marched in, swishing my arms, and stamped as best I could. Stood to attention, gave the salute and stared ahead. He told me to stand at ease. Then, with a big smile, he came over and shook my hand. He pointed to the drawing hanging on the wall and said how much he liked it. It seemed the colonel had a sense of humour. He thanked me before dismissing me. I again stamped my foot, which brought me to attention, marched two paces backwards to the door, stamped the foot yet again, saluted, about-turned, stamped again, and got the hell out of there. Relief.

I was given the evening off. I decided to go back to Sea Point. At the train station the MPs were checking for guys in uniform who were going AWOL and who obviously wouldn't have a pass. But in the navy we didn't get issued with papers. They stopped me and asked for my pass. 'Excuse me?' I said. 'Do I look like a native to you?' Remember, this was in 1983. 'I haven't got a pass. I'm in the navy.'

I had one star on my arm because I was an able seaman, which is nothing – it's a lance corporal – but they didn't realise this. They weren't sure of navy rank, being in the army. They all thought I was a lieutenant. They saluted me and backed off.

We did guard duty at the base in Durban for a couple of weeks. At one stage there weren't enough people to guard it. It had a gate in the front and a gate out the back, with barracks and a little headquarters inside. It was fun, because you were in town.

Everybody would club together, somebody would phone dial-a-pizza and they'd deliver it to the gate. One corporal sent me to withdraw money to get more pizza. The ATM was just down the road, half a block away. When I got there, somebody must have withdrawn but not taken the cash. There was about eighty bucks in the slot. I looked around, but nobody was there, so I took it back to base. 'Here's money for pizza.' We had a bonus that night. All had lots of pizza – one of the highlights.

In the block of flats opposite where we stayed lived a couple of ladies. Ladies of the night, I think. The guys who did the late-night guard duty got a nice boob flash every now and then. The ladies would stand by the window, do the dance thing and then it was up with the shirt and we'd go, 'Yeah! Give us more!' I think one of the corporals went to visit them one night because, when he stood in the shower the next day, he had scratch marks on his back. 'Where were you?' we asked. He just laughed.

Standing guard at the base – what a drag. In the early nineties the threat was minimal, but guarding the base was still required. When we were issued our rifle they gave us a half-full magazine sealed in a plastic bag. We'd sign for this bag from the corporal. It was not to be opened and, if it was, you'd have a lot of explaining to do. We weren't even allowed, as far as I can remember, to have a round in the chamber. We'd be posted to certain areas around the perimeter. At night the place was deserted. Standing beat, all alone in the middle of the night, I'd ask myself what I'd do if attacked. Rip open the bag, pull off a few rounds and sprint back to the guard room?

A section stood guard for four hours at a time, sometimes at the gate, or in the furthest and remotest corners of the base. Groups rotated out, then split up and trundled off to their designated spots. Then we'd come back and get four hours off until the next shift. We'd rest or try to sleep in these scaly, siff bunk beds at the main gate's little guard room. The corporals on duty would watch this tiny black-and-white portable TV, with bad reception, or the radio would be on.

Standing duty at the gate meant marching up to the car, stamping your foot and doing a chest salute. You had your rifle, slung over your shoulder, placed against your chest and with the butt folded in. You'd let the car's occupants sign themselves in or out, then you marched to the gate, opened it, let the car through, closed it again, marched back to your spot, stamped your foot, stood at ease and waited for the next vehicle. It was a laugh to see the PFs coming back in the evenings, drunk as lords, and scribbling their names into the register. Some could hardly hold the pen, let alone sign.

Late at night some of us would sneak into the chapel, which was hardly ever locked. We'd arrange to meet there and then catch a small kip on the pews. We'd be alert for any noises or sounds. Talking was obviously a no-no. We kept quiet and let time tick by. Someone would keep chips and tap the door if he saw a corporal on the hunt, which would give us just enough time to get the hell out and vanish into the shadows.

I remember the one night vividly. I was down at the far end of the base at the vehicle compound where all the Samils, Buffels and recovery vehicles were parked. It was two o'clock in the morning. Those orange floodlights, on high poles, were burning brightly. It was belting down with rain. A gale-force wind was blowing and it was freezing. A real Cape winter's black southeaster. It was dark, except for those bright lights, which made everything black, brown and orange. The raindrops were almost horizontal with the wind, and were illuminated into long streaks. I needed to shelter from this storm. My poncho and I were drenched. You're supposed to roam the area, but I thought, 'What the hell am I doing here? Forget this! It's pouring, I'm wet, it's two in the morning, it's howling with wind and I'm stuck in the arse-end of the base.'

I huddled up in a dark corner in the doorway of a workshop and lit up a smoke. The taste was good. It warmed me. I watched the smoke turn orange, get caught in the wind and sweep around the corner. You got slightly loopy in a situation like that. I stared at the rain and spoke out loud in an attempt to regain some sense and reassure myself, because, as surreal as it was, it was a little scary. I said, 'In spite of this, this is something to remember, because it won't last forever and one day it'll be nothing but a distant memory.'

You know when you see an image you feel you'll never forget? That was one of those moments, and I purposely burnt it into my memory that night. Alone, cold, wet and smoking a cigarette in a dry, deserted little corner of Youngsfield Base, watching the streaking orange rain come down.

I ended up at 2 Mil NCOs' mess. Was first at the officers' mess but that was too stressful so they sent me to the NCOs'. That was still too much for me, so they put me with a one-liner in stores, the cushiest position on base. He was a bastard. I freaked out with this oke. Destroyed his storeroom. Completely freaked out. Did the whole effect of grabbing razor blades when guys were watching. Turned my bed and threw my kas over. Got given a shot. Calmed down. I remember waking up in a passage and blotting out again. Eventually came to in the army hospital. A nurse was taking my pants off. 'This is pretty cool,' I thought. Blotted out again. It was the injection they'd given me.

It became an official thing after I had this crack-up. They gave me civvy clothes and wanted me to go to gym. Could chill out there. Had a duvet on my bed, a hi-fi in my room. *Streshanteering.* I stayed on base and could go home over the weekends.

Then I decided I wanted to join the Permanent Force. I wanted to become a canary in the air force, as I was singing in the Cape Town Choir at the time. The air force had cool uniforms. I thought it would be great to get a salary for singing, for using my tenor skills. Get a pay cheque to sing and travel around wearing a kiff uniform. But I stuffed that up for myself with all my messing around, so you can imagine my request reports: denied, denied, denied.

After my freak-out episode, and having had enough – as in *enough enough* – I went on a quest for zol. I had to find this thing called dagga. I'd heard about it and went looking at Wynberg station. I saw this coloured chap, poor and out of it, and reckoned he'd know where to score. I asked, 'Have you got any dagga?' He whipped out these *stoppe* and packed a neck. I didn't even know how to smoke a cigarette, let alone a bottleneck! I didn't know how to inhale or even the slightest technicalities of it. He told me to take a hit. His hand smelled of kak. I didn't get it right. By the time I got back to base I was freaking out, not because I was stoned, but because I stank like a hotbox.

After Basics I was transferred to 2 Military Hospital where I ran part of the rehab centre. I was in charge of general orthopaedics. Rehab was a big unit with chemotherapy, orthopaedic and psychological units. There were social workers and physiotherapists. I felt I added a lot of value to the system. Every week we had discussions about patients regarding their rehab progress. I saw quite a few that had come back from Angola or the Border who simply couldn't handle the stress. They'd be sent up for six months, come back down for a while, and be sent back up again for another six months. Young guys.

I also started a sports rehab and jacked up the cardiac unit. Did a lot of extra work outside the military set-up and became team doctor for various sports teams. Eventually the man in charge of 2 Mil gave me trouble. The colonel couldn't handle the fact that I was so dedicated to my work, starting new projects and trying to help all the guys in rehab. We organised a lot of sponsorship for them and he was totally against it. He did me injustices in many ways. He didn't like me much.

I was a full two-pip lieutenant because of my qualifications, even though I was only a National Serviceman. I was approved by the SADF and selected to join PF, as there were vacancies, but he was against that. He didn't want to offer me a job. At the time, I wanted to join. It would've been to my advantage. I'd just got married and needed a better income and more security. I needed his official approval but he wouldn't give it. I said, 'There are vacancies in the unit. Why can't you give this to me? There's my CV. There are the forms.' He started screaming and swearing. I said, 'Listen, You're a commander. You've got no right to swear at me!'

'You're a troep!' he yelled.

'No. I'm a full lieutenant! You can't swear at me!' That's a standing order in the military. You're not allowed to swear at a fellow officer. 'Carry on swearing and I'll walk out of this office.' But he carried on. I turned and left and asked his secretary if I could use the phone.

'No. It's not allowed,' she said.

'I'll pay for the call myself!' She still refused. I left and made a call to the brigadier in charge of the medical unit for the Western Cape. The next day I was summoned to the colonel's office.

'How the hell do you find the right to call the brigadier?' he screamed.

'Well, you keep on swearing at me and I'll do it again! What right do you have to discriminate against me?'

He always transferred people all over the place, and I ended up in Oudtshoorn for six weeks. I eventually went to the same brigadier to discuss the situation. He sympathised but said there was little he could do to change the colonel's attitude. He did, however, pull me out of Oudtshoorn. I was then transferred to SACC for six months.

The colonel was eventually transferred to Nelspruit and demoted to commandant because of the many injustices he'd done to a lot of other officers. He didn't want to understand people's feelings and didn't give a stuff about anybody else.

One oke's spectacles were about three millimetres thick. Could use them as a magnifying glass. He was a nerd. As soon as we'd go out on patrol – the moment the Buffel started – his eyes would close and he'd be asleep. The corporal would klap him on the helmet. 'Hey! Word wakker, jong!' We'd hardly be away and he'd be dossing again.

I once played a nasty prank on him. On Sundays we could have siesta time. Rest, park off or relax – no being chased around by the corporals. You could officially let your guard down. This oke always took his glasses off before he snoozed. I took boot polish and smeared them with it. We got one of the corporals to come in. One oke shouted, 'Kaserne! AANDAG!' Everybody jumped up and he, half asleep, grabbed his spectacles and suddenly couldn't see anything. His head turned left and right, up and down. It went all over the place. We pissed ourselves. Then he swore like anything! He was mad at what we'd done to his glasses. When a nerd loses his temper it can be a scary thing.

I walked around with my arm injury during the three months of Basics. When I came back from pass the doctor had a look. He sent me to the army surgeon, who decided to operate. The injury was more serious than first thought. Today, the scar makes it look like I was assaulted with a machete! That's what an army op looks like.

Our G3 group ended up helping the support unit at Lohatlha, which was basically all the admin guys, guys on control towers and the ones guarding the base. They didn't actually use us for anything else because we just knocked the system as far as we could. I don't know why they didn't simply kick us out. In my squad there were only seven of us who were really terrible. One guy who stood out for me in our group had been in the process of becoming a Catholic priest, but had given up. Then he responded to his call-ups. He came to our squad from Bloem. They tried to convince him to carry a rifle, in spite of knowing his background. Here's a man of faith who believed in peace, and he got abused for it. The way they treated Priest really got to us. In the middle of the night they'd spray him with the fire hose. Always called him a moffie and kicked him around. It was continual harassment. They singled him out because he was a pacifist. He was a small, thin, complacent guy. Most of us rebelled because of the way they treated him. We all liked Priest. Sometimes he'd sit with my guys and cry. He said he just wanted to go home and didn't want to be there.

Another guy who also stood out for me had a very serious physical deformity. His left arm was elbow-length, with a deformed hand. He had to carry on as if there was nothing wrong with him. He was G4. The poor guy should've been made G5 and sent home from the start. He should never have gone in. They picked on him as well.

I took my anger at the whole messed-up system, and the way Priest was treated, out on the more senior ranks. I wouldn't salute them. I refused to conform. As a result I was beaten up a lot. Had a few serious opfoks. You got to know the pole very well in that situation. You'd get a pole of about six feet, put it on your shoulder and off you'd march all day or until you fell over from exhaustion or dehydration.

They once brought in some navy trainees, who arrived by bus. The driver happened to be a lieutenant, wearing all this rank and insignia that I didn't understand. My lieuty asked me, 'Well? Aren't you going to salute this man?'

'I don't salute bus drivers, Lieutenant.' So back I went to my comfortable pole, even if I was G3. Where, and to whom, could you complain? Where? Especially in Lohatlha.

I did my fair share of AWOL – three times and never caught – but realised I was missing out on a lot of fun when not in the unit because the others were pulling things down, while I wasn't, so I always went back to help them. They'd phone and say that they were going to do something bad. Once I went back because they were going to polish the sergeant major's office. 'Okay. Wait 'til I'm back.'

I hitch-hiked back and did the extras – usually standing guard. But standing guard to us meant going past SAWI, buying a case of beer and getting drunk at the guard gate – leaving it open. So whoever wanted to go in our out was free to do so.

We eventually polished the office, but with black shoe polish. Everything was polished: his table, his chair, everything on his desk – including his papers – the floor, the walls, the door, the windows – everything. They tried sending some of us to DB, where we also didn't cooperate. All they did was swear at you, make life miserable, spray you with water and scream at you to stand to attention, but eventually they had to send you back to base. There was a system that a certain number of troops always had to be within the unit at any given time.

At one stage I was in DB for a week. Walked around with a sand bucket all day, every day. I'd been arrested for possession of acid. One guy had split on me. He wasn't a friend – he liked the army. He was G1K1. He saw that there was something other than alcohol making us happy. They searched my kas and found my stuff, which I'd just brought back from pass. This screwed things up for me. Returning from pass was now very difficult. Before, I'd easily been able to smuggle in my drugs, but now, thanks to him, I was searched every time. They moved this rat away from us on purpose. They were afraid that we'd damage him, but we wouldn't have done anything. Being pacifists we didn't believe in violence.

I also refused to go to church. That got them writhing. You had to go to church in the army. Instead, I slept in on Sundays. I didn't open my bungalow door for anybody. Sometimes they'd break it down and drag me out of bed. Beat me up. Next day I'd go and get my wounds patched. I didn't make it easy on myself, but it had to be done.

Within a couple of months after Basics I faked epileptic fits just to get out of the army. I read about it and put it to the test. It didn't work. Once

I knocked my head pretending as though I was passing out – I connected with a lamp pole and got concussion! Ended up in 3 Mil for two weeks. They sent me on a week's recovery pass back home.

Then, when I came back, they made me barman. I was never short of booze. The liquor prices were horrendously cheap. My whole pay basically went into the bar. You had nothing else to spend your money on except sweets and cigarettes. We'd get as drunk as skunks and then play chicken. We'd place a lit cigarette on our forearm. He who pulled away last, won. You can still see the scars on my arm. That was our entertainment. It was also 'damage to state property'. You could get charged for it and sit in the cells. We were so bored. There was nothing to do. My commanding officer got concerned about my alcohol abuse and sent me to 3 Mil's psychiatric unit to dry me out for two months. When I came out I was really thirsty. So I drank again. They sent me back. I won't say it was the army that made me dop. I just did so because I could, but I also knew it was another way to beat the system.

I got my ear pierced but never wore the earring inside the camp. Once again they charged me with 'damage of government property'. For a pierced ear! Wonder what I would've got for a tattoo?

We were in the guard room. This one guy was depressed. His girlfriend had phoned him earlier. Said she'd met somebody else. He picked up his R4 and said he was going out on base patrol. We heard the shot. He'd only walked about ten paces. I ran out and saw him on the ground, with his head wound, all because his girlfriend left him. They never admitted his death to be a suicide. That's how logical the world was in which we lived.

Towards the end of my service about thirty of us were selected into a platoon. We drilled in slow marching for three days solid. It was a crash course. We'd been chosen to do this particular march at some guy's funeral. A slow march was quite difficult to do correctly and in unison, especially for those of us who didn't enjoy ordinary marching in the first place. The right arm was kept straight and to your side while the left clutched the rifle grip on your chest. As one foot shot forward, you skimmed the boot's sole gently over the tar, pointed the toes out and stepped. Then the other foot was thrust forward and the same procedure followed. It was very easy to lose your balance if you weren't concentrating. This, and the fact that it was at someone's funeral, made it a difficult task. You didn't want to mess up and knew you had to do the best you could.

On the day, we dressed up in white puttees, white gloves and blue cravats. Looked smart. We were issued our R4s and then went by bus to Parow, a suburb in Cape Town. After arriving, our corporal *tree'd* us *aan.* We stood to attention in front of the coffin, which was draped with the old South African flag. I recall seeing a maroon beret on top, but I can't say whether it was a Recce's, Bat's or medic's. All they told us was that he'd been accidentally shot in the head by another soldier while they'd been cleaning their pistols. That's all I remember them saying. I don't know whether he was an officer or not. We all reckoned it was suicide, but some-one piped up that he wouldn't receive a military funeral if that was the situation.

The procession began. We slow-marched in the front, while family and friends followed the hearse behind us. The formation slowly made its way around the block towards the Dutch Reformed church, where our platoon was halted. Curious onlookers gathered, but kept still and silent. I could see that they acknowledged, respected and understood. The coffin was taken inside the church by members of his unit.

During the service we sat in the bus. Some guys joked and buggered around, yet I sat alone and kept quiet. I wasn't in a mood to be boisterous. Afterwards we had *tee en koek* in the church. The jokers scrambled in, almost elbowing one another out the way to be first in line, while the poor family watched. I thought, 'You callous bastards. Can't you show some respect?' The snacks had been supplied for us by the family as a token of thanks. This basic acknowledgement was humbling.

I don't know if I should admit this, but slow marching in a funeral procession for a complete stranger, just being there, alongside his family in their sad moment, I found very moving. It was one of my proudest and most treasured moments, not just within the army, but as a human being. Yet there was no joy.

There was an army dentist on base. He was a PF lieut, I think. I made an appointment to see him and explained that my tooth was really sore. He wasn't bothered and shooed me away, telling me to come again another day, in spite of the fact that he had no other patients. He couldn't have given a toss for troepies' teeth, only PFs', but I was adamant because it was genuinely painful. I explained this to his assistant, who checked. She realised I wasn't lying. Only then did he have a look, and said it was a wisdom tooth that needed to come out. I was reluctant but wanted it done. If you couldn't handle it in the army, then when could you? So I agreed. If I'd known what was about to happen, I wouldn't have.

He injected the gum with anaesthetic and, before it had even taken effect, grabbed his pliers and pulled and tugged, and pulled some more, but the tooth wasn't budging. He was quite a fat dude. He was also grunting. By now I was gripping the chair with white knuckles. It was a hot day and the beads of sweat forming on his forehead began falling on my face. Then I heard a crack, but the tooth was still firmly stuck. He then put his knee on my chest and tugged. He certainly wasn't gentle, like a civvy dentist would've been. By now my eyes were as wide as saucers. The pain was bad. Finally I heard another crack and out it popped – after about ten minutes of tugging. My face was wet from his sweat. He asked if I would like the tooth as a souvenir. Swallowing the blood, I said, 'No, shank you, Looshenant,' as the anaesthetic finally kicked in.

I spent the remainder of the day repeatedly applying wads of cotton wool to the inside of my mouth. The good thing was I didn't have to pay a cent for the procedure. I had no money and no medical aid, so thanks to the SADF and the taxpayer, I had my wisdom tooth out for free.

It amused me that there were so many ex–Royal Navy guys in the PF. Their Afrikaans, if they could speak it, was shocking. In the navy, instructions would be one month in English and the next month in Afrikaans. We'd joke that at least every second month half the navy didn't know what was going on! These guys would chuck the notes in their desks and wait for the next month's English version to come out. This wasn't exactly ideal from a work point of view.

We were called out to ferry a whole lot of Buffels from 44 Para Battalion, north of Pretoria, to Bloemfontein. I was allocated my Buffel. You had a list that required you to do a pre-check on all the various basics. Indicators flash, lights work, brakes appear to function, battery's okay, engine runs – that sort of stuff. One of the requirements was to check the water. Behind and underneath the Buffel was a big water tank with a tap for the troops to fill their bottles. It also served as a landmine barrier. So I checked that, too. Made sure it was full. Opened the tap and water flowed out.

Time to go! We were all driving along in convoy. A while later I heard a loud whistle and then an explosion. I'd blown the head gasket! When the list said, 'Check water', it meant check the *engine*'s water! I didn't know this because I drove Samils. A Samil is air-cooled, like a Beetle, which is why it's so indestructible – you don't need water to keep it running – but a Buffel is water-cooled. I assumed they worked the same.

A staff sergeant tiffie arrived in his huge recovery vehicle. It's a kick-arse, hardcore truck with a big crane on the back. He tells me he's not going to hook me up and tow the Buffel on its rear wheels; he'll straight-bar me instead. The bar's about three metres long. He hooks it up. There are still a few hundred klicks to Bloem, which means a few hours' driving, at least.

Now – if you're driving a six-ton vehicle with no power steering and no power brakes and the only thing that works are the flashing hazards and all you see is this brick wall ahead of you and you can't see left and you can't see right – you shit off. All you're doing is concentrating on that straight-bar, because it swings and whiplashes your vehicle, which you have to counteract. When he takes a corner it's like water skiing. You go wide, come out on the other side and then have to bring yourself back in. Then there's slack on the bar and suddenly he clocks it. *Kwang!* Come around another corner, slide to the other side. *Kwang!* It's about to rain and there's lightning in the sky. On downhills he overtakes other trucks, never mind the cars! *Kwang!* Hours and hours of this. It's probably the most hardcore thing I've ever done. *Kwang!*

We find our way to base. I'm freaked out of my mind. I'm as white as a sheet because I've only just managed to make it there alive. I notice two empty bottles of Klippies in his cab. He'd been dopping and having a jol. He certainly wasn't bored. This was his fun. His kind of stuff. *Gee gas.* Hardcore. This is where he separated the mice from the men. It was scary – very scary – long-haul surf-skiing with a six-ton vehicle.

I went to the bungalow, still shocked out of my mind, and the guys tuned me the corporal's pissed off because my bed and kas were looking shit. 'I don't care,' I said. 'I'm going to sleep on the floor and the corporal can go bugger himself!' I just didn't give a shit. I'd nearly died a few times that day.

One night the major, the captain and my sergeant major decided to have an informal braai with their wives and some friends. Having no rank I was naturally expected to make the fire and do the braaiing, which was fine, as I enjoy doing that. Used lekker, dry rooikrans and had a raging fire in no time. Had a couple of beers. Small-talked with the rank. Everything was relaxed. We watched the coals burn down, and then it was time to *gooi* on the chops and boerie. The major tuned me he'd do his steaks himself, for him and his wife, his way. Cool, no problem. I was to learn something that night.

All the meat was sizzling away nicely, and thankfully I hadn't messed up – had it all under control. When it was almost done, the major opened his Tupperware and hauled out two *makhulu* rumps, drenched in oil and crushed garlic. There was so much garlic I hardly even saw the steaks. He stoked up a few coals to get flame going, and said, 'Kyk mooi, boet,' and threw them on.

Now, let it be said, I'd always braaied the traditional way. Let the heat cook the meat. I was to be exposed to the flame-grilled method in a big way. The flames leapt up and consumed these steaks. They literally caught fire and sizzled and popped with lots of white, billowing smoke. I was amazed. I'd never seen anything like it. 'What the hell is he doing?' I thought. 'He's destroying them. They're gonna taste really kak!' After the flames subsided he turned the meat over, and once only. They caught alight again. Within seconds he took them off, waited a while and gave me a piece. It was the most delicious piece of steak I'd ever tasted. Juicy, tender, rare and garlicky. Not burnt at all. From then on I was converted. No more dry, tough, tasteless meat.

It wasn't too kak being paraat in those days. You'd be walking from one part of the base to get somewhere else and see an officer approaching, say a one-pip or a three-oh-three. As you walked past you'd salute, wait for them to return it, and whip your arm down afterwards. On your own it was easy, but if there were two or more of you then it took more coordination. You made sure you were in step, which you had to be anyway, whenever you walked as a pair. As the brass approached, the one who'd decided to call the salute went, on the left foot, 'Twee, op.' You pulled the salute. Kept the tips of your first two fingers on the edge of your right eyebrow. Walked past. Then on the left foot again, 'Twee, af.' Smart. Together. A sloppy salute could get you a blast, or worse.

Military rule also stipulated that you didn't salute without wearing a beret, but strekked instead, and didn't have to salute if you were already with a higher rank. Only the highest rank of the group saluted. Also, if you were sitting down and an officer walked in you strekked by stiffening your back and straightening your arms to your knees, with fists clenched. Lekker paraat, ek sê.

There was no way I believed I should cooperate with the army. They weren't paying you properly, they gave you stress and they treated you like shit. No respect for no money, so why should I work?

Everybody was zikking whatever they could from the stores. Tents, spades, sleeping bags, clothing – whatever. Everything just buggered off the base. You should've seen the stuff that disappeared out of that storeroom. The storeman was on his last two months and so pulled things out for himself. I became his replacement. When guys had to hand their stuff in and were missing things, like a pikstel or a blanket, I was in the position to overlook it. The replacement costs would come off their salaries. Suddenly the okes all saw the point of now having you as their buddy, in spite of having treated you like shit the whole time because all you were was a storeman – unlike the cook in the kitchen. He was a buddy from the start. He gave out the chow, so everyone was his buddy. You'd give him five bucks for his bottle of Tassies, and for the next few days you'd get extra pudding. But as a storeman nobody gave a damn. They only realised at the end. Suddenly you were being bribed. Not even I saw the potential until this happened. There were cigarettes and booze flooding in.

Guard duty at Simon's Town was one day on and five days off. At first they didn't trust us to stand guard with rifles. They issued us with torches and whistles, instead! So, if terrorists had to attack using petrol bombs and AK-47s, we could blow a whistle and throw a torch at them, then run. Eventually they issued us with rifles without bullets, which we could hit them with in case of an attack. What were they thinking? That was our great defence – rifles without bullets, and whistles and torches.

Over weekends certain PFs would steal from the Defence Force's vehicles. They'd drive their cars in on a Saturday afternoon, park them next to the military cars and exchange the batteries, spark plugs and whatever else they needed. It was usually VW Golfs. The navy could never work out in their books why these cars, only a few months old, were konked-in and falling apart. Those guys supposed to be guarding the base over weekends were the same ones pilfering and pinching stuff to get their own cars going. In my mind it was bizarre. We conscripts were there for a short term, but for these guys it was their career. If they were caught stealing, quite rightly they'd be punished. It was stupid of them. That's all they did on a Saturday afternoon. They'd get bored. There was such a waste of things in the military.

A ship would go out for a tour of duty. When it came back we'd do the books. Usually a disproportionate amount of jam was used. It was crazy how much had been consumed. It was later discovered why. Different jams were packed in a box. If one particular sort was liked, they kept them aside and threw the rest overboard. Dishes, too. Who wanted to wash dishes? Much easier to chuck them over the side. They'd come back after a week and there'd be no cutlery left. All ditched on the way. On it went. As Logistics Command we had to supply them and couldn't work out why they were using up so many supplies. Eventually the situation was brought under control.

During my time with the navy there was a big savings drive. They wanted to be more economical. I was in charge of ordering stationery for my office. I heard it through the grapevine that whatever was ordered would be halved. I just went ahead and doubled my orders for pens and papers, and so on. If I wanted, say, ten pens, I'd ask for twenty. They'd be adamant and say, 'No! We're only issuing ten.'

So in the end we were happy – we got what we wanted – and they were happy, because whatever showed on their books was exactly halved. It was a false sense of economy. Like I said – bizarre, my two years' 'Natural Circus'.

I was in the January '85 intake. Went in straight after school. Basics was in the Ordnance Services Corps at Discobolos, 1 Maintenance Unit, with Bravo Company, which was taken up as Quartermaster General troops. This meant that after Basics you'd be posted to various depots around the country. After doing a driver's course at Wonderboom I got posted to SADFI in Voortrekkerhoogte and was made a purchaser's clerk. For some reason my name appeared on the SADFI list and I was subsequently transferred. Luck of the draw, you could say.

SADFI drew its troops from all the armed forces: army, air force and navy, but not Medical Corps or, of course, MPs. From the army they drew only from Maintenance Unit and Ordnance Services Corps troops. SADFI personnel were based mainly in Voortrekkerhoogte, where they specialised in functions such as marketing and retailing.

SADFI did retailing in various products, consumables and insignia. In Voortrekkerhoogte there were furniture stores, supermarkets, shops, a dairy and so on. They also had a purchases division that supplied all the insignia, flashes, Tupperware flashes, badges, patches, stable belts, unit buckles, balkies and such. All of that went through the purchases division. We'd put the orders out to civilian contractors, who'd manufacture the items, and we'd resell these to the various corresponding units. The bulk went to the stores but some items were sold to canteens. They provided a lot of stuff for guys who'd lost something and had to replace it without the hassle of going to stores. We also provided commemorative and unit beer mugs, wall plaques and other souvenirs.

SADFI operated a cash-and-carry type of shop, which supplied the canteens. Permanent Force members were the main buyers. We supplied the supermarkets, which had civilian tellers, where people could purchase whatever they needed. The managers were either retired SADF personnel or ex-SADF members who'd resigned from their commissions or positions. The various unit canteens purchased all their alcohol, cigarettes, cold drinks, chips, chocolates, sweets – any consumables they needed – through SADFI.

Guys used to wonder why things were always so cheap. It was because mark-up wasn't the issue. SADFI wasn't profit-driven; it was there as a service. National Servicemen also worked at these places, so there were no salary issues. Civilian salaries were paid by the Defence Force and not from the outlet's own pocket. Buildings were provided by the military. All of this equated to low overheads. Also, SADFI would buy products in huge bulk. It was both wholesaler and retailer. In turn, the supermarkets and canteens then also bought in bulk. The final outcome kept prices to an absolute minimum. Remember how cheap beers were?

I was at VTH from May until November, until they posted me out to Grootfontein in South West.

THE BORDER

You say I've got a pretty good memory about it. Ja, well, it's just stayed.
I had a year and a half up there to think about it. There was a lot of
time spent just sitting around doing nothing. My time there was very
interesting, but extremely tiring, and an intensive period of having little
sleep for long periods of time, which wasn't great.

I smaaked those Ratels. Named after the Cape honey badger. You think it's
a nice, soft, cuddly little creature? No ways, brother. He'll rip you to pieces.
But the Buffel – terrible things! Horrible! Top-heavy. Too many accidents
happened on those bastards.

Our gear wouldn't last. The sun faded our clothes. I didn't have long
sleeves. I'd cut them off. I never wore socks or underpants – threw them
away. It was just extra washing. Who needed that? Always kept my hair
very short. Still do.

Concrete beacons represented the designated area of the borderline,
because, between the Cunene and Kuvango Rivers, there was no river
separating South West Africa from Angola. They formed the invisible
dissecting line, which ran for about four hundred kilometres. The beacons,
which were placed every ten kilometres, were called on the map to
determine your grid. They were mainly used for the National Servicemen
doing general patrols. In certain areas the beacons were only stones, placed
in a cone-shape, because there were a lot of dry shonas around that
became covered by water in summer.

When I was in the army, in 1971, it was only really the PFs who were flown up to the Border area to start building and operating permanent bases. The first guys to go up from the air force were mostly radio operators and helicopter pilots. The northern border was still manned by the police, who were basically acting as military units. The terrorists were dealt with as criminals.

They were interesting times. The war was on the verge, with little skirmishes here and there over South West, but we knew it was going to become full scale. SWAPO was only then getting organised. When the Portuguese pulled out in 1975, everybody wanted to take control of Angola. The army went up in about 1975 to replace the police, and it became a full-scale war.

I was all over the place: Angola, South West, the Caprivi Strip. I still have a letter that followed me all around the Border. One week I was at this base and the next week I was at that base and the following week I was at yet another. When I eventually got back to my main base in Bloemfontein, they gave me my well-travelled letter. It had followed me, but was always just too late. It also went all over the Border, following me for just over three months. It was a letter from my folks.

Out on patrol we had our little Noddy Cars. You had your driver, your gunner and your group commander. I was a group commander. We were on patrol, seven days at a time, and then returned to base. One day's relaxation then off you went again. Fired a couple of rounds. On to the next base. On and on and on. This was all on the South West side.

We had one or two Noddy Cars blown up by landmines on the side of the road. No major problems. Fortunately we were taught how to drive. We didn't have any major casualties except for a couple of rather bad injuries. There were no deaths in my unit that I was aware of, but one Bedford went up. Four guys killed. It was stupidity on their part – they went out for a joyride and hit a landmine. They were troepies who wanted to go to a cuca shop. They weren't my guys; they were infantry. Their guys went to pick up the mess. 'Died whilst on service' is what their parents would've been told.

It was about September '75. We caught a troop train from Bethlehem to Windhoek, which took five days. It was a steam train. No baths, no showers, no nothing. By the time we got there we were covered in soot. Had solid, black rings of gunk around our necks.

We went into a camp at Windhoek, where we had a shower and some food. Climbed onto Unimogs. I was one of the drivers. We drove to Ondangwa. It was quite a big place and had a runway. Our first night we had to stand beat. The ou manne came back and tuned, 'The terr's gonna slit your throat while you're sleeping and piss on your face, *roof*.' Tuned us all that kind of shit. By then we were wired – even the ends of our hair – we were wired for anything to happen!

I had a mate – we still know each other – who was also from my part of the world, in Durbs. He and I had to guard the 44-gallon drums of fuel. It was the middle of the night. Suddenly, *clang!* The drums had shrunk with the cold. They made those noises and after a few times of this you're sort of freaked. 'Hey! These fucking drums, china!'

Another time we were sent out of the camp to protect a small beacon used for radio comms. There were four of us doing bush beat. Two ous kipped, two ous pushed beat. We were parking off in a little bivouac and we were more relaxed because we'd realised that there weren't terrs under every blade of grass, jumping up and throwing things that went bang at you. The other two okes were kipping. It was quiet and dark. Then we heard something. 'Boet. What's that sound?' I whispered.

'I don't know.'

We slid our safety catches off. Something sounded as if it was very slowly leopard-crawling towards us. We heard the brush moving softly.

'Let's shoot this fucking thing.' He could hardly hear me, my voice was so strained. Next thing this damn donkey walked into view. 'Aargh, FUCK!' We'd almost blasted it to pieces with our R1s. I don't know who got a bigger fright – the two okes dossing, me and my buddy, or the stupid donkey.

The whole of Charlie Company went up in January '76. I became platoon sergeant. First we went by train to Grootfontein, which was a massive army camp. From there it was on a convoy up to Oshivelo from Groot-fontein. I was in a parked Unimog. Every ten minutes or so these long convoys of about one kilometre long passed by. They were lowbed trucks with heavy equipment and Noddy Cars on them. I knew I'd never witness something like that again. Never.

Then it was off to Ondangwa and on to Eenhana where, as we were nearing it, a landmine was tripped. There were these road graders up there. The driver sat in an armoured capsule. This Ovambo driver was grading the road and went over the landmine. When this thing went off we were still in the convoy. We turned our Mogs around and went back to the site of the accident.

When we arrived, smoke was still coming out of the hole. The grader's front wheel was parked off in a tree. This Ovambo dude was still sitting in the cab. He couldn't jump out in case any other mines were around. Eventually the engineers got him out. In the meantime he'd turned Caucasian. He was white! 'Ag, baas,' he said, 'Ek't gedink daai goed gaan net vir wit mense af.' I can laugh at it now, but back then it was my first, real wake-up call. I thought, 'Jussis! This is for real!'

After that we moved on. The road was quite wide and had palm trees alongside it. As we came around this bend, all I saw were two clear bubble-shapes, with two helmets inside each one, coming at us. They were Alouettes. They flew low over the road towards us. I just saw everybody ducking in the Mogs. They liked to fly low so as not to get shot at. It was the first time I'd seen anything like it, and all this on my first day at the Border!

Later we were on Ops Trampoline near Oshikango. On the other side of the border post was a small town called Santa Clara. The army got the idea of Ops T from the Israelis. It was a nine-metre corridor: three metres of sisal, planted one metre apart, then three metres of haak-en-steek thorn bush, followed by another three metres of sisal. Sisal is the stuff used to make ropes and hessian. It's like a cactus – it grows outwards with broad leaves that have thorns on them. The idea was to make a natural fence barrier in order to slow down but not necessarily stop insurgent crossings, then patrol it daily with helicopters. The terrs would have to cut through it with pangas once the plants had taken hold.

At St Petersburg, during World War II, the Russians planted this stuff as a defence from the Jerries. They sent in tanks, and the furthest that one reached was ten metres because the leaves shredded, which bound the tracks fast. The tanks stopped dead.

We planted this barrier below our side of the kaplyn to stop them simply waltzing over the border, skipping over fences, and causing kak on our side. While planting them we were told we'd stop when we got to Addis Ababa, not just the entire length of the Border! Ous walked in a row a metre apart with hoes, while others walked behind and threw in the plants. Guys behind them got on their knees and packed the soil. There was a platoon of us, a few officers and the Springs Regiment, who were campers. There were a lot more of them than us. The kaplyn was a long, graded, straight dirt road.

The Israelis used this natural barrier successfully, but in their part of the world they didn't have the rain that we had up on the Border during the summer. They didn't take into account our little swampy areas caused by the rains. The shonas gathered water from the rain, which killed all the plants, as their roots rotted. Eventually the terrs could walk right through and out the other side. So, after planting the cacti for forty klicks, Ops T didn't work.

I was keeping records of all our travels as we went along Sector 1Ø. Although I was with a mechanised unit, we didn't do mechanised patrols at that time; instead we just walked patrols. During that period I kept very detailed notes of everything we were doing. The descriptions themselves weren't long – just the dates of when and where we went, how long we were there for and a few keywords to jog the memory. I wrote this all down on the back of an old writing pad.

It's interesting to look back again and see what we did in a period of even the first week. The distances we walked were incredible. We did things from suddenly moving in the middle of the night for some particular reason, to coming across captured terrs.

It was Friday 13 February, 1976. I'm not a superstitious guy, but during the day we got a call-out. The bokkoppe had found a landmine and, as engineers, we had to pull it. A few of us hopped on the Unimog and argued about who was going to do the honours. When we were a couple of kays away, I said, 'Hey, guys! Remember – it's Friday the thirteenth!' Now nobody wanted to touch the thing. When we arrived the bokkoppe were doing rondomverdediging. 'You ous! Hurry up! We've been here for hours!' they said.

'Well why don't YOU pull the bloody thing, then?' Then they shut up. We checked what the fuss was about. There was a slight groove in the dirt, with two logs above a hole. My buddy had the mine detector. I secretly said to him, 'Hey, if there's nothing there just give me a signal and we'll pretend there is.' Now all the bokkoppe were standing around watching us do the sweep. My buddy tuned, 'Jeez, there's a noise here! It's a definite!' They all jumped backwards. I called them back. 'Hey, ous, come look here. So, buddy, do you think it's an anti-personnel or anti-tank?'

'China, this thing is *big*,' he said. 'Must be anti-tank.'

'Okay, here we go!' and I jumped into the hole. A whole bunch of them hit the deck screaming. I thought they were going to beat us up, they got such a fright. After they calmed down we worked out what it was. A floppy's car got a puncture. They'd taken two logs and stuck them under the axle, dug a hole, pulled the wheel off, put a new one back on, thrown the old one in the boot and driven off. They obviously didn't have a jack. It was clever.

Anyway, that horrible Friday the thirteenth was a strange day. Later my buddy and I were on cover defence. As we walked along the periphery we noticed a little kraal with wooden sticks outside to keep the wildlife out. There were huts inside. As we walked towards it I just went cold. Goosebumps. 'I don't like this. Let's leave. Come … move!' We left. He asked me what had happened. 'I don't know, but I had these most horrendous, cold shivers.' It was uncomfortable there, and it was only the two of us. Nothing happened, but it was a very strange feeling.

During the evenings we stayed in an abandoned mission station that had a little school hall. In the mornings we did opstaan and in the evenings we did klaarstaan. The best time for terrs to hit was as the sun set. They then had the whole night to run, whereas in the morning, if they ran, we had the whole day to follow their tracks. One part of the building, where the kitchen was, had a verandah where the food was served and where we'd stacked sandbags as defence. It was thigh-high, so if shit happened you could kneel and shoot. One afternoon some guys went to get supplies and came back with post. For six weeks we hadn't received any. Post was helluva important to okes sitting on the Border, unless it was a 'Dear Johnny'. Later that evening our captain called out, 'Ouens, julle het pos.'

We were all in our spaces, quietly reading our letters. Then, at 18h55, they hit us. The first RPG hit the verandah area on the corner of the building. There was an oke with us, who, to my knowledge, was the first Jewish guy to get killed on the Border. He was covered with shrapnel holes, but didn't die straight away. One of the Springs campers had half his head taken off. There was another Durban boy, called Roly, who sat holding a finger to his own neck to stop the blood pumping out. We also tried to stop Roly's bleeding by putting our thumbs in the wounds.

We had what we called 'go-karts' – green plastic boxes with a plastic lid over them. About six were placed together over deep trenches where you'd sit and do your business. When you finished your dump you threw the lid down – *whooph* – and the force of it blew all the kak smell out, along with the flies, all over the ous squatting there. I used to get *mal* when that happened. It was a *lag*! We threw lime over to help with the stink. I think it made it worse. When they hit us the 'go-karts' were full. We'd been there exactly a week. You had a hundred guys shitting every day, so there must've been about seven hundred dumps in the trench. When the contact started, some of the okes threw the 'karts' off and dived into these trenches to try and shoot back.

I remember the captain running around, just in his underrods, shouting, 'Skiet daar! Skiet daar!' and he's firing his 9-mill anywhere into the bush! A Bedford that was used to fetch supplies was parked between two bunkers. It had big gas bottles on it that we used for cooking. The truck caught alight. The lieut told me to shoot the petrol tank to stop it from blowing up. I told the okes in the one bunker to give me firing cover. I ran, dived inside an outer bunker closer to the vehicle and fired three shots into the tank. First shot – nothing happened. Second shot – nothing happened. Same for the third. I shouted to the lieut, 'Nothing's happening!'

'Jy't gemis!' he screamed. Then the gas bottles took off like giant rockets. I screamed back, 'Okay! I'm coming back! Give me cover!' I ran low. I've never since been lower off the ground other than sitting! The ous stood and fired all around me. I dived into the trench and remember saying, 'Jussis! It's hot out here!' and with that I turned and a whole sandbag lifted up and dropped on me. My okes marked the spot where the firing had come from. Next morning we dug out .50 Browning casings from that spot. We also found a grouping the size of my fist on the Bedford, but I'd shot the wrong side. Shot the toolbox instead.

There was an oke who shouted to me, 'Kyk daar!' I looked to where he indicated and, can you believe it, there was a terr standing on top of the small school hall – directing fire! I hadn't seen him. I aimed and shot. The oke went down. He didn't walk out of there. The only thing they found the next day was his bush hat with a big hole in the back, so a round obviously went through his head. The cap was a plain Yank–olive green, but styled like ours. We didn't find him. The terrs had grabbed their pals, dead or injured, and taken them away.

Two Pumas landed and deployed trackers and other squads. We wanted to join the chase. 'No, you're not going,' they said.

'Why not?'

'Because you okes are now *mal.* You'll shoot them because they killed your friends.'

'Well, ja, that's exactly why we want to go!'

'Nope. Sorry, manne, bly hierso. As julle beweeg is julle in die kak!'

In the casevac there were more than two fatalities, but I can't recall how many. Certainly under ten. I think maybe five. We covered them in tarps. The wounded and dead were flown away. Then there were follow-ups. Whether they got them we were never told. I think they did. You heard rumours but no one came over and officially told us anything. It was estimated that the terrs hit us from twenty-seven different firing points.

Black okes couldn't shoot properly. We tried to teach them. The new ones would look down the side of the rifle, and up and over. They had no idea how to shoot. Their initial training was lacking. They were with us for a short while in 1976. I think at that time they were known as Bravo Group, before 32. They could, however, drill with precision! It sounded as if it was one person drilling even when there were thirty of them. Their drilling was unbelievable.

There was this hunt for insurgents. Then the biggest adventure I had in the army started when it was discovered that they'd come through from Ovamboland, over the lower kaplyn, and into South West proper. This was the sectional boundary, south of Ovamboland, not the Angolan and South West jati. It ran east, from Oshivelo, and was made from two high chicken-wire fences with a clearing in between that was swept every morning to see if anybody had crossed it. One morning they found twenty-one different spoors, which split into several smaller groups.

We went to where the spoor started and had 346 officers and troops, choppers, dogs and the berede chasing them. Bushmen would track for us, but we were warned to watch out for them. If the spoor got hot they tended to lose interest because they'd be up front in the possible line of fire.

They divided our battalion up into smaller groups, with a company here, a company there, and a central unit coordinating the process. It was well organised. Sometimes we'd park off for a week or so, doing nothing, just sitting on a farm waiting to be called. Sometimes we joined up with other sections and tracked both sides of the spoor if we weren't exactly sure where they were heading.

In those days we carried Brens and R1s. As a corporal I was given a small section of twelve guys, plus Frans – a raw Bushman. He was older and spoke a bit of Afrikaans. He walked with a stick and carried a .303 with five rounds, which we fired off on the first day, trying it out. When we took a break he'd lie in a tree and stare at the vapour-trails of commercial jetliners high up in the sky. We'd tell him it was an aeroplane and that there were people up there. No comprehension. He'd say it was a moving cloud.

Frans would track the spoor and gauge where they were going. The chopper would drop guys off about five kays ahead – stopper groups – who'd ambush all the possible waterholes. Another section would track across from another angle until they picked up spoor, then they'd radio us and Alouettes would pick us up. We'd carry on the chase like that. At one stage there was a third chopper chasing them. It picked up the spoor and saw them, but desperately needed to refuel so backed off. They refuelled as quickly as possible, using drums of avgas carried on Unimogs. The one pilot, a young officer with blond hair who must've been in his early twenties, flew the thing sideways amongst the trees. He landed it straight next to the drums. 'Wow. I wish I could be a pilot,' I thought.

Frans was amazing. You'd get these dry water pans with glaring, white pebbles. You couldn't see a thing. He told me there were three tracks. One was an older man's and the other two were younger men's. We couldn't believe it. I saw nothing – Fanny Adams! There was nothing but pebbles. I learnt that when tracking you always look in the direction of the sun. It brings out the tiniest of shadows and you see a spoor much better. You can even walk backwards along it.

We'd been really close behind them. It was on a dry riverbed. We picked up some of their stuff, which they had discarded as they ran to lighten their load. On this particular day a chopper had dropped off a policeman wearing a safari suit. He seemed to be quite a nice, oldish guy. He was running with us and we went up the side of the riverbank. The edges, where they'd run up, were fresh and sharp. Frans started to lose the spoor. All of a sudden he said he couldn't see it any more. He knew he was going to be right in front if we walked into them. When the terrs couldn't run any more, they'd ambush. The police captain put his shotgun down old Frans's web belt and twisted it upwards so that the barrel stuck into his back. Now he couldn't get away. The policeman told Frans to go forward and pick up the spoor. He said he'd pull the trigger if he didn't. About two klicks ahead of us another group got the spoor. The insurgents ran up to a koppie, where the gunships got them. We were too far away to see what happened, but we saw puffs of smoke before hearing the 20-mills.

The bodies were carried down the hill and put in bags. I wasn't there when they did this. That night, when the groups met up and parked off, everybody wanted to have a look. As Frans said, it *was* an older guy and two young ones. How he saw it is beyond me.

The two younger ones were in about their early twenties and the older guy was in his late thirties. Surprisingly enough he still had fat on him even after all the months of running. Their tongues were completely swollen from having had no water. One guy's leg was hanging on by a small piece of flesh, and another's eyes were still open. The gunship had pretty much mashed them. I remember we looked at the one's boots because they had a distinct chevron pattern. I can't remember what clothes they wore, but all three had AKs.

I heard a story that night. One of the gunners said that when his chopper had landed, the policeman with them had run over and shot one in the head with his shotgun, even though the terr was already dead. Sick, but it's true. At the time it was a big joke. Most guys laughed when he told it. At nineteen, what did we know?

My feelings for the terrs changed that night. They really did. I had more respect for them for having gone through all that shit, but I never said anything. I don't think I was the only guy who felt like that. I never felt they deserved to die, but I didn't have any scruples about it. If you had contact, you'd shoot. It's fair game: he shoots at me, I shoot back. That was the mentality. I didn't even feel that taking them out with a gunship was a bit much. But the reason *why* we were shooting at each other was a completely different issue. That you can debate. I didn't want to be there; I didn't want to be in that war. None of us wanted to be there. And the terrs had been running for their lives. I realised how they must've really believed in what they were doing. I wouldn't have done it. The chances of getting away if you were a terr coming over and getting back were nil. They were volunteers, so they believed in their cause. I would never have volunteered even *with* a massive army backing.

The remaining splinter groups were hunted every day for over three months. I think some got as far as Windhoek. We hardly ever saw the other tracking groups. My section mostly chased from the areas around Otjiwarongo up to Outjo and on to the west of Etosha Pan. They eventually got all twenty-one of them.

Right at the end of my service I was in hospital with kidney stones. Somebody came into the ward and said they'd got the last guy – the leader. He'd managed to get back into Ovamboland but had walked onto a dry water pan, where the Bats got him.

There was a curfew in Ovamboland. Any movement after sunset was a no-no. Up north, the locals didn't register 'the Border'. They didn't see it that way. There's this side and that side of the jati – simple – and they travelled at night.

They threw a standard ambush on this innocent old man wearing his Sunday Specials, who came along on a bicycle straight into a *doodsakker* – the area of an ambush from which there's no escape, depending on how it was laid out. I didn't see his body, but they paraded the bicycle around the next day. Imagine a bicycle looking like a cheese grater. It's just pipes and wheels, but there weren't three centimetres of that thing where there wasn't a hole right through it. So you can imagine what hit *him*. Everybody was laughing.

Should he have known better than not to break the curfew? Perhaps, but the issue's not that simple. He'd been riding his bicycle for decades around the place, and also at night. It was his country, his part of the world. Fortunately it must've been instant, but to find the bicycle episode funny was tragic. Not just for him, but for the guys laughing about it as well. I began feeling it was wrong. The whole thing was wrong – the whole war was wrong.

I clearly remember that the Soweto riots started while I was up there. Somebody said, 'There's kak in the States.' I had a big argument one night because they were expecting Cape Corps troops to join us. This guy said he wasn't going to go near them. I said, 'Hey! They're fighting for the country – *your* country!' He wouldn't accept it. I remember his surname, the prick.

After I witnessed what happened to those three guys and that old man, I wrote a letter to my girlfriend saying how I believed the war was wrong. I just felt sick about it. Then it dawned on me – you're always getting messed around by the army. Always disorganised. Hurry up and wait. We were buggered around. That's the way it was.

While we were after these guys, and during a briefing, I suddenly got this pain. I felt sick. Peed blood that afternoon. That night I was sick again. I got a lift with a chopper back to Ondangwa to the siekeboeg. Chewed some pills. Didn't help. Three young doctors, fresh out of varsity, began chatting to the pilot. This one doos – a real Dutchman, not a South African one – told the medic just to give me a Codis, nothing else. I had a big pain. Didn't know what it was. I just lay there for three days. Then they put me on a Bedford down to Grootfontein, and there I lay too. They couldn't find anything wrong so probably thought I was gyppoing or had nothing serious. They put me on a Bedford back to Ondangwa but, again, I felt extreme pain. So it was back to Grootfontein for another week. One night a doctor came round. He shook me awake and asked what was wrong with me. I laughed at him. 'You're the doctor. You tell me what's wrong. That's why I'm here!'

I was supposed to go back the next day. Then a sister came round. She asked where I was sore, so I explained it again. 'The pain starts from here and goes down to my balls.'

'You've got kidney stones,' she said.

They put me on the Flossie the next morning, but by this stage the pain was gone. Everything was lekker. Going down to the States. Before I left I called my sister and told her I'd see her the next night. It didn't work like that. When the plane arrived, the ambulance was waiting. Typical army! I ended up in a ward in 1 Military Hospital in Voortrekkerhoogte.

I went into the air force at Valhalla, then got posted to Dog School and became a 'doggy'. I then went down to Langebaan and eventually up to Ondangwa, to 95 Technical Airfield Unit. We protected the base. The two anti-aircraft stations were manned by infantry while we did the perimeter posts and outer-perimeter protection. I can recall at least ten posts – guard towers – manned with two guys each. About twenty-five guys alternated every few hours on a continuous cycle. Four hours on and four hours off. We had the old R1s with night scopes on them. The air force guys protected the airfield itself, but within that perimeter were the Parabats,

ADKs, TDKs, medics and various other units. Our unit was in the region of four to five hundred okes. Ondangwa was a big, big camp, almost like a small military town. We did a lot of construction work as well. Just before leaving we started building concrete staff houses for PF air force guys.

Both my brothers went up and both were wounded. One was wounded while on camp. The vehicle hit a landmine and he was thrown out. Injured his shoulder – nothing serious. I can't remember what vehicle he was in. I know it wasn't a Buffel, though. Maybe a Bedford; I'm not sure. He was in the Engineers so did a lot of landmine lifting.

The other brother was with 101 Battalion. He was on the Border for eighteen months as a National Serviceman. Their camp got mortared and he picked up some shrapnel in the forehead. Again, nothing serious. The guy next to him, a sergeant, got a big piece of shrapnel between the eyes and a lot of blood all over his face. My brother reckoned that when he saw this guy lying there he thought he was gone. Finished. It turned out he was only unconscious.

My mom phoned me at work to say that my brother had been injured. I got a huge shock. We didn't know the details. Normally, if it's a serious injury, the army lets your parents know. He'd phoned his girlfriend first, to tell her from Windhoek, and she in turn had phoned my mom, which was the wrong thing to do. We didn't know he'd be arriving home later that day, so it wasn't too bad.

My stepbrother was in the air force and he did plenty of camps up there. He was Permanent Force. He'd been a fireman in civvy life. He went in January '76 and I went in July '76. He was made a corporal due to his prior service as a fireman. Took me six months to catch up with him. We served together at Ysterplaat.

Once, my three brothers were on the Border at the same time. This was about 1980. My mom's nerves were wrecked. She took it badly. It just worked on a person. She was very jumpy and worried all the time, and always listened to or watched the news for any death reports.

We assembled in Bloem and took every single vehicle up that we could. We drove in this long convoy for three days up to South West, then all the way north to the Border.

Our base was at Oshivelo, with 61 Mech. When we arrived, the rocket launchers were obviously already there, fully kitted out, and deployed to us on our arrival. They couldn't penetrate dugouts or concrete bunkers, but against troops and trenches in the bush or out in the open they were very effective. They weren't designed to penetrate, but to explode above ground.

We went out four vehicles at a time. They'd know where a target was, or suspected activity. We'd drive out to however far we were needed. Our lieut was in charge of the battery. He'd be the TA. There were about three or four of them, and in a separate vehicle. I never got involved in TA stuff. There'd also be an observation post which was the CO of the battery. He plotted the coordinates and gave them to the TAs, who relayed them to us. We'd line our sights using a theodolite and aiming sticks. All the orders would be repeated and confirmed, like pilots do, before firing the rockets.

The whole idea was setting up, firing and getting away as quickly as possible. Arrive. Get coordinates. Pop the button. Get the hell out of there. Gone! After firing twenty-four rockets a huge dust cloud was left. They'd be easy targets because of the visibility. We'd be heavily drilled about demobilising them. Get the launcher levelled as quickly as possible, and go! You didn't want to hang around and attract fire. That was the biggest negative thing about it. We wouldn't stay out in the bush with our rocket launchers. We'd go out and then immediately return to our TB.

When using the 5.5s we'd dig in, camouflage and stay for a few days. Weeks, if necessary. It was pretty boring parking off in the bush but, in typical army style, they always made you do something. Always kept you busy, either cleaning the guns, cleaning the sights or doing mock drills. When we dug in, it was a few kilometres from the Border. We never really knew the actual distances. You just knew you were close by.

The only time we made fires at night was back at home base, obviously. Otherwise we used an Esbit. You'd dig a little hollow in the ground to boil water and warm up rat packs. Inside were three tins of food, coffee, condensed milk and other bits.

In 1981 I was an instructor. We were in Oshivelo. One time I had to do chicken-parade. The sergeant major told me to take the troops down the white dirt road about three kays away. Israeli army officers were about to arrive and we were preparing to display a full-on mechanised attack for their approval. They'd come through to see how we operated. The place was to be spick and span.

'Right! We've got to clean up. It's very simple. You okes don't pick up what I pick up, then it's ten push-ups per piece.' I walked behind and noticed a few things they'd missed. I got to the end of the road, lined them up and started counting. I got to fifty and said, 'That's 500 push-ups.' With that amount, I decided it was easier to chase them around instead, which I then did, ignoring the little mound I'd formed in the middle of the road – the fifty things I'd picked up. The Israelis arrived and there was this pile of rubbish – beer tins, stompies and bottle tops. When the sa'majoor saw this it was my turn to get chased with a sandbag up and down the road, and just after I'd chased my okes! They all stood and watched and really enjoyed it. Had a good *lag*.

When I was with the guys in Oshivelo, giving training, someone picked up an 88-mm dud and started hitting it with a tent peg. Blew his whole head off. All they found were the frames of his glasses and one tooth.

In 1982 some guys I knew got hit. We were at 1 SAI together. They were following the tracks of SWAPO insurgents. The tracks split, and split again. As their Ratel came around a turn, these terrs put seven RPGs into it. It was one of the troop carriers, not a commanding one, and carried about ten okes. When we got there it was ugly. The okes were powder. Burned. The sad part is that the corporal in that Ratel had already klaared out but had decided to come back for short service for another year. We chased these terrs, who headed straight back to the border. We did stopper groups. Every hundred metres there'd be three of us. This was Etosha Pan. We went over the whole area checking for tracks. The infantry also gave chase, hit them just before the kaplyn, and got some. We'd put stellings on the other side of the border but there were plenty of gaps for them to escape.

I spent eighteen months as a driver on the Border and had a number of run-ins with the military law side of things. Every time we went over the border into Angola it was fine to smoke dope and have order groups with 32 Battalion's captains, lieuts – whoever – all smoking and saying, 'Well, here's the village. We're going to do this and that, and you guys are going to stay over there and wait and resupply us when we come back with the Ratels and Casspirs.' It was all fine. Got stoned. Came back out, across the border and down to Grootfontein where we got arrested for smoking dagga, so it was a very stupid situation.

I don't know if you've read the book *Acid Alex* by Al Lovejoy? When we were in the army together he had a different surname. He and I both got locked up in the same DB in Grootfontein. This is dinkum. You can read about it in his book. I'm the oke who comes to the door.

Alex was also a *waterkop*. We used to load boxes and drive trucks. Alex once said to me he felt it was all a load of crap. He wanted to fight a war and didn't want to be a box thrower. I told him that the easiest way to do so is, on one of our drives, to go up the Caprivi Strip to Omega Base – the Bushman camp – go through the back, over the fence and then he'd be in Jonas Savimbi's camp. Those boys fought all the time. So he decided to AWOL from Grootfontein, caught a lift from one of the HSI truck drivers and got dropped off in the Strip. He walked across the Angolan border and joined UNITA.

At the time we were working for a clandestine group, called HSI, run by a colonel in the Parabats. They captured weapons from inside Angola and we drove them through to our side. HSI would order us out of our trucks, drive away and return a while later with empty trucks. They dropped the caches into holes in the ground and covered them up for UNITA to use.

Alex, in the meantime, had AWOLed and joined UNITA, and now wanted to make war. They sent the colonel and nine HSI drivers to look for him. I got sent back to Grootfontein where I got bust with dope again. They had guys watching us all the time, and not only MPs. They locked me up in DB. About two days later, there was Alex. They locked him in the corner cell. We had these camper MPs from Durban guarding us, who were there for sixty or ninety days and felt nothing for us. They were full of shit the whole time. Always lashing out. They started tuning Alex through the door, 'You're a traitor! You're a deserter! We're gonna hang you! We're gonna shoot you!'

We heard him knocking on the door and asking for food. 'Troep! Shud-dup! Hou jou bek! One more word from that cell and we'll kick your arse!' All of a sudden we heard this growl and then a roar. The whole cell door, frame and all, ripped from the wall. Here comes Alex! He ran down the passage, grabbed a panga – which we cut the grass with – and ran after these MPs, swishing it around, but as he got to the office a sergeant stepped out with a gun. Alex noticed and dropped to the floor to give himself up. The guy would've shot.

It was us two and six other guys. DB in Grootfontein was two inspections a day, three hours of drill, three hours of PT and the rest of the day you were a bandiet working for them. Helped in the mess, cleaning two thousand varkpanne, or cut grass. Basic labour. If you smoked, it was only two cigarettes a day.

They used to take us to a camp called the 'opfok kamp'. There'd be a thousand sandbags, stacked in a pile, which we were told to move over the hill. As you got to the last ten, they'd say, 'Why don't you put them all back where they were?' Afterwards they'd stand with their foot on the edge of one of those red fire buckets, which was filled with water, and say, 'Okay, guys, you've got two minutes for water,' and slowly tilt it over. You'd run to try and catch it before it lost all its water. We shared what was left. It was about 42 degrees Celsius. Your boots were white. Your clothes were white. You're caked with dust, sweat and salt.

61 Mech consisted of one company of infantry, about thirty Ratel 20s, six Ratel 90s of our own anti-tank platoon, one battery of artillery – being six G5s – and an armoured squadron from 1 SSB, using twelve Ratel 90s. Quite a formidable force. The unit had by that time built up a considerable reputation with its successes in previous operations, such as Sceptic in June 1980, Protea in August '81, and Daisy in November '81.

It was my first time on the Border. We'd been there for about four days, familiarising ourselves with the activities on the base and how things were done, and also getting to know the guys from the armoured and artillery groups, who we'd be working with if we were to go north on ops. There was nothing really going on. Things were much calmer on the base – nothing like back in the States. It was December and the summer rains hadn't come yet. Insurgents used the rains as a cover to infiltrate south without being detected. It rained mostly at night, like your typical Highveld thundershowers – just more intense. In the day, though, it was as hot as hell – 45 degrees Celsius. It was madness to be out in that.

We'd already been assigned our vehicles, as well as new weapons and ammunition, which you had to carry at all times. This was the Border, and you just couldn't wait for action! After all, this is what we were trained for, for almost a year. We soon lost that feeling when nothing was going on and boredom set in. There was nothing much to do. The only thing you tried to do was keep cool. Apart from morning parade, or brunch and supper, you had lots of time to yourself. The canteen opened in the late afternoon when it got a bit cooler. At least then you could down some cold beers, which were always available, and watch some old videos on the telly. They were quite organised at 61 Mech.

Then it happened. We were urgently called to the ops room one evening. They'd received a signal that bootprints were found on Charlie kaplyn. The trackers patrolling it found telltale signs that insurgents were on the move. They estimated about ten to fifteen had crossed and were moving south. The rains had begun a day earlier. Platoon 1 and my Platoon 3 – about nine Ratels in all – left the base just after midnight so we could be in position and start patrolling the area at first light. The rest of the company would follow later the next day.

We reached the area just as the sun was rising. The anticipation of action was building and the excitement was running high. We patrolled for about three kays up and down the kaplyn until the trackers picked up a trail that we then followed. The first thing we came into contact with was a herd of elephants – a strange sight.

The bush was quite dense, so for a few kays we bundu-bashed with the vehicles. Suddenly one of the trackers indicated that the spoor was fresh and the terrs were about a klick or two ahead. We dismounted and proceeded on foot for about half an hour. We had become more anxious and alert – mouths were dry and hearts were pumping at a rapid rate. We expected something to happen at any time. This was it.

Then, out of nowhere, they were dead ahead. Contact! The section fired a burst straight into them, dived for cover and then fired single shots in their direction. Just as suddenly, everything went quiet. It was all over in a matter of seconds. We looked around. Nothing was moving. Cautiously we got up, checked ourselves for casualties – thankfully there were none – and surveyed the surroundings, just like we'd been trained to do. We'd caught them totally by surprise. There were five dead terrs where we had the initial contact, and another three who had dropped everything and tried to run but had only got a few metres. One was badly wounded. He'd taken a hit in his shoulder and three in the legs. Between them they had four AKs, one Makarov pistol and an assortment of anti-personnel mines. Nothing else. No food and no water.

There was a lot of excitement between the guys at first, especially between those of us who'd made the first contact. But deep down the feeling wasn't all that good. We stayed at the site for a few hours waiting for the choppers to come and evacuate the dead and injured terrs.

A buddy and I sat under a tree, sharing tins of bully beef and mixed veggies, when he said, 'Look what crap we're eating. Our families are sitting at home having a roast turkey, with all the trimmings, for lunch.' It was Christmas Day, 1982.

I was all over the Border. Up there for eighteen months. Katima, Calueque, 2Ø, wherever. Although R4.00 sounds like absolutely nothing today, I used to get R4.50 danger pay per day up there, so I was never short of bucks. Got paid R134 a month. Used to fly home whenever I got back to base in Grahamstown. It was big bucks in the early eighties. I used to help my mom out with it.

They naaied us ous. The eighties' intake and the intake prior to that they just screwed! Then they started realising that it was causing more trouble than it was worth. Guys were starting to go bos. Ous were drinking and AWOLing. When I was there an oke went missing for three weeks. He was found *trapping* around South West with a pair of shorts – nothing else. He'd had enough. He went off his head up there. He was a fully trained soldier. He threw his rifle away, took off his clothes and just started walking. He was living with the locals. The Ovambo people weren't an aggressive nation; they were actually a very cool nation when you got to know them. They drank *mohangu*. It's like the African beer they brew here – but more potent, depending on how long it ferments. You had to drink it in the shade. He'd been drinking this stuff non-stop. He was gone. We bought it for ten cents a litre in those days. I would add sugar with it to beat the taste.

I used to carry about six water bottles. We put *mohangu* in a couple. When we bedded down at night, just before sunset, we'd have a couple of shots just to ease the situation. Out came the joints. Bugger the lieuty – he was a kid just like I was, so who the hell was he to tell me what to do and how things worked out there? 'Suck the joint yourself otherwise we'll fuck you up.' He had to go along with us otherwise it's *nag* for him. Smoked a lot of zol on the Border, just to ease the brainwash and the rondfok.

I did a lot of walking during that time. It was from pillar to post. 'Get your gear! Let's walk!' Walked twenty kays, and after a while your mind starts telling you, 'No, man! Enough! I'm not even going to see an angry cow out here!' Also sniffed that stuff in canisters they put on boils. They'd spray it on you and it would make them ice cold. I used to sniff it out in the bush and just giggle. Giggled at anything. No matter what happened, I'd laugh at it. Messed my brain up a bit. We scaled the medic out. He'd walk patrol with us and I was pretty good buddies with him. 'Come, boet, just give me one of those tubes. I'll organise some cigarettes.'

'Ag, man! I'll get into kak.'

'Ag, fuck you! Just give the fucking thing here, man!' I'd snort this thing and, I'm telling you, this stuff used to get me going because every day was the same out on patrol. Walk, walk, walk. The same thing, the same thing, the same thing. So your mind told you to do something different. It's human nature. In actual fact it made you skelm. I thought of ways out of having to do the same thing every bloody day. It didn't last for too long – it was just a naughty streak in me.

We'd make these little swimming pools. Some were round, concrete structures. Others were sandbags and plastic. They were actually meant as water containers. You could drink the water and swim in it. Some ous would just jump in kaalgat and gave min. They'd be numb. That place made you numb.

Spent a while hanging out with the motorbike ous. Used those Yamaha XT 500s. Real thumpers. They also used the Kriek, which looked similar, or maybe was a modification of the XT. There were a couple of berede with us as well. Very lekker, good ous. I used to ride their horses bareback. We helped them clean the roads and did fieldwork together. Before we left the base, the roads would have to be cleared with metal detectors. They'd take the bikes out at night for runs, ommie vyand te wys ons is daar! Whether you were daar in your mind was another thing. I was stoned most of the time. Lots of the ous were.

I think most of the NCO PFs were alcoholics. And the officers, as well. Every single one of them drunkards, and a lot of them moffies. They were sick. Dazed, in a way. ''n Hoender is fokkol!' with a big *knol* in your face. You'd just have to stand there and take it. 'Engelsman! ENGELSMAN! Wil jy my opfok?' this two-pip lieuty screamed at me. He didn't like me. I told him to repeat things in English and the dickhead couldn't. Couldn't even say my surname. It's a Scottish surname. 'Repeat it in English, please, Lieutenant!' Jirra, he took off! He changed colour. I got naaied that day, good and solid, with a sandbag, for a good couple of hours. The more he hammered me the more I just laughed at him, and thought, 'You're a poes in my eyes, man!' Bugger him! What could he do? Mess with *me*?

You started to learn that. In the beginning you're all nervous. After a while you sommer told him, 'Grah! In your face! You're a poes as well, man! What can you do now? Nothing!'

He told me to salute him. 'Who? Must I salute *you*? Screw you, my bru!' and I walked off. One pip, two pips – made no difference. Even a captain made no difference. Told him to piss off, too! I said, 'I'm the doos that's doing the dirty work. Not you. You're telling me to do it, then I've got to take it to the platoon to tell them to do it, so who's the doos? Me, man! I'm the poes in the middle that's got to bloody well handle your shit, and their shit, so up yours, man!' Then they started realising that I was right. In the end they realised they weren't going to get anywhere with me unless they gave me a bit of bypass, as in, 'You must help me if I help you.'

My group of guys stuck together. In the beginning they started to single us out. 'You! You go there because you're a *hardegat*. And you! You go there because you're a *windgat*.' But, when it came to doing the job, it was us ous who did it – not those rank wankers! And I'd always want something extra for it if there was maybe the odd bottle of brandy I could get out of the mix. They'd say, 'Okay. Ons sal 'n plan maak.' Then I'd get the job done and want my brandy for the ouens, which we'd drink, and out would come the zol. I stole a 13-socket and smoked the *boom* out of it. Was like a little neck. *Phfff!* Sjoe! I'd get whacked, hey, but it was good. They were good days. Bugger the ou who caught us, because we'd bliksem him. We didn't force the ous who didn't smoke, but they started checking that we were getting happier and happier, so we said, 'If you want, bru, go ahead. *Rook*.'

The 32 troops also smoked a lot of zol. Can you blame them? With the shit they saw? The officers and NCOs drank a lot, too. A few were alcoholics. One or two smoked a joint but it would have to be like, 'Hey. Don't tell anybody. Keep it quiet.' Very strict. They were scrutinised, especially the officers. You wouldn't get in if you didn't have the credentials. You'd also have to speak Portuguese, to some degree, which of course most did. There was this one major. Sjoe! That ou! You wouldn't get a thing past him! He did all the Romeo Mikes. They were the guys who kept on moving. They didn't stop. We worked with him for a while. When you got to know him he wasn't a bad ou, at all. Now *he* was an alcoholic.

So, in early '83, we spent three months with Buffalo. At that stage a lot were ex-Angolan terrorists. I was no better. I was a terrorist to them, as well. At that stage I was a one-liner. We were seconded to help out. They were a small unit then. They needed trained ous because they ran amok and sommer shot you as well, those ous. They weren't very disciplined. If we hit a contact the plan was to control them. They'd fire all over the place. That's how they worked.

We were out doing bush patrols for with them for ten to fifteen days, sometimes longer. Sleep, shit, eat – everything – with your mate. I had to help the signaller send codes. Had to learn all that kak. Still got it in my head today, all alphabetically worked out, as in a, b, c, d and e. The guy back at base would have a list in front of him. He'd work out my codes – it would be a sentence, meaning, 'We're here. Everything's all right. We're all accounted for.' Next radio call, '0700 tomorrow we're moving out.' Then I'd tune the radio into some music and we'd all get stoned. The lieuty would come over and say, 'Julle moet wag staan vanaand!'

'Ja, Luit'nant, *jy* gaan wag staan vanaand.' *We* certainly wouldn't stand guard. We'd just dos. If the shit hit the fan we couldn't have given a toss. We actually wanted the shit to hit the fan because we were getting bored. We wanted it! What'd we been trained for all that time? To walk around like a lot of donkeys? We wanted it! We used to make a fire at night, wait a few hundred metres away and watch. If anybody went near it the plan was to blow it to pieces. It never happened, but that's how much we wanted it.

When we had contact it was quick, very quick. Gone! It wasn't like people thought it was. It was over before you knew it. Mainly after hours, like night-time and early mornings. Hit and run. We'd retaliate, then wait for first light. 32 would go in and find specks of blood, but not a single soul. The terrs carried each other away, and injected themselves with all types of shit. They were just as bad as we were. They were doing heavy stuff for the adrenalin, obviously. We weren't allowed to go through the area. There'd be a lot of dowwerds. Our stuff didn't always go off, especially those snotneuse. If you picked them up they could blow your face off, so we weren't allowed to touch them.

The terrs were watching us more than we were watching them. They knew the terrain. They could walk twenty kays barefoot. *We* sure as hell couldn't! You couldn't see them because they looked local. A single oke would walk past you with the cattle. Greeted him. Meantime he's the ou. *He's* the *ou*! You didn't know that – they all looked the same.

Sometimes the terrs were run over by Koevoet Casspirs, then tied onto the vehicles and pulled back to base to show the guys. Rather see one of them than one of your own, though. They once put an insurgent in the hole for a week. Covered it over with metal so he couldn't get out. Didn't feed him. Tried to make him talk. 'Doesn't want to talk? We'll make him talk.' That boil stuff I used to sniff? Blindfolded him and sprayed it around his neck. He thought his neck was being cut. There were many ways to make them talk – terrible things. Your mindset was different. We were told different things; we were programmed.

At the time it was fine. You were getting your own back. 'Swart kaffer.' *Dwah!* Kicked him senseless. After his brain was a bit zing-zong and he'd lost a couple of teeth and had a few rifle butts in the stomach, his Afrikaans was better than mine or yours. He told you exactly what you wanted to know. You all got rewarded for that afterwards. Lekker chow. Drink. Kept a close eye on him so he didn't run away. After a while it was uniform him, sign him in, and he was one of the guys.

I witnessed this and was sometimes involved. Punched and kicked. I had to. What could I do? Whinge? Moan? Say, 'No, ag, shame, I don't want to do that?' Jeez, sure I would do it! I was aggro, man! *Aggro.*

Towards the end of June '83, after our Secondary Training as ops medics was over, we left Potch for Windhoek on the train. That was the worst part of my National Service. It was a three-day trip. No bathrooms. You could shit, but not wash. It was shocking. The food was terrible. I've never been so bored in my life. *Jirra,* I didn't enjoy that train trip!

From Windhoek we drove up to Grootfontein in Samils. Stayed in a deurgangs-kamp for two nights, then went to Oshakati and got posted out to different units. I ended up at Ondangwa. The air force base was east of it. We were more the Okatopi side. There were four of us medics there. The camp itself was mainly for campers that came for their service. We also ran a sickbay for the locals – like a clinic – at Ondangwa. When we weren't on patrol we'd be running the clinic. It was cool – I must've literally delivered over twenty babies. Did all sorts of things; it was good fun. I actually enjoyed it so much that I wanted to stay on. I wanted to join PF, but there was no money and the Dutchmen were ruining everything. If it was a completely professional army, like overseas, I probably would've stayed.

We mainly did motorised patrols, which were lekker, in Buffels, which was dead right. We didn't have to walk too much. Did walk a few patrols with the campers, though. I'll never forget it. It was in November. The rainy season had just started. It was pissing down and the campers each had a poncho that they got from somewhere. I don't know how. I still had this stupid raincoat. We were on a seven-day patrol. Two days in, it stopped raining. Everything had dried out but the MAG gunner kept his poncho on. The okes tuned him, 'Take it off, you poephol!' When they almost forced it off they saw he'd carried only the spare barrel with him. That's all that was sticking out. He'd intentionally left the MAG at home – he didn't want to carry that heavy thing! He wasn't too popular and got heavily *kla'ed aan* by the sergeant. The other okes moered him. When we got back, the camp RSM went berserk. Whenever we got back from patrol, the sa'majoor would organise every oke a braai pack and six beers. While we chowed our full, this other oke got nothing and had the RSM to deal with. He was mal, and used to shout and swear and throw stuff and threaten to kill people. He'd moer the okes, too. He had no problem with punching them. He was an absolutely berserk guy.

When we went on patrol we'd be in four Buffels. The drivers and I were whites, along with a short-service sergeant and a lieutenant. The others were all black guys. Not 32, though. Our role was to speak to the locals and find out where the baddies were. It was usual to go out for seven days. Slept out in the bush and laagered at night. I loved it. I loved the bush. At the time I didn't realise or care about the danger part of it. It was exciting. We were outdoors and we had guns. I enjoyed it.

I think my scariest moment was when the guy sitting across from me in the Buffel fell asleep and accidentally shot his snotneus. It hit the floor, hit the side, came up, hit the roll bar and dropped between the seats. It has to go five metres before it will explode, but it didn't. I was the only oke with my seatbelt on but the first oke out of that Buffel! If that thing went off I knew what would happen. I thought, 'Okay. Best get outta here!' I was lying in the dirt on the side of the road before the vehicle had even stopped!

We had a good time up there, even though we'd have to deal with troops who'd had contact. We'd often go on casevacs. One of the things I remember very clearly was the local militia – black okes – but I don't know what they were called. They were on the shooting range. The group before them had shot a snotneus that hadn't gone off. While they were picking up the doppies some oke picked it up and it went off. About nine guys were badly injured. We flew in to pick them up.

I never ran around shooting at baddies. Instead, when people got injured, we climbed in the Pumas and went to fetch them. We'd give them drips. The general procedure was first to make sure the ou was breathing, stop the bleeding and then administer whatever first aid you could. There really was nothing else but first aid. We kept him breathing and got him back to the field hospital as quickly as possible.

I became a two-liner, but once lost my temper while drinking beer and ended up back as a one-liner. Some infantry lieutenant was giving us a hard time. This oke was telling us what we should be doing, which we didn't think was a good idea – he'd just got there; we'd been there for eight months already. He started shouting. I said he shouldn't shout. It turned nasty. I ended up smacking him. I lost a line for that – that was all.

As medics we were given a bit of leeway. We didn't stand guard, which was really cool, because we were on standby all the time in case of casevacs, or whatever. Generally the rank treated us a little better. We didn't get jaaged as much because we were there for a specific reason.

I was on the Border for fourteen months. Came back for pass three times. Twice for a week and once for fourteen days. We were obviously told not to divulge any troop movement, which I knew nothing about anyway, so it was stupid to tell me that. All I know is what *we* did, but they didn't say you couldn't tell anybody this.

I was based at Ruacana for fourteen months, from November '83. During that time I had leave on three occasions. I was Maintenance – blue berets – and worked as a clerk at the quartermaster stores. Issued clothing, mostly. Boring stuff. At one stage I was in charge of rations, which had its advantages. You could always score something for extra food. Everybody was always asking for food. There were about four different types of rat packs, as far as I can recall.

The first time we went up was in October, 1984. We were based at Eenhana, and were trying to win the hearts and minds of the locals. That was a complete fiasco because of the whole logistical problem. We made this huge braai for all the chiefs of the Ovambos. We even went into Angola and knocked down trees with a Ratel, to use as firewood. A Kwêvoël took the wood back. We thought we were going to have to make a huge fire for all this meat. We'd supply the meat and feed the chiefs, but they were supposed to bring their own livestock to feed their people. They didn't, so we ended up just braaiing for the chiefs. There they were, the hungry locals, standing around staring at the chiefs and high-ranking officers filling their mouths.

People think the Infantry was easy stuff. It wasn't. We did some crazy things. Saw some crazy things, too. At a later stage we shared a base with Reconnaissance guys. Our tent was quite close to them. There were bunkers, reinforced with sandbags, interconnected by tunnels. These could be defended if the base was attacked. One bunker had a steel gate, which was locked at all times. It had AKs inside. I saw some of these guys arrive late one night and take the AKs out, very quietly. They disappeared into the bush.

When they came back a couple of days later, three terrs were spread-eagled on the front of their vehicles. I saw them coming in with the short version of the Casspir – the Wolf. Koevoet had Casspirs, and there weren't many where we were. They said they were going to get these guys to talk. When they left, these terrs were very much alive. When they returned, they were dead. It was plainly evident they'd been driven through the bush. I saw them coming back with bodies that you couldn't recognise any more. They cut the bodies off and left. We never saw those Recces again after that. That was within my first three months on the Border.

_____

I was in the Infantry and went up in 1985. Was based in Nepara in the west of Sector 2Ø. Our base was called Mike Fox.

Nothing happened. It was very quiet. I personally saw nothing in the line of action. I never went into Angola. We just hung around and walked foot patrols. We built another base – Alpha Fox – for campers. At night we'd drink, braai or stand guard. One of the other platoons allegedly had some sort of contact where they'd captured a couple of guys, but that was rumour. The guys talked a lot. There was a lot of talk in the army.

The Border was, in many ways, preferable to being down in the Republic because it was – technically speaking – a war zone, so you didn't have unnecessary bullshit. You were out on your own. You looked after yourself. There was no running around and being treated too badly. We didn't see the regimental sergeant major for six months! I saw the company sergeant major infrequently. There wasn't that strict discipline the whole time. Back at base in Grahamstown it was a different story – they'd be on your case continuously.

The army was the first place I came across where there was no racial segregation. Up on the Border you simply didn't have facilities for apartheid. We slept and ate alongside black guys. We used the same toilets as them. When we arrived we replaced a Zulu battalion and we, in turn, were replaced by a Bushman battalion. It was very intermingled up there.

At Grootfontein, pretty far from the Operational Area, I was a forklift driver for SAWI. I'd been medically classified as G3K4, so couldn't be operational. We'd offload the trucks and load the cargo into various storage containers that they had on site. Old ship containers were used. Everything was stored on wooden pallets. Then we'd reload the provisions onto the trucks going out to their different destinations.

I stayed at Grootfontein for two months before being posted to Oshakati the following year, in 1986, until uitklaaring. I started as an orderly. On a monthly basis I'd take the orders for all the canteens and PF families' household requirements. You worked from a set order-list. You'd get the order and see that the goods were sent out on the next transport to wherever they had to go.

Then I was placed in charge of the liquor and cigarette distribution. It came in handy for the base parties. All the cans and bottles were stored to one side, all ordentlik and accounted for, but stuff inevitably 'fell by the wayside'. Booze and smokes would be stockpiled, kept as a supply and then brought out at the right opportunities.

I didn't bugger around much but, once, on New Year's Eve, I shot a couple of rounds off into the air. I was busted by the MPs but a buddy of mine talked them out of charging me.

Of note is that we had six 'rehabilitated' SWAPO members working with us. They were captured, held in POW camps and then released to take up position and employment with SADFI. There were also a number of Ovambo civilians who were ex-SWAPO members.

SADFI also took part in operations. Supply trucks were sent along with the convoy to supply goods to the forward bases. We'd have mobile canteens, as well, which were like portable tuck shops. They were Samils with a large rectangular container on the back. A flap opened up, a stand was placed out and the troops lined onto a ramp. The drivers had to be SADFI members.

I was on the Border for eighteen months, based at Ondangwa, in '85 and '86. Going didn't bother me much. In the beginning it did. I knew it was war over there and the possibility of getting shot, perhaps even killed, was likely, but after a while I accepted it – I *had* to go and actually *wanted* to go.

I wore the blue beret – was in 5 Maintenance Unit as a driver, and went all over the place. Drove the Kwêvoël most times, which was better, because it was armoured. It had the mine-proof V-shape at the bottom. It got extremely hot inside with the Border heat, causing a greenhouse effect. There were no windows. You could only open the small flaps, the spring-loaded gun ports, which we'd jam with empty Coke cans to stop them closing back in. Took food and fuel, or SAWI canteen goods in a mobile tuck shop – like sweets, cold drinks, chips, smokes and chocolates. Drove them into Angola or various camps around the Border.

Drove electrical equipment to Rundu once, hundreds of kilometres away, but the rest of the time I drove around the Sector 1Ø side. The road from Eenhana to a camp called Nkongo was about an eighty-kay stretch. It was a terrible road – full of bumps, with those corrugated-iron ridges. My whole vehicle would vibrate, which made my back and stomach pretty sore. In fact, my truck even started falling apart. The spare wheel came off. I heard it fall, checked the rear-view mirror and stopped to retrieve it. The whole convoy stopped. If one vehicle stopped then the whole convoy's supposed to stop. We kept our eyes on the rear-view mirror all the time because we didn't have radio comms. At times, driving around up there was pretty mellow and relaxed. You could smoke cigarettes in the cockpit, if you wanted.

Took supplies to Windhoek twice, in a Samil 50, and stayed for a week at a time. That was interesting. It was the first time I'd seen Windhoek. There was a SWATF base there, and we stayed with them.

Accommodation at Ondangwa was fine. We stayed in prefabricated bungalows. Never got given a rough time. Compared to Basics it was easy. The corporals were much better. Different corporals. It was all different people on the Border from those during Basics. The food was all right – it wasn't too bad. Much better than Basics, though. It wasn't anything special; it was like the food your mom would've cooked. Not restaurant food, but not prison food either.

Klaared in at Grahamstown, July 1985, 6 SAI. Went to Ruacana for six months and Eenhana for a year. Both bases were quite serious because we were right on the cut line. Eenhana was the most northern base with a runway, apart from Rundu, where they could still put Flossies down. The terrs used to rev the base. Don't know how often it was. Felt like once a week. They'd come along, throw a couple of mortars at us, turn around and run away. Then all the Koevoet guys would go chasing after them and bring back their bodies the next day. Fortunately I was only there for the low-intensity stuff.

On a Sunday evening we used to have church parade, but first would be the situation report. There'd be this big board in front of everyone. They'd go through any kills for the week, and say, 'Right, one in that sector, one there in that sector, and one there. This is what we must aim to achieve next week.' Then the dominee would stand up. He was the highest-ranked man on base, or always the equivalent of the highest-ranking officer. He was God himself, sort of thing, this big Afrikaner. We used to pray that the government made the right decisions and the 'Swart Gevaar' was squashed and destroyed. The prayer used to end with him hoping that we got lots of kills for the week, all in the name of the church.

We used to share a mess with the officers at Eenhana. It was both an officers' and an NCOs'. We, as one- or two-stripers and one-pip lieutenants, would have to drink with all these serious PF guys, who sort of forced us to drink. I suppose we could've opted out if we'd wanted to, but we wanted to enjoy ourselves as well.

The system was so clever. We used to have little girls writing to us – six-, ten-, twelve-year-olds – children. They obviously had to write in class. It was mostly Afrikaans, and it was always, 'Liewe dapper soldaat …' Esmé Euvrard used to read messages on her radio programme encouraging people to write or send parcels with the Southern Cross Fund, which used to deliver these letters up to us. You'd open this letter from a seven-year-old girl telling you how wonderful you were, that you were saving them and so on. Then you'd feel compelled to write back. It was always a big joke to ask, 'Have you got older sisters and can you submit photographs, please?'

I didn't really have leave. Came home to Cape Town after Basics and again after second phase finished. Then went up to the Border and only came back twice more, which were for sports passes. My company commander was the Orange Free State power-lifting champion. A huge bull of a man. He and I put in a sports pass to run the Comrades one year and the Two Oceans another year. I didn't expect anything to happen about the requests. We were out on ops, in the middle of nowhere, when suddenly this helicopter landed and I was told, 'Korporaal! Get on that helicopter. You're going to Cape Town.' I was flown back to Eenhana. From there we took a Dakota to Grootfontein, a small Safair to Pretoria, and then a civilian flight to Cape Town.

In 1987, during my first year of National Service, I was hit by a landmine on Oom Willie se Pad, a sand road just off the chandelier, about eleven kays from the border on 54 Battalion's side. It wasn't even on a routine patrol. It wasn't supposed to happen. We were doing aanvullings.

We'd just come off a patrol and were supposed to rest for the day, but our sergeant major was so steeked that when there was a gap out he would take it. So out we went again in our five Buffels, doing aanvullings to other sections, supplying rations and water. We were supposed to sweep or cross-cut over the road, but we travelled straight. This was the lieutenant's decision – a one-pip National Serviceman. The reason was that it was getting dark and we had to be back at base before this. We shouldn't have travelled on the road, but alongside it – bundu-bashed and crossed over and so on – but he was in a hurry to beat the dark.

There was the driver in front, on the left-hand side, and two of us in the back. I wasn't strapped in. You weren't allowed to be, in case you needed to jump for action. I was standing in the front and to the right. My buddy was standing rear-left. We also weren't wearing staaldaks, as they'd been taken away. The force of a landmine plus the helmet on your head was a dangerous combination.

We drove in the same spoor. You weren't allowed to deviate, but we were travelling faster than normal. The first Buffel must have missed the mine by inches because we, in the second Buffel, detonated it. The right front wheel got the blast. The driver was strapped in, of course, and only hurt his arm and knee. The other guy got thrown out and landed on soft sand. All he sustained was ringing ears. But I went over with the Buffel. I have no idea how I could've remained inside. I heard a bang and saw smoke, and that was it. It just went dark. I felt no pain. I was out of it, unconscious.

I was later told that the Buffel went into the air, rolled over and landed on its side. It was totally destroyed. Front suspension gone, wheels gone, tyres gone. Pieces of tyre were found for kilometres around, hanging on steekbosse. I was casevaced in a Koevoet Casspir. Koevoet were in the neighbourhood. They came to do rondomverdediging just in case it was an ambush.

When I woke up I was in sickbay at Nkongo. The next morning I was taken to Ondangwa, where they examined me. From there I was sent to 1 Mil in Pretoria and then finally to 2 Mil in Cape Town, where I lived. My cheekbone was fractured and my nose had three reconstructive operations done on it. There was a piece of shrapnel inside, which got it looking the way it looks now. I had no feeling in my top jaw. My arm was badly cut. I was bruised. It took nearly five months in hospital to recover. I wasn't discharged or offered counselling. Then they sent me back up to the Border. After that I came back and did townships.

In 1988 the RSM of 54 Battalion promised me R12 000 compensation. Never saw a cent – just my danger pay. You got your monthly wages, but on the Border you just used up your danger pay. They tried to cover up the whole situation. The base OC went to clean the area and disguise the fact that anything at all had occurred. Nothing happened to the lieutenant. He'd made a decision, and that was that.

[*The following narrative is, date-wise, neither in sequence nor told by a National Serviceman, but relates to the previous account. It is told by Dennis Croukamp, who spent sixteen years in the Rhodesian army, including four years as a Selous Scout specialising in demolitions. He joined the SADF after the fall of Rhodesia.*]

In early '81 I was housed with 101 Battalion in Ondangwa. Colonel Breytenbach was brigade commander of 44 Parachute Brigade, which had left a pathfinder company with 101 Battalion. There were a lot of Americans and Canadians, a few Poms, a South African and a Portuguese – a whole 'United Nations' group. This was the pathfinder company; Breytenbach's little Special Forces group he'd put together.

We'd been there a couple of weeks. The colonel introduced me to the commandant. He said to the commandant if he had any problems he could speak to me as I'd solve them for him. A fine predicament! Then the colonel left the area.

Later the RSM called me in and said that the commandant wanted to see me. After I reported he took me to the adjutant who took me to the commandant in the ops room. He showed me a map of the road [Oom Willie se Pad]. 'Engineers are sweeping from both directions, meeting in the middle, and by the time they get home the landmines are going off again. What can you do about it?'

'Commandant, can I give this some thought?' I went back to my little camp within a camp and did so. I came back the next morning. 'The best I can do is put up nine OPs along the road, in the bush, but only at night, so we're going to need night-vision equipment.' He agreed and arranged everything. I went up to Oshakati to draw the equipment. The storeman asked me for a permit.

'A what?' I asked.

'You need a permit to draw these things.'

'No, I don't have such a thing,' I said. 'But we used them in the Rhodesian army a lot!'

The line didn't work. 'No, that's not good enough. You've got to get a permit!' So the whole operation was postponed while the equipment was delivered. In the meantime they gave the guys a quick course in using it, as only three of us were ex-Rhodesian. Eventually they sent a sergeant to give us the course, but by the end of the day we'd actually taught *him* how to use his own night-vision equipment! He blew the first one by taking the caps off in broad daylight and switching it on! He cooked it. From then on we showed him how to do things. I don't think he'll ever live *that* one down. He couldn't speak a word of English, either, so I translated to our guys and from our guys back to him.

The commandant gave us three Buffels to drop off the call-signs, which bundu-bashed about ten kays away from the side of the road. The first OP was only dropped a few kays away from 101 Battalion, where the road junction was. A couple of days later and still no one had heard or seen anything. I told the call-signs to stay in their hides until about two hours before first light and then to move onto the roadside and wait. Those that couldn't had to OP at night and withdraw during the day again.

Early the next morning the first OP, five kays away, came over the radio and explained to me what he'd just witnessed. I then dashed over to the commandant with the RSM following me and the adjutant following him, both trying to stop me. It was like I had to make an appointment to see the man! I explained to him what had just been explained to me. He wanted to speak to the OP. We dashed off to his ops room. 'What's your frequency?' he asked. I didn't have it on me so the whole little ops-room group rushed over to our little ops room in the camp within a camp.

The OP explained that when the minesweepers were just out of sight down the road, the local ladies tilling the soil on the land nearby would dig up a mine, hop across the fence, plant it in the road and resume as usual. It was that easy. They lifted out a mine, which they'd stashed next to something that could be easily identified, usually right next to a fence post.

The commandant rushed back to his ops room and summoned Koevoet. Their commander flew in by helicopter while the rest of the column followed. By the time they arrived we'd all been briefed by the commander, who'd also spoken to my OP over the radio. Koevoet tore off down the road. Wherever they saw people tilling the land, two guys would debus from the vehicle and run across to them. After a few slaps here and there, they recovered over two hundred landmines from these women that same morning. Problem solved. We then recovered my troops.

The next day I got a message from the RSM that the commandant wanted to congratulate my troops. The following morning we lined up. We weren't even a platoon size. He wanted to know where the rest of my men were. 'The rest?' I asked. 'This is it, Commandant.' Then he wanted to court-martial me because I didn't have platoon-sized strength patrols out in the field! It was a standing order in Ovamboland required for standard infantry troops. It took an intervention from Colonel Breytenbach to wind his neck in. He told him we were Special Forces, and that was the end of it.

The problem had been going on for years. I can't put a time on it. Oom Willie's little blue bakkie was still there, about fifteen to twenty kays away, along the road from Ondangwa. It was the first vehicle to have been hit by a landmine on that road. Oom Willie was a local, white South-Wester – that's obviously where the road got its name. The road ran from Ondangwa to the border. One must remember that those roads just got wider and wider. The Buffels wouldn't destroy the fence itself, so, if there was a fence on one side, the road would gradually expand outwards. Sometimes they were a kilometre wide of clear land but would occasionally be restricted into a channel. Only our vehicles could travel along those, which the ladies would naturally target. The roads were very soft soil, so the mine could easily be recovered from its hiding place and reburied in the ground within seconds. I have no idea on the actual figures and whether they're available or not, but these caused many casualties.

[*WO II Sergeant Major Dennis E. W. Croukamp, BCR*]

It was beautiful up there. Going to the Border was interesting – that's probably not the right word – but we had an incredibly exciting time, especially for a little city-slicker like I was. I had never seen anything like it.

INTO ANGOLA

We always got newspapers a week late. One day I read a South African newspaper that said we didn't exist and weren't in Angola. Pik Botha stated 'categorically' to the United Nations that there wasn't a single South African inside Angola. It was quite a shitty feeling to know we'd been there for a couple of months and then simply be dismissed like that.

We built a foofie slide from a bridge that was blown just outside Ongiva. The Cubans sat on the other side of the river and applauded while we did tricks. We used to wave at each other. Not one shot fired. Not one word said in anger. If we'd gotten across the river we'd probably have traded stuff. Then one day we came back and they were all gone. Nothing left. It was weird. Very, very strange.

When I was in Angola, during the mid- to late seventies, we were running around in our Portuguese uniforms and takkies; Afrikaners speaking terrible English because we, the South Africans, weren't supposed to be there. We wouldn't speak Afrikaans to each other but had to speak English instead, and of course our English wasn't that brilliant. But, ja, we got through.

When I went in it was on a bigger operation. The armour had their own infantry support, but we usually had another infantry unit with us, like the Cape Town Highlanders. One guy got his Honoris Crux as a result of the action we saw. He was a captain in the CTH. It was a mortar attack on our base. A couple of tents were hit. Fortunately nobody was injured. We'd had a party that evening and some of us were inebriated. That saved a couple of our lives – we were where we shouldn't have been. We fired off two 90-mm rounds and that was the end of that little encounter.

We saw some horrible sights and that. But, you know, it's like if you see a motor car accident – you become a little bit harder as a result. You definitely did in Angola. You picked up people's pieces, and all of that type of thing. It wasn't very pleasant, and you became a little bit callous, picking up both the terrs' pieces and your own. It was basically random shootings and landmines. I don't mean to get political, but you had both MPLA and FNLA and, unfortunately, when you were in a situation, you didn't bother to ask them who or what they supported; you just wiped them all out.

32 had a winter and a summer camouflage, whereas the Recces never had recognised uniforms and wore anything available. They made use of whatever they could. Used stuff that was discarded as unserviceable – stuff that was thrown away at the back of the stores. They would rummage through it and take what was needed.

Bravo Group originally wore old Porra cammos and then SADF browns. When the States began supporting them financially, they consolidated into a recognised unit, becoming 32. Because they were going so far into Angola – at least 200 kays – they used their own camouflage to distinguish themselves from other operations that might occur with National Servicemen, or whomever.

We were sectored out to the engineers, who used to lift mines and caches. We did cross-border ops regularly – but little, subtle ones, not major things. We were never involved in anything big-time. It was always 32, 101 or Koevoet who went and did the proper stuff. Infantry were the dustbin-men, anyway. We just tagged along and cleaned up the mess, sort of thing. We'd trail behind in our Buffels, and then wait. Helicopters and gunships flew over the top of us. There'd be at least ten Buffels as well as the support vehicles. Sometimes there was also support from the armoured guys in their Noddy Cars.

When we went out on ops there were about 150 of us. Out there you might meet about ten of the enemy, if something *were* to happen. The odds were definitely in our favour. Definitely.

My National Service was during 1980 and 1981. I was in the Mechanised Infantry and carried an LMG with a two-hundred-round R1 belt-feed. You'd change the barrel when it glowed with heat. We had a spare barrel in the backpack.

In '81 some of the Ratels were hit while inside Angola. An RPG hit one and blew it into a balloon shape. Terrs fired from behind and it went straight in. Sometimes they'd shoot point-blank, which was a stupid thing to do. All the crew and occupants were killed, but the terrs were taken out. Some SWAPO were picked up after they pleaded surrender. Our ous said, 'No ways. Stuff that! Give us information! If you don't, then on the Buffel you go. We don't care. We'll tie you up with wire if we have to. We're going to drive and if you scream we hit the brakes.' They were tied to the Buffel, above the engine compartment. It only hit me later how bad it was.

There was nothing left inside that Ratel. There was nothing to remove. When an RPG penetrates, it bounces around inside and sets off every bit of ammunition it hits. It's fireworks inside. The last I remember the Ratel was still in Pretoria. They painted the thing silver and kept it as a monument.

While up at 61 Mech we found out the real story behind the silver-painted-Ratel incident. There was also a twist to the tale.

The unit was preparing to go into Angola for either Ops Sceptic or Protea, I can't remember which. Some say there was an Ops Smokeshell, but Smokeshell happened during Sceptic, in June '80. Smokeshell was the area named where PLAN had a huge base in Chifufa.

Anyway, before they left, the brass would find out if there was anyone who felt they couldn't go due to injury or welfare reasons. Usually there wasn't anybody but, this one time, three guys were having a really hard time dealing with situations back home. It could've been anything from sick parents, marital problems or a death in the family. They went with their problems to the unit chaplain, who in turn recommended that they stay behind to guard the unit or otherwise be sent home on welfare pass. Their problems were genuine and had been well documented already.

However, the company's commander, at the time a Captain H, was having none of it. He was apparently sick and tired of their problems, and insisted they participate. Instead of joining their respective platoons up front, they would help out with the rear supply vehicles, in particular one of the Ratels assigned to carrying extra ammunition for the ops.

During the ops, the company was attacking a SWAPO base when, in the confusion, their Ratel became separated from the rest of the supply column in the dense bush that made up most of the assault area. They came to a stop in a clearing. Suddenly the Ratel was surrounded by about seven terrs. The poor ous tried to fight their way out, but the Ratel became almost stationary. It was bogged down in soft sand, which then made it an easy target. The first RPG blasted through the driver's window, killing him instantly, and exploded under the turret, taking out the commander and gunners' legs, and then ignited the 20-mm HE and AP rounds. Two more RPGs ripped through the left side, blowing-up in the engine compartment and two giant diesel-fuel tanks, causing a massive explosion. At the same time another RPG hit the right side, near the back. The guy in the tail gunner's turret got blown out. He actually took out four terrs before the blast took off his legs. Nobody is sure if he survived. By that time everything inside the Ratel had caught fire or exploded. It was carrying a lot of extra ammunition, like I said, such as M26 and M79 grenades, RPGs, 20-mm rounds, claymores, R4 rounds, and so on. The Ratel became a massive inferno.

When the recovery squad arrived, there was absolutely nothing they could do. All the guys, obviously, were dead. The heat was so intense that they couldn't get closer than ten to fifteen metres away from the burning Ratel. It only cooled down after three days.

After the company had obtained the objective and had overrun the SWAPO base, word got out to the guys that their buddies were dead. It was especially hard for them because, in the actual contact, there were hardly any casualties – nothing but an occasional flesh wound and cuts and bruises. They immediately became very pissed off with the captain.

The next day, when the company was doing mopping-up operations, the captain took it upon himself to go into a trench which led off into a bunker that hadn't been properly cleared. He tossed a grenade in the doorway, waited, then went in – but didn't notice another doorway leading directly to the left of the first, where a wounded terr was hiding. A couple of troops who were nearby heard shots and ran towards the bunker as the terr was trying to run out. They took him out, went into the bunker and found the captain. He was dead, although I don't think there were many in the company who gave a damn.

[*Note: I asked for an opinion regarding the Ratel incident from a 2 SSB gunner. His comments follow.*]
Depending on whether the Ratel was crewed or fully bombed-up, it would be an average of nineteen tons of vehicle. That armour was thick. The front plate alone was 1.5 to 2 inches. So, for a Ratel to balloon from the impact and the heat contained within, it would've had to have been an intensely large explosion. It may have been the result of a HEAT missile, which is equipped with a titanium tip that punches its way through the target's armour plating. Once inside it explodes, which causes a massive amount of heat and pressure. These projectiles must've come from tanks. I would say that that's more likely.

An RPG is not an accurate device. It needs at least fifteen metres for the projectile to arm itself, and it's a little weak. It could definitely stop a Ratel, but causing it to balloon is odd. What could've happened is that the RPG exploded inside a fully bombed-up Ratel and a couple of the 90s went off inside – that would cause it to balloon, for sure. If memory serves correctly, there are about seven kilograms of TNT in each round. If a couple of those went off inside, then there's no question.

In '82 I did cross-border ops but, being artillery, we stayed way back. '82 was conventional warfare.

There were Mirages flying in and out. MiGs were also flying above us. They were the only real threat in quelling our rocket launchers. They'd have two MiGs. One flew low in an attempt to attract our attention, while the second flew higher up. They'd fly in sorties. It was an attempt to keep us quiet so we wouldn't be on the move. It worked. There would certainly be no movement on our behalf at all. I think they had an air force base higher up at Cuito Cuanavale, a city with a large military base in eastern Angola. The Recces would sit there and watch every time two MiGs took off. We'd get a radio message from them. We'd throw our cammo and cover the mirrors and windscreens to make sure that there were no reflections. Then we'd just sit in our trenches and hope a bomb didn't hit us. They dropped bombs, but some never went off. They'd stick in the ground and we'd find them afterwards. For three months we sat there.

In mid '81, the previous intake, who hadn't even fully trained in second phase, were sent in with campers to assist in Ops Protea with the 5.5s. The guys went 350 kilometres inside.

I did lots of unofficial cross-border ops as a driver in Maintenance – blue berets. Some drives were with 32 Battalion or 61 Mech. As truck drivers we'd support the Elands or Ratels or whatever armoured vehicles were being used. They'd go ahead and we'd follow as a support unit in the back with bladders of diesel for their vehicles, or carry oils, ammo and food for the guys. Drove a Kwêvoël, which was an armoured Samil. If one got hit by a landmine or RPG, the drill was to stop the trucks. First truck went left, second truck right, third truck left, and so on. Hop out your cab, onto the bonnet, up onto the roof and down the back towards the next truck. You didn't jump out because there'd be claymores or anti-personnel all around you. If the troops all bailed out then they'd get klapped. You'd find cover, *gooi* cammo, get ready and wait. It was all structured, all thought out, by their side and ours.

On ops I was king. The guys would come past: 'Please, man, we need another couple of rat packs.'

'Sure. What colour do you want?'

'Green!'

'For two yellow ones I'll give you a green.' That's how it worked. I was their support. I had their ammo, their oil, their fuel and their food. Not all at once, though. Different times I had different loads. In the back of these Ratels were about ten troepies each. I was now their best buddy. They'd look after me and my truck. That truck had to be there, otherwise there was no water or provisions for them.

The horrible thing was, while in the Ruacana area, we used to support Koevoet. They'd go across the border and take no prisoners. In their whole time, of about twelve years of fighting, there were only two prisoners known to be brought back and put in interrogation – which is impossible. The rest got killed. They had the highest kill rate of any unit, more even than the army, which meant that they should, as a consequence, have had the highest number of prisoners. So why only two? Their kill rate was so high because they stole kills. They'd listen in on the radio and as soon as spoor became hot and a contact seemed imminent, they'd race to the area and pounce. It was the army ous who'd do the long slog and follow the terrs. Koevoet and 101 would take the glory. What they then did was take the bodies, tie them over the Casspirs' wheel arches, and drive back across the border and through Ovamboland. The sight of bundu-bashed corpses was a signal to the locals – 'Join SWAPO and join your buddies over there.' It was a visible deterrent. The official explanation was that it was both un-pleasant and unnecessary to travel with putrefying, bloated corpses inside an already crammed armoured vehicle. As a support driver I was now part of this convoy. It was the most horrible thing that we ever had to experience.

I went over on Ops Super in early '82, which was quite a big one. We supported mainly 32 on that one. We went to the Caprivi Strip, where all the Recce camps were, as well as Buffalo for 32 and Omega for 201 Bushman Battalion. We'd support them from Mpacha, refuelling their helicopters with avgas bladders.

On one ops I had an accident. I was the diesel-tank driver, right at the back of the convoy, followed only by a lieuty. We had no radio comms. They'd stopped the convoy of thirty-eight vehicles. It was lined so far back it carried on around a bend instead of being on a long, open stretch where you could see. It was just dust. I came around the corner and saw that the trucks had stopped, but had nowhere to go. It wasn't like the path was open and wide and I could pass. The roads were usually built up from ground level. I hit the anchors but knocked over a trailer carrying phosphorous grenades off the back of the truck in front. It rolled down the slope flanking the road. The collision ripped open three of my truck's compartments. Nine thousand litres of diesel were lost. Everybody came running over and freaked out. The 32 ranks went completely mad. The guy in charge was a PF captain. I got fined R20 for 'belemmering van 'n operasie'. They said I tried to defeat the ends of an operation; that's what I was charged with. The reason why they charged me for attempting to stop the operation was because, out of 12 000 litres of diesel for the vehicles, I'd lost 9 000.

The first time I came back home I saw Pik Botha on TV, who said, 'I categorically deny there are any South Africans in Angola.' Strange, because I'd just returned from there.

I'll tell you something about Koevoet. It was a private police wing originally formed in '79 out of nothing. They traded with the SADF for the vehicles and supplies they needed. Their orders were taken from Oshakati, but I wouldn't say they had an HQ there. And, regarding Koevoet, those things you heard didn't happen. There may have been the odd Mad Max between them, but they didn't do that shit as a rule. They definitely brought back the body counts, sure, because they were the 'Sheriffs of the Bush'. That bull you heard was disinformation propagated by the terrs to the international media. So maybe a few terrs got in the way of the vehicles and they ran them over, but so what? It had to be done. Was the driver going to stop and let them get away? Please, man, get real. And as for bodies on the fenders, would you want them inside a vehicle that's hot, with no body bags? Would you want to wash out the mess? Anybody who turns their nose up is thinking as a civilian. They did their jobs and they did them well. I don't care what anybody says about stealing kills. Stealing kills? Let them take the kills! They were far better trained than the ordinary troepie. They had the fire-power and the vehicles. Do you really want a troepie to go hurtling into the bush after insurgents, carting webbing, helmet, water bottles and a rifle? No way! Let the proper guys come in with expert local trackers, Brownings and Casspirs. Then the real business gets done, and thoroughly, too.

Those stories got blown out of all proportion. It would be a real dare-devil story you'd hear in a bar. You used to hear a lot of that crap in the bars, especially down at Grootfontein transit camp, from all the people coming through.

We weren't supposed to be in Angola. In fact, we were listening to the radio while inside Angola with Pik Botha insisting that no South African troops were inside!

Just after our arrival we had kills, so we came down for Christmas, which was very nice. I was part of a section that had contact. I don't really want to tell you about it. It's hectic. It brings back memories. You've caught me off-guard.

We'd been inside for about a month, on the west side of Angola, over the Cunene River. We went across with rubber ducks and then marched over mountains. Non-mechanised. Just foot. It was thick bush. There were no roads to follow. No water. We had serious problems with water. There were two platoons, spread over a large area, with three sections per platoon and twelve guys per section.

Intelligence reported about seventy terrs supposedly in the area. We'd been ordered to set up an observation post. We were on top of this mountain and heard helicopters. While standing on the mountain one of those gunships almost shot me. I was looking out over the valley. Suddenly it came out of nowhere and the gunner pointed his guns at me. He was so close – about ten metres away. I took off my bush hat, which had Dayglo in it, and showed it to him. He dropped his guns, almost in fright, because he *was* going to shoot. You could hardly recognise us as South African soldiers. After being there for almost a month we were completely black.

Then we saw the terrs running. There were only four, so it must have been a splinter group. The gunships began shooting at them. We went down and gave chase. Three were killed and the fourth got away. I don't know where he got to. We then radioed HQ, who told us to remove the bodies. There were no bags to put them in. We picked them up and moved about five kilometres away, two guys per body. We took turns. It wasn't pleasant, because, after a while, the bodies putrefied. It was hot – about 48 degrees Celsius. Some of the one guy's brain popped out where his ear once was. Their skin peeled off and shit like that, which is why I don't want to talk about it.

We radioed again but were told to keep moving so as not to be found. Finally they came down in the helicopter and identified the bodies as FAPLA, put them in body bags and took them away. Still have an AK bayonet from one of the dead terrs.

The next day we were flown thirty kilometres further into Angola. We had no water. Inside the Puma were dozens of two-litre plastic bottles filled with water. There were a lot of them but they wouldn't give us even one because they were on ops with the paratroopers. So, the Bats got their water while we had to search for ours! The pilots dropped us off by a dry riverbed and told us to find our own water. Crazy. Jeez, it's not like we were trained Special Forces – just National Servicemen.

I went on Ops Askari with the mechanised infantry. There were two parts to the op. I was in the first phase – November, December '83, in the beginning. The ous in the second phase came back in January '84.

There was a Valkiri driver and his co-driver – a Number One and Number Two – who got in to start it one morning. A rocket went through the compartment, but it wasn't primed and didn't explode. The sergeant and I were there at the time and were the first two okes to help them. The one guy had been killed instantly, and I didn't think the other guy, the driver, was going to live. The back blast had burnt him really badly.

Funnily enough I met his brother about six years ago. We were sitting drinking beer, and I don't know how or why this particular story came up, but he said it was his brother. It turned out the guy had lived. He was fine. He'd moved to Cape Town from Durban. He was killed in a motorbike accident the year before I met his brother. It was sad that he went through all that recovery just to die like that.

At Cuvelai the Bats walked into a minefield. Three or four had their legs blown off. They were doing a recce. We went to that casevac. Those ous were tough, *jong*. They basically fought the battle by themselves, in the beginning, until we got artillery, tanks and other support there. The Cubans had a lot of hardware.

Went in by convoy three times, taking supplies to various infantry camps, usually to 51 Battalion and 53 Battalion. Just drove through the bush. That was an experience – bundu-bashing. Tried to drive in a straight line as much as possible – one behind the other – because of mines, but obviously snaked around large trees and major obstructions.

I personally never had any encounters with landmines, but I knew a guy who did. He was in a Kwêvoël 100. They'd delivered their supplies, so the vehicle was empty, and they were on their way back along a dirt road. Luckily the truck wasn't going fast. It hit the mine and went into the bush. The metal fender over the top of the front wheel spiralled up, and, when they found it, it had holes all over it. The wheel was gone.

When we went out on convoys, the roads were swept in the early hours of the morning. Engineers stood in a line and walked with their metal detectors. Some of the terrs got clever and planted the mines beneath metal pipes. The engineers would detect the pipe, ignore it, and move on. That's probably what happened in this guy's case.

There was obviously lots of dust when driving. We kept quite far apart to prevent it from interfering with the vision of the vehicle behind us. The number of vehicles in the convoy varied, but it was usually about ten Kwêvoëls. Some took petrol, some took SAWI consumables, while others carried ammunition, supplies and rations. We had what was called *beskerming*. Buffels or Noddy Cars, in front and behind the convoy, carried infantry in case of ambushes.

Most of the time we slept in our trucks, on the platbak. I remember the stars – clear, bright and infinite. It was seldom that there were clouds. The rainy season was summer. When sleeping in the back of the truck, I'd be quite glad when I heard the rain tapping on the cargo's canvas sails. We'd cover the cargo with the sail and then throw a cammo net over. If I drove a diesel tanker I'd sleep in the cab on the floor. Stretched myself out between the seat and the pedals. It was very uncomfortable, but what else was there? On a Kwêvoël were two single seats, with a big depression in between, so you couldn't lie on it like you can on the back seat of a car. Those diesel tankers were heavy at the back. You had to be careful when taking a corner otherwise it leant to the side. When coming to a stop, you felt the weight of the diesel moving the truck back and forth. It played with the momentum. You had to take it easy.

The first time, I went in about eighty kilometres to a town called Nehone, a ruined ghost town. It was the first time I'd seen an Angolan town. There wasn't a soul living there. No women, children or even animals. All the buildings were destroyed. Political slogans were painted on the walls. These once-beautiful Portuguese buildings were originally painted in various colours. The strange thing was, the only building completely intact was the church. Above its main entrance was a round porthole, about a metre across. The stained glass was smashed, but that was the only damage. Inside the church I felt a strong spiritual presence. Funnily enough, the interior hadn't been ransacked.

Driving back we entered Chiede, also deserted and damaged. Somebody mentioned that all the towns in Angola were similar, having a distinct Portuguese style with brightly coloured walls, but always desolate and in ruins.

Heading back to South West I checked a Buffel that had hit a mine – it had obviously happened a while before. I saw a big crater in the ground, and the Buffel was sitting upright on its bum. Other Buffels were in the area. Never saw the occupants so I can't say if there were injuries. The driver was out. We didn't stop, and carried on past the scene. Never seen anything like that before or since. There were moments like that.

There was no debriefing. None. When we got back to base at Bloem, every time there was a bang of some sort, the guys were on the ground, thinking it was an attack. No jokes. The same thing happened even after leaving the army. It may sound clichéd, but it's actually true.

THE TOWNSHIPS

In 1988, after six months on the Border, I came back and went into the townships. Natal, Grahamstown and East London. Had a few ambushes and attacks. Shot at a few so-called terrorists. Unlike some, we weren't told not to shoot. If you had a situation, you went for it.

On the Border we knew our enemy was north. In the townships the enemy was invisible. You didn't know where they would strike from.

I am so glad I didn't do township patrols. Some of my intake stayed behind and did townships. I would've hated to do townships. You didn't know who the enemy was. At best, up on the Border, the enemy was pretty good at blending in. They could just strip off their kit and suddenly walk around in shorts and T-shirts, as though they were wandering farmers, but in the townships everybody was a potential enemy. You weren't wanted there. You were a hated white face. People living there, even the women and children, would be defending the so-called terrorists – who are our leaders today. It must have been awful.

Nothing in our training prepared us for what we saw once there. It was chalk and cheese. When you're there, physically, on the ground – especially during night patrols, when everything's dark and you don't have torches on – it's different. There is that fear in you. Nothing prepares you for that. Nothing.

I was with 6 SAI from July '84. We did plenty of township patrols. Did one trip up to the Border, and were supposed to do more, but they needed us in the townships. We were the first guys to go inside in the Eastern Cape, which we saw extensively. Port Elizabeth, Uitenhage, Despatch, Kenton-on-Sea, Adelaide – you name it. After adding up the broken periods of service, I worked out that I spent altogether about a whole year in the townships.

We'd sit on the back of the Buffels. It was horrendously boring. Hours spent on the back, doing nothing. On patrol were us, Echo Company, and a platoon of campers. The highest authority with us was a one-pip National Service lieutenant. We never saw anybody higher than that on patrol.

In that time we only saw one major incident. Our platoon sergeant shot and killed a guy. It was the usual scenario: we noticed an incident, so we went to investigate. Of course, when the people saw the Buffels coming, they scattered. Then they congregated again. We had an Afrikaans guy with us, a local bloke, who could speak fluent Xhosa. He told them it was an 'illegal gathering' and ordered them to disperse. They didn't. We did the usual minimum-force procedure after the verbal warning: tear gas, then rubber bullets and then on to live ammunition. The cops with us had their shotguns. The crowd began chucking rocks and bricks at us. When you saw stuff flying at your vehicle, you didn't think about it, you just responded. You were too busy pointing stopper guns and trying to get your rubber gas masks on. You were otherwise occupied. The platoon sergeant and platoon commander opened fire. They were supposed to fire over the heads of the crowd and into the hills. The sergeant pulled off a couple of rounds into the ground, but one bullet flew up, ricocheted off a wall and went through some guy's neck. Killed him. The crowd ran. That was it. End of gathering.

When we returned to camp there was a proper debriefing on who saw what, when and why, by the platoon commander himself. Whatever happened to the sergeant after the eventual inquiry, I can't say. It was only finalised long after I'd left the army. He was a white PF and rumoured to be ex-32 Battalion. I never saw a cammo beret or anything to that effect, though. One heard things, but how much of it was actually true is a mystery. A lot of what one heard in the army was hearsay. He was one of those okes who was always screaming and shouting, the type of guy who's on your case the whole time. But we had respect for him because he taught us a lot of things – like how to get on in the bush. Lots of little tips, but such important ones. You could pick up pretty easily the difference between the guys who were narrow-minded, nasty, malicious little men, and those who also screamed and shouted, but did so for a reason. You had respect for those ones. Different styles of leadership. The sergeant was a little strange. He used to get drunk and then stagger off to Rhodes University, where he'd rev the students. They'd gang up on him and beat him senseless.

We once got a report about some sort of unrest in a location just outside Grahamstown. We went in and saw a person lying on the ground. He'd been stabbed. We gave him first aid as best we could. The ambulance wasn't prepared to go in, and waited on the main road for us to escort it in, but we couldn't get to the main road without leaving the guy behind. We tried to resuscitate him. It was a no-win situation. He died in the end.

After the withdrawal from South West in '89, the army brought 32 down to Pomfret, an asbestos mining town in the Northern Cape. They lost support from the South African government and just fell to pieces along the wayside, but couldn't be left behind after we pulled out. Then the Defence Force tried using them in the Natal townships, but they were too aggressive, having been trained in a guerrilla-warfare capacity. To suddenly come into the urban aspect of a conflict just wasn't going to work.

One of the unfortunate situations was to involve black troops from 32 Battalion after our withdrawal. Many were used for service in the townships; places they didn't want to be and didn't know how to handle. They were all experienced combatants. Some were in 32 from an early age. All they knew was life in the bush with 32 Battalion.

I speak under correction, but, from what I understand, the SADF felt that they couldn't leave them on the Border after the Angolan conflict because they would've been targeted as traitors. They were then deployed around South Africa and sent into the townships. This was a big mistake. They weren't familiar with any of the languages – they couldn't speak Zulu or Xhosa or Sotho. They resented being in the cities and townships and wanted to be in the bush. They wanted to fight an enemy they knew, and one who was a valid enemy – not a civilian enemy. There were a few nasty incidents – rape, violence and some open fire; incidents where they just lost it. They'd never been ragged or sworn at or treated with contempt by their so-called 'enemy'. Some, albeit very few, retaliated and dealt with it by opening fire. When asked why they did so, they explained that they simply didn't waste time on trash like that. Township duties were not something they'd been trained for. It wasn't simple, conventional warfare. They weren't welcome in the townships by the locals, either. The majority were non–South African blacks fighting on the side of the SADF and SAP. Perhaps they would've been happier, and more comfortable, if they were used out in the grama-doelas to patrol the Republic's borders.

My township patrols in 1990 were very interesting. They were in the last six months before klaaring out. We did them, but not the way the army wanted us to. We abused the system and did shebeen raids. Knocked on a guy's door, pointed a gun in his face. 'Where's the shebeen?' And he'd tell you! We'd go there and demand, 'Where's the beer?' Got back to the Casspir with crates of beer. Told the crew, 'Keep quiet. It's coming with us.' Then we'd get motherless again.

At the time there was an upheaval about Mandela getting out of prison. Everyone, including us, was anxious about what would happen next.

We were the peacekeeping force at the time. In '91 the political situation between Inkatha and the ANC was pretty bad. We were in there to keep them apart. The one side would be the ANC and the other would be Inkatha. They were literally separated by a little dirt road a few metres wide. That was it. That was their border.

For six months we did these patrols, staying in TBs, and went all over Natal. At first we were in Umlazi but then followed the problems further and further into Natal. We moved wherever we were needed. Our main mission was to disarm the people. When the factions fought each other we went into that area to try to stabilise them. They were well armed and we occasionally came up against some pretty serious stuff. The favoured weapon at the time was the pipe gun. We bust quite a few factories where they were made. Then the locals started complaining that we were disarming them and that they didn't have anything to defend themselves with. That was a big complaint.

Some of the troops were from Natal and could speak Zulu to the locals and communicate with them. Within every group, if there wasn't a black policeman, it would be one of us who could speak Zulu. This was absolutely necessary in order to find out from the local community what was happening and if they had seen anything unusual. We were favoured by some communities, who would sometimes help and inform us about where weapon stashes were. 'Have a look in such and such a place,' they'd say.

Most of the time they wouldn't help. Certain communities were very scared and didn't want to talk. We'd tell them that we were there to help. They probably saw us as a threat, maybe from the whole Defence Force situation in the eighties. We asked if they'd seen anything suspicious, knew who the bad ones were or what they looked like. We even had mugshots given to us by the local police. There was still a fear in the people that the army was around. We still had that kind of authority, in a way. They were scared of us, but it wasn't like the eighties when the blacks saw the army as their enemy. This was later on, in the nineties – black against black – so we weren't really seen as the enemy. We were trying to maintain the peace. But the terrorists, when they saw us, usually ran. They never fought back. You still shat off, though.

There was an incident where we found a teacher who was ambushed on his way home. They riveted him and his bakkie with AK rounds. He went through a barrage of bullets before being torched, along with the car. We found the burnt body the next day and left when the police arrived.

We went into the townships as a whole battalion. Alpha, Bravo and Charlie Company. Each had a different section to patrol, and was about thirty to thirty-five strong. The highest rank on patrol was usually a lance corporal or corporal. We had a full lieutenant and captain, but they remained at base. The captain was the commander. He had his 2IC, the lieutenant. Some of the patrols that went out did have a lieuty with them, but usually the highest rank was only a corporal. Patrols were either on foot or in a Buffel, with about six to ten guys. We rotated twice a day. On patrol from midnight to 6 a.m., then back to base to rest from 6 a.m. to 12 p.m., back out from 12 p.m. to 6 p.m. and then back to base and rest from 6 p.m. to midnight. Then back out again. Six days a week for six months. Day and night. Every seventh day was a turnabout, when we returned to home base in Durban for a day and a half. We usually started getting ready after a patrol on a Friday. Slept that night at the TB, then moved out early Saturday morning in the Buffels to Durbs. There we could clean up and have a decent night's sleep. You'd wash yourself, wash your clothes and get a hot meal. You lived off rat packs for six days, so coming back to main base was great.

In those six days you didn't shower. You lived in the same clothes. Just took a pair of clean socks along. Didn't even wear jocks. Each morning it was a face-wash and shave with cold water from the donkey trailer. That was the worst – not bathing for a week. When returning to main base, the guys that were clean would back away, 'Jeez! You guys stink.' But when you were clean and the following lot came in, you couldn't believe you'd smelled like them. Getting to the showers you took off your boots and stood under the shower in your uniform, with a scrubbing brush and a block of Sunlight soap, and scrubbed your clothes. It was the only way to get off that black grime. Then you took off everything to wash, later, after a good shower. Nothing like a good, hot shower. It took a while to wash the clothes by hand. Next morning, usually on a Sunday and after breakfast, you were on your way out again.

One of our temporary bases in this township was an old soccer field. Some of our guys got hepatitis and were all hospitalised. It's spread through urine. They were staying on a certain side of the field and probably got it from there. The locals must have been using it as a piss pot. It was only the guys sleeping in that specific area who got it. Every one. I never got it, but got glandular fever instead, which is almost as bad. My glands swelled up. I was in hospital for three weeks.

We had a problem in the townships because our berets were green and our infantry balkie was green, yellow and black, so some of them actually saw us as ANC supporters. So the balkies had to be removed, with only the bokkop remaining. I think that's why today's infantry colours are still only green and black.

Patrols were mainly on foot and hardly ever in Buffels. We walked many kilometres during a routine patrol, as far as we could within a given radius. Within the first couple of weeks we worked out how large an area we could cover. Every day we'd walk a different area, and knew that in two hours we could walk from base up to a certain point and take three hours, at a slower pace, to get back. Uphills and downhills were also taken into consideration. You used the roads that you knew. We'd occasionally change the route, however, for safety reasons. So we'd walk to a point, walk back and still be on time to take a break. When we returned, the next lot went out, sometimes passing each other, and we reported back in – all accounted for. That's how it was. It was like that the whole time. In, out, in, out. Six hours on, six hours off, twenty-four hours a day. Day patrols. Night patrols. The worst beat was always from midnight to six. It was cold – generally just a crappy time – and you wanted to sleep.

Some guys carried tear gas and some the smoke grenades. I had tear gas and four magazines. One mag would be in the R4 at all times, with a round in the chamber on 'safe' if we went into an area where we knew real crap was happening and we could come up against fire. The order given was 'stand-twee'. In quieter areas it was 'stand-drie', with no round in the chamber.

I must admit, some of the guys became shit-scared the moment the patrols started, especially when we went between the shacks. Then it was automatically 'stand-twee', just to have the edge if you needed it. You didn't even wait for the command. I wouldn't say it was a frightening experience, because you immediately reacted to your drills. We were drilled for three months during second phase not to fire unless fired upon: 'You don't fire your weapon except when commanded to do so!'

I was the section's sharpshooter. You'd have one in every group. It was usually the guys with skietbalkies, who'd scored 80 or 90 per cent. If there was a situation where you were being fired upon or somebody had to be taken out, you were usually the one who got the command. Not everybody opened up in a wild fire fight. If you got ordered, 'Take him out!', you hoped you had your 'mach-one eyeball' correct, like a pilot's. Precision.

We did observation as well, and watched certain areas – mainly the rivers – with night-vision goggles. There was an area where guys were smuggling weapons over in the evenings. About four of us made a small outpost. One guy was on duty while the other three rested or slept. Four hours' rotation each. All you did was watch through the goggles. If you saw any movement, or anything that looked suspicious, you'd alert the others and radio in.

Our section took out four AKs in the time that we were there. For every one taken out of circulation, the section got a day's pass in Durban. You'd dress up in your cravat and puttees and enjoy yourself. The navy guys had a ferry that they used to cross the harbour to Durbs. We'd take it in the morning and get picked up later in the evening.

Apart from the factions there were also terrorist-type activities. Small guerrilla groups moved in, causing chaos in the little villages and killing people. That was simply what they were doing. If you were in the wrong party and in the wrong place, then, 'Sorry, you don't deserve to live.' We had to put bodies in body bags. We often came across them after faction fights and had to clean up. It didn't happen a lot, but you put the bodies in and took them away. We always had body bags with us.

Even Bats did township patrols. We went into a location just outside of Bloemfontein. Did the usual – drove around in Buffels with a policeman; did the foot patrols. Township patrols were interesting, but being there put the fear of God into me. I just know when I was there I kakked off. I remember coming out of the army and being petrified of crowds. Still can't stand big crowds. We'd be surrounded by people, all the time, and stuck in the middle of bloody riots.

We shot tear gas into these crowds. The kids were so quick. The little bastards would pick up the canisters and throw them straight back into the Buffels. One time a kid picked up a canister, which was glowing with heat, and threw it in from about twenty metres away! We couldn't believe it. Another time the corporal, who was a real wanker, just jumped out of the Buffel. He was the first one out. He saw a canister coming and could've deflected it, but didn't warn us or say anything. He just bailed. We all wondered why he was jumping until we also saw it, but it was too late. Okay, it's not lethal, but it burnt and stung. We didn't have our gas masks on.

So we were in a Buffel. So what? And we only had one magazine each. I don't think they were even full – perhaps ten rounds – and each had a safety pin with a piece of wire and a little red ball on it. If you broke that seal you had a lot of explaining to do.

One thing that sticks in my mind was seeing a black oke with a panga wound to his head. Our medic jumped out to help. Then the cops came and just chucked this guy in the back of their wagon.

At Grahamstown we drilled before the time, before we went into the townships, and did all the training for riots. House entry, room entry, how to arrest somebody – but it was pointless. Although we knew how to arrest, we didn't have arresting power. We usually had an SAP guy with us on the Buffel or on foot patrol. Although he may not have been the highest rank in our patrol, he had the highest authority over us. It was he who had the arresting power. We would hold somebody for a short while but couldn't arrest him.

You'd see interesting things. I'll never forget this. It was somewhere in the Umlazi region. There was this shack, with probably about three rooms inside, and next to it was a little afdakkie. Under this was a green Jaguar. Spit-and-polished! Here was this well-looked-after, beautiful, immaculate Jag next to a dilapidated shack. What a total opposite. I'll never forget it – it sticks in my mind. I doubt whether it was stolen. Sometimes, while on patrol, residents, dressed up all nicely, would slowly drive past in lovely, expensive cars and wave to us.

There were times when we'd have walked for hours, with nothing really going on, so we'd go into the local community halls. The locals loved ballroom dancing. We'd watch the youngsters and elder folk dancing. We'd just sit there, on the side of the hall, watching. Sometimes they looked at us with big, white eyes, but we said we weren't there to disturb them so, please, could they go on. It was nice to pass the time like that.

In the townships there was plenty of ganja. It grew *everywhere* and was freely available. Most of the locals had a little vegetable patch, behind their shacks, growing along with their dope. These bloody things grew about three metres high! We went on a run where we pulled out a whole plantation and later destroyed it. We had a couple of Rasta Reggae guys – our radio operators – who were into the whole thing. In the ops room you occasionally got this nice, funny-smelling whiff, especially when the OC was out of the unit and most of us were on patrol. These guys were making themselves some serious zols. We could see them puffing it up every now and again when they were off duty. They were well connected and had a little TV room back in base. Somehow they organised M-Net. You had to pay these ous if you wanted to watch.

I joined the police force instead of doing National Service. I first did riots in Nelspruit and Soweto in 1986. I was still a constable then. We were in a section of seven constables and one sergeant as a single unit on patrol. Now and again we'd meet up with the army guys. Mixing with them was fine – we were all there for a common cause. I never used to work alongside them, though. We'd do our stuff and they'd be doing whatever it was that they had to do.

Although I personally didn't work with troepies in the townships in 1990, which was Nyanga in Cape Town, the times I did deal with the army guys were good. No animosity of any sort – the guys got along well. By that time I was a sergeant. Every night shift I'd drop constables off and hand them over to the Buffel patrols. They were senior to the troops and had the arresting power. The army guys weren't allowed to patrol by themselves; they had to have a police officer present.

Just before the 1992 Referendum after Mandela's release, we went from Bloem to Natal in luxury-liner buses and arrived near Mpumalanga township, just outside Pietermaritzburg. It hoarded drugs and AKs.

Our duty was to stop the ANC and Inkatha from killing each other. That's what they did. They killed each other. And they raped. And they destroyed. And they pillaged. Our job was like the police's. We were a police force. We said to them, 'You! Don't kill him, don't kill him and don't kill each other.' Police work. Sheriff on the job. Generally it was a waste of time cruising the streets. There we were with our R4s. Their reaction was, 'Okay, you're soldiers, you've got a gun. Don't worry, we're cool.' And they *were* cool – they had to be – because if they weren't we'd bloody well shoot them, if it got to that.

Every incident needing a testimony in court by the troepie involved in the arrest resulted in him being granted a two-day pass. He'd go to Pietermaritzburg. He'd be put in a nice hotel, have a cold beer and a nice hot meal. Sleep, shower, change, look respectable. It's not like we were doing fire and movement. We were maintaining the peace. Policemen. Every time trouble happened and a troepie was involved, he had to give a legitimate account of the occurrence in front of a judge and jury. Everything by the book – civilian law. You wanted these passes, so you were paraat. To help in an arrest if it meant a two-day army-paid luxury pass? Of course, yes!

When I arrived in Natal for ops duties I was six weeks late. I'd been trying to get my jump wings. It took me three PT courses to qualify. The others had already done six weeks in the townships, so I arrived at a time when all the others may have been issued specific orders not to shoot unless fired upon, but I didn't get them. It didn't matter. I was a driver. I wasn't in on the scene and, as a driver, all I had to do was drive. So I drove. That's what I did. I drove. And it just so happened that the night they decided to put me in on the scene, with a rifle, I got separated from the rest of the troop. Obviously … I'm a driver. 'We're gonna do the men's work,' they said, which, as it happened, turned out to be *my* work.

We went out on foot patrol. It was dark, and very hard to see, but in the distance I faintly made out my buddy in front of me, an Afrikaans oke. He always helped me make my bed in the mornings for inspection. Anyway, we were assigned to this small area. I saw him standing there. I also saw this black oke pointing a .22 rifle at him! The oke couldn't see me. He didn't even know I was there, in the darkness. I didn't quite know what I was looking at. The problem was, I couldn't tell whether he was the enemy or the police, because he was wearing an SAP jacket.

I was, however, sure about three things. One, he was levelling a rifle at my friend. Two, he had a police jacket on. Three, I was going to kill him. I just felt he was not part of the system, at all. Most soldiers would say it's not after point three you take the shot, it's after point one, but we were in a difficult situation – it wasn't a battle – so I really had to determine my enemy. It happened that, between two and three, he lowered his rifle. He was lucky. I was pretty good about it because, between two and three, I would've killed him before he killed my friend. I could've killed him. I would've. I came very close.

He then hid the rifle under some canvas and moved off. I went around the corner and ordered him, 'Stand right where you are!' The guy skrikked.

'Waar is jy?' my friend called.

'Hierso! There's a rifle underneath the canvas!'

He comes running up, finds it and runs off to notify the lieutenant. I'm still holding the guy in my sights. The others arrive. The lieuty eventually calms me down. 'Lower your weapon. It's under control.' I stood down. The police were notified and arrived. The oke was arrested. They tried to drill as much information out of him as they could. They beat him up quite seriously before throwing him in the back of the Casspir.

Some time after this, Sergeant Napoleon, the cammo-clad Zulu policeman who was usually with us, got so blind drunk late one night that he was beyond motherless. He had drunk himself stupid. I was woken up and told that Napoleon wanted to talk to me. I got out of bed, went to his room and knocked on the door. 'You're such a runt,' he said. 'Such a shithead. Full of shit. But you're my buddy. And you just bagged a murderer. You caught a murderer, you little idiot. The ballistic report's come back. That rifle's killed people.'

It had an American-made Weber sniper's sight. Good quality telescopic rifle, a .22 with Weber sights. You could shoot a mozzie from here to Timbuktu. It was given a ballistics test and proven to have been used in several murders. Remember the two-day-pass thing? Well, the case was so legitimate I didn't have to go to court, which disappointed me. The oke probably tried to justify himself by saying he was fighting a war.

It wasn't set in stone, your training. There were hundreds and hundreds of different situations. They said you couldn't shoot unless fired upon, but, if it came to it, kill. It's either your buddy who's going down or it's this other 'person'. It's life or death, in a split second. There was no hard and fast rule. Sure, don't shoot a policeman is one rule. But *is* he a policeman?

So, now, tell me where the rules of engagement are – tell me. It's circumstance. He's wearing a police jacket. Do I know what he's going to do? Do I kill him? Those are not my orders! They taught me 'enemy'. Do you think I'm going to follow protocol? With protocol my friend could've been dead. Yet even if someone waved a gun at us, we were taught not to shoot. Life, though – instinct, self-preservation – taught me to shoot. I wasn't trained like the police were to negotiate such scenarios. This was police work. We weren't bloody well trained as policemen; we were trained as soldiers! The idea *is* to shoot! If I had shot the oke I would've had a perfectly legitimate case. He had a rifle levelled at my friend. In court the judge would've slammed down the gavel and said, 'It's all right. Kill the bastard!'

No one can be my judge.

I became the company barber. The sa'majoor found out that I could cut hair so, before I knew it, he went to buy shears. Every couple of weeks I had to cut the entire company's hair, from captain to troepie. They would keep on coming until my arm became numb. I wasn't allowed to cut a number one. It was only short sides and a trim on top. One day I got fed up because of not bathing or shampooing. I liked being clean, even to just wash my face and hands, and I always had a bar of soap in my battle jacket. If I got to where there was flowing water, or a tap, I used to wash. It was the first thing I did. When your hands and face are clean, you feel a little cleaner. Being fed up, I took the shears and cut myself a number one.

I was involved in only two serious faction fights where Inkatha and the ANC would climb into each other, panga each other and throw bricks at one another. Serious stuff. It was an eye opener to see how little life meant. No matter if you were a teacher or a pastor or a kid on the street, if you were in the wrong party and you were in the wrong place, you just got taken out. That's literally how it was.

The one fight was when we were walking patrol in Umlazi. It was a war-party march. These guys were in their respective ANC and Inkatha groups and shouting their jeers very loudly at each other. They were on their way to a stadium and, often, what they did, just to intimidate each other, was head straight for each other. If one group had to move through another area to get to the stadium, they wouldn't take the road around, but they'd go through the opposing group and, automatically, a faction fight would take place. This is what happened during our patrol. Literally within seconds they were at each other: they met in the middle and wound in quickly. The groups didn't walk into each other but ran through each other, like you see in *Braveheart* battle scenes.

We called in extra guys, but the corporal went totally berserk and screamed that the factions were climbing into each other. He yelled, 'Fok! Hier's 'n groot fokop! Hier's groot kak hierso! Stuur versterkings in!' He didn't know where we were. He was crapping. The captain tried to calm him down on the other side: 'Just explain to us where you are.'

We could do nothing as a group of ten. Each faction had about fifty men. We were totally outnumbered. They ignored us. There was nothing we could do, even though we were armed. A lot of them would've gone down. We just stood and watched total chaos break out. Total chaos. They were throwing stones. I pointed my rifle at one or two who were busy picking up bottles and stones, just to indicate to them to drop what they had. They glared at me with these cold war-eyes, as if to say, 'You know, if I had a weapon now, you'd come off second best.' That was the look on their faces.

One guy was slashed with a panga. He came right up to us and screamed, 'You are here to protect me! Look at me!' He had wounds in his front and back. His T-shirt was ripped because it had some ANC member's face on it, so they targeted him. They really climbed into this guy. It was a white shirt, but there wasn't much white left. I don't know where they got their weapons from. If they didn't brick or stone each other, they climbed into each other with sharpened objects. It was brutal fighting – literally stabbing, throwing and clubbing.

These fights usually ended when everybody ran in different directions. When the police or Buffels came they'd split up. Whatever was left would be a total mayhem of wounded people. It would be like a picture from a newspaper: there'd be a spear lying here, a knobkerrie there, a knife over there and lots of sticks and stones and broken bricks everywhere. In that particular incident nobody was killed. There were a few very badly slashed who bled all over the place. I didn't use the tear gas. I sometimes think, though, that if I had used it things would've turned out a little bit different, you know?

Another section was in a stadium where an ANC speaker was talking. Inkatha stormed in and a big fight erupted. My friend said that the most amazing thing he saw that day was how far a little kid could throw half a brick across a soccer field. It hit somebody on the other side. He saw it happen. He couldn't believe how far the kid threw it. Things were hurtling over the patrol from all around. They were caught in the middle, trying to prevent it with tear gas. It all happened so quickly. Very, very quickly.

It was odd to see only women and little kiddies. In some areas, more on the Zululand side, some villages only had them. All the men had left. None remained, whatsoever. Deserted. They had moved out because, if the factions came in, they killed all the men, including boys from about the age of twelve, who could be a threat later on. They just took them out, no matter if they pleaded or begged for their lives. We came up against these guys. They were definitely not local because their skin colour was a different black. Coal black.

Some large areas became completely deserted – empty, not a soul – almost overnight. Just empty shacks. Looked like a ghost town. You saw some of the old folk, here and there, or a little fire, but it was mainly empty shacks. Hundreds of them. It was amazing.

We were on our way back home for showers and a hot meal. We passed a little village, a small community, which had just been attacked. The women, children and small kids were running down the road. The attackers were still in the area. We caught one. He had an AK and a massive ghetto blaster that he'd stolen from one of the houses. He was a short little guy dressed in full army browns about four sizes too big for him. Shorty, in oversized browns, with joller box and AK!

The police arrived. There was some form of interrogation, which we didn't see, but a few klaps were dealt out before they arrived. We then did a house entry after a closer inspection. You could see the house had just been hit. There were bullet holes everywhere. The windows were broken. The door was kicked in. There was no stopping these guys. They would just force their way in, no matter what. Some were beautiful farmhouses, built from clay bricks and made by the locals themselves, situated on the fringes of these massive sugarcane fields.

This car pulled up. A man got out and said his two brothers were inside. I went into the house first. My Number Two went in behind me. We checked all the rooms. The back room was barricaded slightly. We pushed our way inside. Both of his brothers were lying there, dead. 'These are my brothers,' he said. You could see, not just the fear, but the sorrow in his eyes and the heartache on his face. His one brother was twenty-one. The other was just a young teenager. They were laid out on the bed. You could see that they had at first been sleeping, before being totally surprised, and then it was too late. The rounds ran from the floor, over the bed and into the ceiling. The killer had kicked the door in and fired on automatic. He'd killed both of them, just like that.

The thing that got to me the most was, because the bodies had been there for about twenty minutes, there was this sickly sweet smell inside the room. Maybe they gave off a gas or something.

'My brothers. I saw them this morning. Now they're dead. They were killed because they were here, not for any other reason.' I put my hand around his shoulder and said to him that I was very sorry. We went outside until the police came. Opposite the road, the village was burning.

Then, in the distance, we saw the guys running towards the sugarcane field. There were six of them, including a teenaged kid of about sixteen. One was carrying an R1. I could clearly see the silhouette. He was holding it by the carrying handle, which the FN has. He wore a blue overall. The guy in front of him had a .303, and the other a shotgun. I couldn't see what the others had.

I'll never forget this. I stood next to a banana tree and lifted my R4. I was now in the situation where I had my sights on somebody, the one with the FN. There was a fury in me after I walked into that house and saw those dead youngsters. I followed him in my sights. He was about 400 metres away. My finger was on the trigger – I was so close – but the drill came back to me that I wasn't allowed to fire. 'Shit! If you shoot him, what's going to happen? They'll probably be pleased, or instead they might ask, "Nee! Why did you do it?"' The second thing that went through my mind was that, if I did shoot him, I'd be doing society a favour, because it was probably he who'd killed those two brothers, judging by the weapon he had. But the biggest problem I had were his buddies, who would probably come back and retrieve the rifle when he went down – so I would've just killed someone for nothing. That thought, luckily, went through me.

So we went after them, instead, and took them on by foot. My Number Two was the LMG gunner. He and I were the fittest in the unit and the others couldn't keep up with us. We still had full kit on: helmet, battle jacket, water bottles, rat packs, backpack and full magazines. I was the fittest I've ever been, even though I'd picked up a lot of weight from the rat packs. I was fit – super, super fit. I'll never be so fit again.

I was about ten metres away from the youngest of the group. He was shouting. He was screaming. Yelling in fear. It's not surprising. At his age I also wouldn't want an armed troepie chasing me. He knew we were onto him and if we caught him he would be interrogated. The kid was unfit and couldn't manage the pace. The older guys used the bush to their advantage, but he was out in the open. We got very close, but they knew the area so well. The moment they hit the sugarcane plantations, they just disappeared – *fwoosh* – like rats in a field, and split up. My Number Two was giving me cover, if needed. We didn't know where the group was as we approached the edge of the field, and we were unsure if they'd turned around and were ready to ambush.

Unfortunately my corporal shouted a command for me to stop. I stopped only when the second or third command came. I was just so focused on catching this kid. He shouted, using a lot of F-words, 'You WILL stop NOW!' I then complied. Bear the consequences, I thought.

I said to him, 'You're the one who's going to explain to the captain what happened. We just saw a village being taken out. There have probably been more people killed than just the two we found. *You've* got to explain why I was ten metres away from this guy and you ordered me to stop! I could've caught him and we could've had some form of intelligence coming in. *You* can explain why the situation is like it is!'

We picked up a small pistol that one of them had tossed away. About half an hour later we were on the one side of the valley and they were on the other, waving at us, taunting. We couldn't believe the ground they'd covered. They chose all the shortcuts and made a huge distance between us. Then the captain came along and the first thing he screamed at me was, 'Why didn't you catch him? You were right there!'

'Speak to Mr Corporal, Captain. Yes, I was right by him, but the rest couldn't keep up because they're all so unfit!' and off I walked. The corporal got crapped on from a dizzy height. He wanted me to stop because I was getting way too far ahead of the group. He didn't want me ambushed or isolated from the rest, which is correct, but I wasn't alone. I had the LMG gunner with me. As the LMG gunner, he was also fit. Short, stocky little guy.

Unfortunately, communications were a nightmare. What they should've done was bring in an Alou or a police chopper. We could've nailed them. The next day patrols were sent into the valley, but obviously nothing came of it.

A mother came over to our Casspir. She told Sergeant Napoleon that her daughter had been taken by her husband's brother. She was worried because she was unsure what his intentions were. Now, saying something like that meant she got pulled aboard that Casspir, very quickly, in order to protect her. The fewer eyes and ears the better.

She gives us the address. Now we go to Uncle's house. We rock up, and Sergeant Napoleon walks up to the front door and doesn't bother to knock. He walks straight in. We follow. There's zol all over the table, loads of alcohol and a couple of dazed guys in the room. 'Where's the girl?' he demands, but they're speechless – daggadronk en gesuip – so he walks off to the bedroom and, there, on the bed, is this little girl who's naked with Uncle and his girlfriend, so now we know it's down. It's all going straight down.

The little girl is wrapped in a blanket and handed to her mother. They go back to the Casspir. Then we, who're not too sure what the blazes is really going on, are asked to go back to the Casspir too. Napoleon was going to take the law into his own hands – literally.

At the time, things were very difficult. All arresting authority was back-of-hand. The culprits could go to court and stand trial, but that was a long, languid waste of time. So now the law must be dealt out. It meant that Uncle and all his buddies were beaten up. Napoleon kicked Uncle's head in, that night. We just sat in the Casspir while the sergeant moered him. Not just moered him – like hospitalised-him moered. Didn't-give-a-shit-if-he-dies moered. Beaten-to-a-pulp-and-still-thrown-into-jail moered. I wasn't proud about it then, and didn't like what I saw, but he had to be taught a lesson.

The big highlight of townships was Operation Golden Eagle. It was a big show of force. We went in the early morning with Pumas and Alouettes. The Parabats were also involved. They jumped in a different area. We went to a soccer field in the township. Then the armour came in with the Noddy Cars in one long convoy.

We had an area to sweep. It was a big area and a big operation. We covered ground like you can't believe. It was on foot, for most of the day, through rain and mud. The choppers were supposed to pick us up at 4 p.m. at a rendezvous point, but a real Natal thunderstorm came in, so they couldn't. It was really howling. We stood there on the side of the road, completely drenched, like we'd taken ourselves and our kit and jumped into a pool. Totally soaked.

We waited like that for two hours. Eventually a couple of Samils pulled up. We went to a police station to dry up for the evening. Next to it was an old Victorian-style house, which became our headquarters. In the lounge we threw newspaper on the old wooden floor and made a fire in the fireplace using our rat-pack boxes, in order to stay warm. It was cold in the evenings, especially with that storm. You can imagine twenty troepies, in their jocks, all huddled together to stay warm. Our clothes were stacked in a half-circle round this fireplace, so you could at least get your boots and socks dry for the next day. Early morning and we're up again. Out to do another patrol for the entire day.

There were moments that were lousy, but we still had fun. When moving into a new location, the first thing we did was find out where the shebeens and tuck shops were, because you lived off rat packs for weeks. Fresh bread was delivered to the townships every day, so we could get fresh bread – if you were there early enough in the morning, depending on whether you had the early-morning klick from midnight to 6 a.m. You could then chow lekker, fresh bread before going back. Could also buy the two-litre Cokes, finish them and get a refund. We only really stopped at shebeens to get Cokes.

There was a big reservoir in the one area. Often, when on patrol, we'd stop off for a dip. One guy stayed at the Buffel, looking after the weapons, while we all went swimming in our undies to cool off, because it was hellishly hot in the middle of summer. One group had a midnight shift and went down to Balito Bay in the Buffel, parked it on the beach and took turns skinny-dipping, not only for the change, but to get the muck off.

Being in the Buffels was the biggest fear for me, but we were never ambushed, as such. The dirt roads would often have a higher and a lower level parallel to each other. The fear was thinking that somebody would pop in an HE or petrol bomb from up top. Some of the units were hit by shit bombs. That's literally what it was – a shit bomb. They crapped in a bag and threw it. Even though we weren't the enemy, it still occurred.

There was an accident one night. A Buffel overturned, caused by a local who skipped a stop street in his tractor. He hit the Buffel side-on. It rolled down a steep slope, but luckily most guys were tied down with their seat belts. Others managed to jump out. Nothing more serious than cuts and bruises. They'd been getting ready for a foot patrol, which is why not everybody was strapped in. The driver was stuck inside, upside down, still strapped in his seat. It took a while to get him out. They had to turn the Buffel first. The tractor driver was drunk, or stoned, or both. The police arrested him.

We had a temporary base at a local police station and we stayed in tents. An order was given to pack up and move out. Literally a day after leaving, the station was hit in an RPG attack. One of the police vans was taken out. These okes didn't attack while we were there. They knew they'd come off second best if they did. It wasn't two days after that, and we were all back and had to reassemble everything.

When we came back, I saw the bodies in the police 'morgue'. They were still in the garage. Again, to me, they didn't seem local. Their skin was so dark. Looked more like Ovambo types. The Zulu cops had retaliated and taken out the five who'd attacked them. They were shot in the skirmish right outside the police station. The van that got taken out by the RPG, which, incidentally, didn't explode, had one of their own guys in the back. It went right through him and left quite a mess. I just saw the muck and blood that remained. His pieces were all over the bakkie. The grenade entered the one side through the mesh, went through him and out the other side. They just took out one of their own as the van drove by. Luckily we didn't have to clean him up. The police did that.

I used to help them clean their rifles in the evenings. They had R1s, mainly, and big Beretta shotguns. These things were really a mess. We used our cleaning kits and did the cleaning for them. We couldn't believe they actually still fired.

There were some corrupt police. I knew it for a fact – you could spy out things. There was definitely a bad group of them. Not a lot, but there were. You'd see a pair of them walk out into the bush, with an R1 and a shotgun, and ask yourself, 'Where are they off to?' Late in the evening they'd come back, and you wondered what went on. Strange things like that. Things that were observed, Intelligence checked out occasionally. Everything was reported to them. There was a bad contingency in Natal, almost like an involved third party. You could very easily see it. I don't know if it was a covert military wing of some kind, but these guys were causing major crap. Whether it was our own government's operations or not, I can't really say.

One thing I *can* say is that Military Intelligence was a total balls-up. For instance, we were told that we had to hit a certain house. We'd get there early in the morning and cordon off the area only to find that the bust had already happened, and days ago. Military Intelligence was never intelligent enough.

We had another TB, in an open field, with sandbags in the middle and bivouacs around them. The captain and lieutenant slept in the sandbag bunker because, the evening after we arrived, somebody opened fire from far away with an AK, but rounds still hit the field.

'Shit! You guys are building me a bunker,' the captain ordered. He slept safely in the sandbag bunker while we slept in little two-man bivouacs. The captain was a short-term service volunteer and had been in a few years already. He used to ride around looking for us because he knew the guys were gyppoing, or weren't where they should be. It was easy to radio in and say, 'We're fine. Everything's okay.' Some areas were more built up than others and had shopping centres. The one had a fried chicken franchise. We'd pull in, with the Buffel, behind it. Someone would jump off and buy chicken burgers for everybody, or for those who had money, at least. Chow quickly and off we'd go.

It was pathetic, really. Some of the company commanders were in competition with each other. Our lovely captain decided that he liked the Buffels polished. So we washed those Buffels. The army had big cans of liquid floor polish. We polished our Buffels with it, and did those Buffels shine! It was all about the image. Then you went back into the township inside gleaming, shining Buffels.

Our captain and major made big bucks when they started a tuck shop. Of course, when you got back to base, after a patrol, it's a six-pack of Cokes and about twenty chocolate bars. You'd go off and eat yourself silly. I picked up a lot of weight then, as well as from the rat packs. They had a lot of protein, with cheese, chocolate, powdered milkshakes and ProNutro. Just added water. The fish curry was the worst. We always chucked that away. Later on we became very creative – a single dixie with stews of mush and dog biscuits. All kinds of stuff. We came up with some amazing recipes to make that rat pack just a little more interesting. We kept all our Super Cs and gave them to the little kids, who were everywhere – always at least twenty. I kept my sugar sachets for them. You threw them over the Buffel and watched the kids climb into each other for a packet of sugar. The little guy always ended up getting it and sprinted off with a crowd behind him. He'd eat as much as he could before the others caught up. We saw that *many* times. Some guy thought it was funny when he threw a whole lot of condoms over.

At the end of my service there was a heap of confiscated home-made weapons – probably about three metres high – kept in the storeroom. Anything from pangas to spears to pipe guns with shotgun rounds in them. It was a massive heap of scrap metal. The factories that we hit sometimes had loads of the stuff, which went straight into the room. It was picked up later and the stuff got destroyed.

We found a revolver on one guy. It wasn't a proper weapon – it was turned on a lathe. He'd actually made it. It could take six 9-mill rounds. This was one of the many fancy weapons that were made out of scrap metal. It would probably have exploded at some point.

We found really old, crappy shotgun-type weapons and typical nail guns, known as kwashes, which were hand-held steel pipes with nails and thick rubber bands at the back. The nail hit the shotgun round and sent out the shot. They got creative and made nice wooden butts, which you could place into your shoulder. Sometimes there'd be a lever on the end that would be cocked back and let go – almost like a catty. It would hit the round and out came the bang in the front. If it didn't explode in the shooter's face, then it would do the intended damage. That's all they wanted – the damage done.

By the time I left, things were worse. The locals were armed more. Not with pipe guns but with AK-47s and such. When we were finishing our deployment, some campers took over. We had to show them the ropes.

Another section took them out on patrol, and their Buffel was fired at. The driver came back. 'Shit. We were just fired upon! We were driving along and it went *tack-tack-tack* on the side of the Buffel.' We saw the hit marks – somebody had shot from a distance. The townships were on hills, so the roads were sloped. The gunman had an easy view.

Another section heard the firing and ran to where it had come from. One of the guys almost floored the gunman as he ran round the corner. This guy was crouching, putting a mag into his AK and looking where to fire next. When my buddy, who was with a black policeman, brought up his R4 to arrest him, the round in the chamber jammed when he cocked to get it ready. He had a *storing*. The guy heard him pulling the lever to recock and disappeared in a flash among the shacks. Off he went. My buddy said that when the guy saw him, the policeman had actually hidden behind him and hadn't wanted to do anything. Obviously – the guy was armed with an AK. Maybe the cop hid out of fear, from previous experience.

We stayed at Durban main base for two more weeks before klaaring out. It was December, just before Christmas. In six months I had leave twice, for a weekend each time. Flew from Durbs to Cape Town on the Friday. The Monday I was back in Durbs. Luckily my father worked for the transport services and got concession flights. I made use of one of them. The guys that lived furthest away had it the worst. Some of us just stayed in base. It wasn't worth the hassle for a few hours at home. Guys that lived in or around Durban took along some friends, though.

UITKLAAR

When I talked to my mom and dad about these things, after klaaring out, it didn't seem to sink in. They never asked me what happened.

I remember it was six months before klaaring out when, on 5 January 1976, South Africa first got TV. They'd been flighting and testing for a while, and all the larneys had sat with their sets on watching the test pattern!

Then 16 June happened, and the army wanted us to carry on boxing for them; wanted us to sort out the uprising. We said, 'Voertsek! We're outta here! We're going home. Send in the *roofs*.'

Klaared out at the end of June, 1976.

I cleared out in Windhoek just before Christmas, on 23 December 1977. Got put on a plane, arrived at DF Malan Airport, got home, met the folks and that was it – the end of me and the army. As an extra-twelve-month volunteer I didn't have to do camps. I spent three months at home, after the Border, on my bed. Most of the guys came out all right. You just needed time out to relax. Then my folks said to me, 'Uh-uh. Go and find yourself a job.'

I received the Pro Patria when we came back from the Border. We had a medal parade at our main base. At the *uittreeparade* we were all given our ProNutro. I qualified for my cross-border medal – the Southern Africa Medal, the one with the little leopard on. But nobody was 'officially' awarded that for a while. Especially now. Un-PC, you see. I struggled even to get my General Service Medal, but it eventually arrived in the post a good seven years or so after I'd finished my service.

Just weeks before klaaring out they finally realised that I had kidney stones. The day after arriving in hospital they got them out. I stayed for a further six weeks – they wouldn't release me until I was completely fit. It was the best treatment imaginable. We used to smoke in the ward, and everybody would share or donate cigarettes and sweets.

Ag, man, you won't believe the stories. We were on the ground floor. As you came into the ward, the first bed on the left was an oke from the Cape who had his leg in traction. A landmine explosion had picked him up. He said that his one eye was left hanging on his cheek. He didn't lose it, though – they put it back in. He'd been there for months already, and was the nurses' favourite. He complained all the time. He sprayed aerosol around his bed at night – his leg didn't smell lekker.

Next to him was a guy who'd been admitted late one night. He'd tried to open a can of bully beef with his bayonet. It had slipped and pegged into his groin.

Then there was a guy next to him who'd been in the squadron that I'd trained in Basics. He'd gone over to some admin job in the Infantry. Some of them had stolen a grenade from a dump. There was this thing you did where you'd hang hand-grenade pins from your boshoed. The stupid numb-skulls unscrewed the base plug and pulled out the fuse, which is really delicate. It could go off just from the heat of your hand if you didn't handle it properly. They threw it in a box of other primers and it exploded. He had burns all over him. Served him right, the stupid idiot.

Next to him was a Parabat who had arrived a month before me. He was a very quiet guy who used to walk in the garden. We didn't speak to him much. He'd returned for another operation on his leg. He told me that they'd been in a contact and he'd been hit. They'd shot him with one of those Chinese-manufactured PPShs. It had a drum magazine. When fired it sounded like frozen peas being dropped into a pot. *Drrrr!* It had a high rate of fire. He first got hit through his hip; rounds went clean through his rifle. He crawled to a tree for cover but was hit again, this time through the legs. The radio had been shot up, so the guy manning it fiddled around. He took silver cigarette paper and did something that just managed to get their grid reference through to base. The Bat said he was losing consciousness as he heard the choppers coming – 'The sweetest sound ever.'

On the other side of him was a guy who'd been with me in Basics. Afterwards he went to Berede. His horse had stepped on a landmine near Eenhana. When I got to hospital he'd been there for a while already. One leg was amputated and the other needed thirteen skin grafts. That Christmas of '76 was the first time they'd let him out. He came back later for more skin grafts. The night he came back, just after we'd had dinner, he went funny. All of a sudden the nurses were there and hauled him out immediately. He died that night. Had a heart attack. There was talk of a malaria-induced heart attack. And after all that pain he went through. He was nineteen.

I can't remember the other two ous in the corner.

Then there was Staff Krokodil, as we called him. He had long hair. He was a camper, and had been bitten by a crocodile. It bit two holes in one leg, one hole in the other and a hole in his hand. They'd come back from a patrol on the Caprivi and had stopped at a spot on the river where they often swam. He felt something grab him, so put down his hand. He knew it was too big to be a barbel. The rest of the attack he couldn't recall. His mates shot the crocodile. They showed him photos later – he said it was massive.

He was a fun guy. He'd walk around the ward and make jokes. Whenever a new patient was brought in he'd sit in the office, in front of the ward, and wear the doctor's coat and stethoscope. He'd pretend to be the doctor, while the nurses played along. They'd dress the new guy in his bedclothes and stand next to Staff as he gave his diagnosis. 'Okay! Prepare him for heart surgery!' The new oke would skrik himself! We'd all be there, watching this and *lagging*.

Next to me was an ou from Nigel. He was a strange guy and full of tattoos. He had a plastic tube coming from his head, which was taped to the side, and all his hair was shaven off. He had another tube in his dick. The nurses would tickle it to see what would happen, sometimes when he was awake. They left him in bed naked because he used to crap in it. He was a bit nuts. One night my sister came to visit, and she asked me if he was blind. 'No. He's just not lekker upstairs. He fell off a Bedford onto his head.' He'd been badly concussed but was a little stupid, as well. He'd walk down the aisle stark naked, and we'd have to help him back to his bed. Whenever he asked for a cigarette, we'd tune, 'Nooit! The smoke's going to come out of the little pipe on your head.'

Then there was a guy who'd been shot through the stomach, from Brakpan. He looked like a walking skeleton and had bedsores. When they turned him over to rub cream on him he'd scream in pain. After his op he had to start eating, but it was very painful. He used to cry. The nurses would sit there for hours and plead with him to have another mouthful. He'd refuse and just wouldn't try; he was one of those ous. With a stomach wound, a person naturally loses weight from not eating and, of course, you have to start on solids again to get better. At night he'd ask us for a cigarette, but he wasn't allowed to smoke. We'd say no. He'd plead for one. 'Okay, but just please eat something tomorrow.' He'd agree and get a smoke. But then, the following day, he wouldn't try. This went on and on until one night he asked again. Somebody said, 'Ag, just piss off and die, man!'

The guy next to him had been shot in the stomach the month before this oke – the exact same thing. After I arrived he was there for another few days before he was discharged. They'd both been there for months.

I was really annoyed. It was now January and I should've already klaared out and been spending time with my girlfriend. I had some bucks, as the army had paid me out. I'd made plans, but they wouldn't let me go. I had a catheter. My pee was too orange and still had blood in it; I became depressed. Old Staff Krokodil asked me what was wrong, and I explained that the colour wasn't right. 'We'll fix it,' he said. He filled the bag with diluted Oros. They came round the next morning and took the bag away. They saw it was clear and finally released me. When they emptied it they must've thought my pee smelt really sweet!

After I was discharged I peed blood for quite a while before it went away. I returned to visit the guys. I smuggled booze in for them. They told me that the stomach-injury guy had died the day after I left. He'd just given up. The ou who'd injured his leg in the mine was asleep while I was visiting. His leg wasn't smelling any more – they'd cut it off. Gangrene. Sad case. He was about twenty years old. So, ultimately, when I klaared out it was a complete anti-climax.

I was supposed to be at Lion's Head Commando. After a couple of years they wrote to me and asked if I wanted to be honourably discharged. I said, 'Yes, thank you very much.' That was the last I heard of it. I think they had closed down the commandos.

I received my Pro Patria at a parade at Wingfield, but a couple of years *after* I had finished. I didn't have any browns at the time. I'd thrown them all away, which, of course, you weren't allowed to; you were supposed to keep them all. I had to borrow some.

We were the last guys to do a full two years, from January 1988 to December 1989. The July 1988 intake klaared out a few months later, just short of two years.

I should've studied first. Perhaps it would've been easier to get stuck into studies when my head was still fresh from school. But, the thing is, no one could've predicted that our service would be shortened. The two-year guys didn't realise it was all coming to an end, otherwise very few would've gone. They would've studied or tried to get an apprenticeship.

After three months of doing nothing in the Northern Transvaal, we came back to the base in Bloemfontein and were told that our National Service had been reduced to eighteen months. I remember the day. We were about to go in to lunch when they *tree'd* us *aan* and said that we were going home soon. We'd had no idea – we'd klaared in for the normal two years' service. We went crazy with happiness. Suddenly everything was better, the sun shone brighter and the grass was greener – but then their attitudes towards us changed. They called us 'aerobats', after Jane Fonda's 'aerobics', and made derogatory remarks. Bitched that we were not the same as them. They branded us as false Bats because we weren't going to do the full two years due to the war being finished in Angola, and so hadn't done the exact same training as them. Apparently our training was less tough, even though we kakked. I don't know how the PT course had changed. How would I know? We were just told by our seniors that we were all wusses. I didn't care. Ours was the same – I don't think it was any less tough.

Because I did my Basics at Technical Services Corps I wore the Tiffie badge, which was a brass lightning bolt behind a rearing silver horse, similar to the Ferrari logo. We wore black berets. Youngsfield was Ordnance Services Corps, which had a round badge with waved lines and an arrowhead above, and blue berets with red, white and blue balkies. Strangely enough, as I was a tiffie in Ordnance, I wore the blue beret with a Tiffie badge and an Ordnance balkie. Nobody bothered me about this or told me to change it for the nine months that I was there. Two days before I klaared out, a staff sergeant ordered me to take the Tiffie badge off and replace it with the Ordnance badge for the *uittreeparade*.

On klaaring-out day, Mevrou, the two civvies and I had a chicken skottelbraai in the media department's tiny coffee area. We weren't really allowed to sommer have a braai, which is why we had it indoors. Mevrou took charge, as usual, and did the cooking. Afterwards I said goodbye and was actually quite sad to see the last of them. We'd all got on well and had some good times.

At the *uittreeparade* there were three of us – out of about a hundred troops – who were told to sit out because they said our GSMs hadn't arrived. The medals would be sent in the post instead. In 1992 nobody qualified for the Pro Patria. The Border War was long since over and, apart from the townships, no other Operational Areas existed. We sat with the audience and watched the colonel pin the little medals onto the other guys all standing to attention. A GSM may not mean much for some, but it was important. It was awarded in recognition of service in the army, and it was intended to acknowledge service in the townships.

Afterwards we were marched, for the last time, to the gate. We fell out and threw our berets into the air and laughed and cheered. Some immediately *gooied* their newly acquired medals over the wall of the base, making out as though they were the manne – trying to show that they really didn't care about receiving them. I bet you they went hunting for that little medal later, though. I took down some addresses but never made contact in the future. Then I got into my car and drove away. That's how my National Service ended. And, needless to say, the medal never arrived.

Later that year I was notified in the post as to what Citizen Force Unit I belonged to. I didn't give it a second thought – being the end of 1993 I knew I'd never go. The letter was just the army doing the formalities. A few months later another letter arrived in its official tan envelope. It stated that a farewell dinner was planned for the disbanding of the unit, as they were stepping down, and that I was welcome to attend. I didn't go.

APPENDIX A TO
CHAPTER 5 OF SALO GS1/115

Telephone :
Queries   :

SOUTH AFRICAN DEFENCE FORCE
CLEARING OUT CERTIFICATE: NATIONAL SERVICEMEN: SA ARMY

NO: .... RANK: .... NAME: .... CORPS: ....
INTAKE: ...... DATE OF BIRTH: ....
UTILIZATION (MUSTERING): ....
CF/COMMANDO UNIT: ....

POSTAL CODE: ....   TELEPHONE: ....

It is hereby certified that the above-named member completed his
initial service satisfactorily in the SA Army over the period
mentioned below:
FROM (CALL UP DATE): .... TO (CLEARING OUT DATE): ....

Enquiries regarding the pay which the member received during the
above-mentioned period are to be directed to:
Chief of the SA Defence Force (CSF) — For attention Chief Paymaster
Private Bag X137
Pretoria
0001

RESTRICTED

[The unofficial certificate below was handed out to troops in Sector 2Ø in 1982 and 1983 by Military Intelligence personnel as a joke. (Whether it was issued before and after those years is unclear to the author.) While it is tongue-in-cheek and is not meant be taken too seriously or literally, beneath the humour lies a subtle yet ominous warning to family members that their son or brother may have problems readjusting to civilian life.]

NOTICE OF RETURN

```
Issued in solemn warning this ........ day of .........
TO: Parents, Neighbours, Friends and Relatives of No: .....
Name: ...................... Rank: ..................

    1) Lock your daughters away
    2) Fill your fridge with beer
    3) Get his civvies out of the mothballs
```

Very soon the above-named soldier will once more be in your midst, dehydrated, demoralised and eager to assume his place in society as a human being entitled to liberty and justice, while engaged in a somewhat delayed pursuit of happiness.

In making joyous preparations to welcome him back to civilisation, you must make allowances for bad environmental situations that have been his lot for the past ___ months, therefore show no alarm if he prefers to sit on the floor instead of a chair, always kicks his boots against the steps when he enters the house, wears a towel and sandals when visiting the neighbours, has a fit when he sees bully beef and dog biscuits and always salutes anyone who looks important, even the postman. His diet (to which he has become accustomed) should, for the first few weeks at least, consist of dehydrated potatoes and other vegetables, and a small piece of corned meat. Fresh or rich foods, especially milk, should be avoided at first and then gradually introduced into his diet.

Do not allow him on the roads unaccompanied, as he has
almost completely forgotten traffic. Do not be surprised
when he shouts any obscenities at traffic attempting to
cross a green light, as he is probably unaccustomed
to traffic lights by now.

Do all his purchasing for him, gently establishing in
his mind that threatening, arguing and bargaining with
shopkeepers are taboo in civilisation. His language may
be a little embarrassing at first, but in a relatively
short time he can be taught to speak some English again.
Never ask him why the boy down the road has a higher rank
than him, and never make flattering remarks about the air
force and navy, as you will only have to begin the
English lessons once more.

For the first few months be particularly careful when he
is in the company of women (of any age). After seeing
them wooed on the screen by handsome men, he thinks that
he is a master of the art himself. His intentions are
good and will be sincere, but dishonourable.

Keep in mind that beneath his tanned and rugged exterior
there beats a heart of gold. Treasure it, as it is
probably the only thing that he has left. Treat him with
kindness and tolerance and the occasional carry pack of
good beer or a little bottle of rum, and you have every
chance of rehabilitating this hollow shell into the man
you once knew.

(Signed)
Rehabilitation Officer
Section 20

CAMPS

You knew you had to go to camps when you were notified in the post by registered mail. You had to go to the post office and sign for the bloody thing. It told you where and when to report. If you wanted deferment you had to make a representation by a certain date, with proof, such as a letter from your employer. You had about three months before having to report.

The fact of the matter was that you had to go. If you got registered mail, you'd sign for it, and there your call-up papers for camps would be. At one stage I just refused to accept any registered mail, but, once a year, you'd get this call-up. You had to report on such and such a date and if you didn't, you were AWOL. Then they'd come and look for you.

After coming home from camps I had no problems and fitted straight back into society, but I'd be sure to take my annual work leave then, just to relax, sleep late, grow my hair long and not shave. I did that for three weeks. Took my leave and then went back to work. Got my little medal. Pro Patria – For Country.

After my two years' service I never received my medal, not even in the post. Nothing. One assumes that everybody was automatically issued their Pro Patria. I know I was supposed to get it. When I went for camps I could've asked them, but it never bothered me – at that stage, for me, it was worthless. Now it means more; I don't know why. I never even worried about it until a few years ago, when I found my father's and grandfather's medals, which my mother gave to me. Then I started thinking about it, and thought, 'Where's mine?'

When I klaared out at the end of '71, we weren't obliged to do camps. Some guys were later called back, especially air force radio operators, even though they were officially exempted.

I klaared in from June 1975. Did eighteen months because National Service was no longer for only one year. We had a choice: it was either eighteen months or two years. The difference was the pay. The first option was something like R900 extra when you reached the end of your term, but two years was about R1 700 extra. I didn't do any camps.

I didn't have to do camps. For some reason – I don't really know why – they gave out what they called credits. If you'd been on the Border for a certain amount of time you didn't have to do camps due to these accumulated credits. That's what they said to us, anyway.

As I had volunteered for the extra-twelve-month option after my one year's service in 1976, I wasn't obliged to do camps. Eight years later I got my first call-up. I simply went to the authorities to show them my clearing-out papers. It was proof enough to exempt me.

I started my one year's training from January '76, but did an extra twelve months voluntarily. You had to do the one year first, and had a choice of doing an additional six months or one year. I did two years in total because I got a nice lot of money out of it. I think it was R3 500, which, in those days, was a fair amount. That was over and above your forty-six cents a day. For the year, plus the extra six months, you got R1 800. And then your Border service got you a little bit of extra danger pay.

At the end of 1977, when we had our last forty days to go, it came out that everyone had to do two years' compulsory National Service from then on. No choice. Although I had already done two years, I then had camp duties as well.

After my two years' service I joined the fire department, in 1982. I never worried about camps or even thought about it. I received no notification of call-ups for camps. Then one of my associates got his. We went to the personnel division and asked what we had to do. After giving proof of our employment as civil servants in the fire department, the lady pulled out some forms to fill in, which we did. They were posted away and that was it. Never did a single camp.

I didn't do camps because I was a teacher. For almost ten years they always called me up during school terms. It was crazy of them to expect me to go in February. I explained that I was teaching at a private school that couldn't find a replacement in my absence. I told them to call me up in holiday time and then I would go, but during school I would not – could not – go. They always exempted me. My camps were supposed to be at SAS *Unity* at the Cape Town docks, which I don't think was a very serious base in the first place. Eventually National Service fell through.

I never went back for camps after leaving the army. I was supposed to, in 1992. The previous year a white guy had been raped by blacks in the Parabats – my old unit. My dad refused to let me go and said to stuff my call-up papers. He was right. I thought, 'Bugger that! I don't want that kind of crap in my life. For what?' I tore them up and threw them away. That was the only call-up I ever got for camps.

General Service

I did my first camp, in 1965, at 2 Mil Hospital. It was supposed to be for three weeks, but there were so many people that after only two weeks they told us to give them their stuff back. And that was that, the end of my National Service. However, when the military situation changed and became more intense, a lot of doctors and medics put their names down for camps. I was trained as a medic, so I put my name forward – they needed us. So after ten years I went back in. A lot of chaps actually did. I did camps in '76, '77 and one on the Border in '78.

On our last week at camp we went to say goodbye to the intake following us. 'We wish you all a merry Christmas and we hope your new year starts with a bang!'

I was in the navy in 1967. After the nine months' National Service we had three camps over the next ten years. Two weeks each. The force never lost you. I still have my discharge papers.

When I first went in I was able seaman second class. When I left I was still able seaman second class.

I left school at seventeen, and turned eighteen during my National Service. I went into the air force, starting in '77. At the end of '77, when we had less than forty days left, they changed the law. Said it would now be two years. You had to do it. Then, at the end of that, they changed it again by adding camps as well. You could complete some extra camps straight after the two years' National Service, and be paid off and dismissed, or you could complete the second year and do your obligatory camps at a later stage, spread out over a much longer period of time. In total – I added it up – I spent close to four years vir Volk en Vaderland: two years' National Service and a total of two years' camps.

Most of my camps were spent in the Pienaar's Rivier, Hammanskraal area. From time to time we would spend a while at Waterkloof Air Force Base, as well, just outside of Pretoria. It had that silver Spitfire with the clipped wings outside. My anti-aircraft unit was based there.

Towards the end of our National Service, in Hammanskraal, we had building teams. This one corporal drove his Bedford tipping truck too fast around a corner on the gravel road. The truck was loaded with sand, and slid down the embankment on the side of the road. The guys sitting on the back all leapt off in time and escaped relatively unhurt, but one soutie held on as it turned over. His legs were caught under the truck and were badly damaged. Somehow his friends managed to pull him out, but by then the damage had been done. One guy ran back to camp, alerted the others, and this poor oke was taken away by helicopter to hospital.

Later, while on camps, this same guy did clerical work – but on crutches! He permanently needed them for support. Why he still had to do his bloody camps is beyond me. Couldn't they have let him off? That's the kind of waste that I hated; his life was buggered up for nothing. Another stupid accident while on National Service.

Sometime in the late seventies I did my three-month camps, but I never returned to South West. Before then, I had my option of doing another six or twelve months over and above my initial one year, which meant that I wouldn't be obliged to do camps. I chose not to do the extra time because I had the most beautiful girl waiting for me back in Durban. I think eighteen months was R1 800 and no camps. If you decided to do two years it was R2 700 and no camps. That was huge money. When I klaared out I bought my first brand-new car – a Beetle, for R1 800 – and if I'd done six months extra it would've paid for it. If you convert that into today's money, a brand new Beetle is R140 000.

So I ended up doing camps. My first was February 1978. The reason I remember it is because I'd started my articles as an auditor and was doing stocktaking. There weren't even fax machines in those days, let alone cell-phones. There was a message for me when I got back to the office to phone my HQ. Got the call on Monday. By Tuesday I was on the trucks on the way to the Natal border of Mozambique. The Rutherford family had trading stores up there that had been shot up. We were ordered to go into the area and stop the terrorists coming through from that side.

While I was studying to become a chartered accountant I did another three camps. Our HQ was in Soldier's Way, Montana House. Did at least two camps there. Then it moved to Point Road. Today the camp is a paint-ball arena. There are no roofs and half of the walls have fallen down. It's a ruin.

In the early eighties I did a few camps, but all in Langebaan, and then no more. Langebaan Air Force Base was about twenty kilometres away from the navy base. I usually did one camp a year, and for not longer than two months at a time. In some years I'd ask for a postponement and go later that year or the next.

On my second camp I became a full corporal. I was a guard commander, which meant that I sent troeps to the watch towers to guard the outer perimeter and man the gate – that sort of thing.

I managed to bail out and get into the brass band. I was a musician, so I played the trumpet at 1 SAI and the bagpipes with the Cape Town High-landers during a couple of camps.

I also played at the odd funeral. On one occasion, I took part in the funeral of a guy who'd been killed by a phosphorous grenade. Some guys had gone down to De Brug. The corporal had been showing them how to throw the grenade when it went off. He was being negligent. About twenty-six of them got burnt and some died. To witness mothers and girlfriends trying to throw themselves onto the coffin was something else. Then you had to play the 'Last Post'. It was very difficult.

Some parents were told, 'He tripped over a tent peg and died.' What nonsense! They weren't told what had really happened. They were told ridiculous stuff that we would laugh about. I mean, who trips over a tent peg and dies? And how many of them were supposed to have done it? I'm not kidding. Some of the accusations were insulting.

Did camps over a ten-year period with Koeberg Battalion. When I did my camps I got another stripe – platoon sergeant. Made more bucks. Did seven camps, starting every January. Every flippin' January! Christmas would go past, no worries. Then, on the first of January I'd get this big brown envelope. 'Oh well, here we go again.' You couldn't refuse.

I was tired of it, and angry – but really just moerse tired of it. Every year! That made me mad in my head – the guys just tuning you to come in, the whole time. You knew: They blow the whistle; there you are. *Doonk!* And if you didn't go they'd be at your door – the MPs, the RPs or the SAP – and they'd flipping well lock you up without even hesitating! You were being watched without your even knowing it. They knew where you were, and must've caught thousands of ous like that. I didn't want to disgrace my name. I thought, 'I'll just go, go, go and go until whenever.'

My first camp was in 1989, in Durban. There was a massive parade in the streets, led by the pipes of the Irish Brigade. It was all for show – a show of force. As an Ordnance Services member in 5 Maintenance, I was attached to the brigade.

We were then sent to Lohatlha for the next two months. At that particular time I was assigned to the kitchen staff. I had to prepare and serve meals, one day on and one day off, while the rest of the maintenance unit resupplied forward units during manoeuvres and mock air attacks. On our days off we went into the koppies with binoculars and watched.

On my second camp I was allocated to Umkomaas Commando, stationed in Richmond, where I did general clerical duties. On weekends I manned the Marnet – a radio-operated communications system linking the local farmers. The area was very volatile, and a lot of farm attacks had taken place, so we had to have continuous communications with the farming community. While I was there the Oosthuizen couple was murdered. They were caught outside their house, stabbed and then shot. Executed. I received that call.

After 1990 the army really struggled to get guys to respond to their call-ups, let alone their camps. The writing was on the wall, and everyone could see it. Things were going downhill from a call-up point of view. The army wasn't going to take drastic steps such as imprisoning people, like they used to, so a lot of guys just stayed away. But I was one of the few that did report for camps.

My third was again with Umkomaas Commando. This was around 1991. After that I was attached to the Natal Carbineers, based in Pietermaritzburg, where I lived, for a fourth camp. It was very short – not even a month. Yet again I stayed on base while the unit was deployed in the townships. I was in the office.

My fifth and last camp was for the 1994 elections – just to be available if something bad was to occur.

The Border

For my last camp, in 1978, I was sent up for three months to Mukwe, not far from Pappa Falls, where a missionary hospital was located. As a medic I did a variety of things. I was stationed at Company Headquarters, which had the area to look after, mainly for the PBs. Things like general sickness, eye infections, scabies, cuts, dog bites, falling off bicycles or trucks and stuff like that. Nothing dramatic. We also had the health and hygiene aspects of the camps to look after, such as checking the latrines. There was a case of geelsug in the area and we had to find out where it was coming from, but we never did. It just disappeared. It's like jaundice – an infection in the liver. I had put it down to someone's latrine disciplines not being as good as they should've been.

I was lucky. We didn't have any contact and I was grateful for that. We were there when those chaps at Katima were shot and killed. They didn't call us for that. They coped with it. From Katima they would've gone straight into Rundu, I'm sure, then on to Pretoria. That's how I estimate it, because they didn't release much information; I only found out most of it when I got back. We were very fortunate that we never received any serious contact casualties. We were very thin on the ground. I had two fellows under me and they were many kilometres to the south.

Finally they said they wouldn't be needing me any more. 'You're in the hospital services so we're klaaring you out.'

'Fine,' I said. 'I've had enough anyway.' By that stage the training – everything – was a whole new style. I was also in my mid-thirties, and my employers were moaning about staff shortages. Thus ended my duties.

In 1980 I reported at the Wingfield camp in Cape Town. You'd arrive with your balsak full of the stuff you would need. Items like sleeping bags and webbing weren't allowed to be kept at home, so we were issued with all of that there. We were supplied with our weapons only once up on the

Border. Then we'd go over to DF Malan Airport and wait in four big hangars that used to house the Shackletons. We'd get into the C-130s and fly to Kimberley. The following day we'd have lunch at one of the army bases, then fly on Safair to Grootfontein. When we arrived it would be the middle of the night and pitch-dark. We'd be loaded onto trucks. We wouldn't know where we were, so we'd look at the constellations for any recognition – Orion's Belt or whatever – and realise, of course, that we were still in the southern hemisphere. Then we'd load onto Bedfords and drive up to Ondangwa in convoy. You weren't really shitting yourself, just thinking, 'Oh, God, here we go again.'

I spent about three months at the Ondangwa Air Force Base. It had three 40-mm Bofors guns mounted on towers to defend against ground attacks. The Recces were also on the base. You never saw them; you only heard them – interrogating their 'guests'. They had their own cordoned-off area and you weren't supposed to go near it.

There were always different guys on each of the camps, but you made friends. Two I knew for long after the army days. When these two first came up they were my *rofies*. It ended up being just the three of us. They'd cram eight people into one tent, with virtually no space in between. Two rows of four metal beds. Anyway, the three of us decided to cause shit. We carried on as if we were mad – not befok, just crazy. We farted, coughed, shouted, screamed and just made a nuisance of ourselves. The other five guys buggered off. We had the only tent with three people inside. We just didn't want anybody else in our tent.

For patrols we'd go out for one night and sleep in the bush, then come back in. Then one day's rest, then one day's standby, and then you'd be out again. Three sections of us rotated within a five- to ten-kilometre radius. When the section went out it was just a sergeant and a two-striper. All of us were National Servicemen. There were no lieutenants or PFs with us, so we took many liberties.

We were bored during the day, so we'd take an R1 bullet, stick it in the barrel and work the head off. We'd pour all the cordite into a termite hill and blow the termites away. Great fun. The number of bullets we wasted! We blew up a lot of termite mounds on patrol. We'd see a pond, and want to have some fun, so we'd take a hand grenade and throw it in, just to watch the water splash up. There were about five seconds after you squeezed the handle before it exploded. The base was informed that we were going to practise, so they knew what the explosions were all about.

Sleeping out in the flippin' rain! If it rained there, it flippin' rained. The summer rains in January, February and March were awful if you were out. We were equipped with night-vision sights – the ones you put on your head, like goggles – to see if anybody was around. You could use them for driving, as well. You put on your sights, stood up and looked. It was yellow, but everything was so clear. You could see the shape of a tree and what was underneath it.

At night it was black, black, black. During the day it was white sand, like sea sand. White, white, white. I had to have my Ray-Bans on all the time because of the reflection. There were lots of palm trees, too.

We made fires and had braais. We'd get hold of some meat and have a braai for lunch. Somebody would organise it from base. I still have my dixie at home. I used to love brewing up tea – a nice, hot cup of tea. The main thing I'd get sent from home was tea, and tins of condensed milk. Apart from sweetening things and making milk, it was excellent for bribes – like a form of currency. Condensed milk: the troepie's favourite.

We used to watch quite a few movies in the evenings. This was between bush patrols, when you were back at base for a day or so. That would make the time pass. They used to snap or melt a lot, too. You'd be watching a movie, in the blackness, and suddenly you'd hear a bang go off or see a tracer flying through the air.

The first time I've seen dogs literally climb a fence was when the PF guys were shooting at them. Stray dogs used to come inside the camp and these guys were just so *gatvol* that they'd shoot them. Those poor dogs.

Because we were in South West Africa, not Angola, I never had contact. In the early stages of the war a lot of guys were killed by our own side. They shot down a helicopter carrying a colonel and a whole lot of other officers because it wasn't identified properly by the anti-aircraft unit. It was on the news at the time. They didn't say who shot it, but they were shot down by our own people.

I reported with call-up papers, a food voucher and a train ticket. I always made sure to have a long chain and a few padlocks. Up there you had to lock up your washing. If you didn't, by the time you finished your shower your clothes would be gone from the line.

There were special trains leaving at certain times. You arrived at the station and all got on the train. Then we'd arrive at Pretoria station. The guys would pick us up in those old Bedfords. Went to Waterkloof, were kitted out, and then caught a Flossie to Ondangwa, which took a couple of hours.

I remember the first time we went up. We got there and they asked for volunteers to relieve another unit, which was already deployed. We'd just have to man the equipment temporarily. The NCO asked for about twenty troops to step forward. He knew some of us had wives and kids and so didn't tell us who should go or not. 'Volunteers, step forward.' Everybody stepped forward together. The whole lot.

My last camp was in '84, some of it on the Border at Ondangwa. Not really deep shit. They chucked some mortars at us, once, and we fired back. That was about all the action we had. I was never really in the thick of things. I was interned with the 250 Air Defence Unit. We had the Hilda, which was the British-designed Tigercat system. When we got it, from Jordan, it was painted desert-cammo with Arabic script all over the back. We resprayed it brown. They were deployed around the base and along the runway, basically just to protect it. The idea was that if the enemy came through with their aircraft, we'd have a defence for the runway and the base. But the reality was that it never happened because they never penetrated so deep into our airspace.

In the morning you'd get up, deploy the thing and then sit and wait. Just sit in the sun, *ballas bak*, and wait for stuff to happen. You'd be deployed along the runway, watching the Flossies and the Daks and all sorts of aircraft landing and taking off. Sometimes, in the mornings, we'd watch Impalas take off. Their wings were groaning with the weight of long-range drop tanks and ordnance. They'd bugger off. A couple of hours later they'd come back with nothing, and one or two a little shot up. Most of the aerial combat was well beyond the Angolan border.

Coming back was always a nice party. Lots of us on the train. You were happy to come back home.

Every time I went back for camps I saw the same old faces, minus a few here and there, and thought, 'Where are the rest of the guys? Why aren't *they* here?' Eventually I was getting all these bloody call-up papers and just tossed them in the bin. 'Bugger this! Why must I go back to do camps? That's it. Done my bit.'

Some guys had lekker jobs, like those loadmasters, but for the average bloke it was just kak. In my time the loadies had about a month of training and flew everywhere on the Flossies. Okes always sucked up to them – they were always everyone's best buddies. You gave them a case of beer and said, 'Hey! You got a space back to Cape Town?' Of course, there was always a bit of space, and they'd sneak on a few of their buddies and fly to Cape Town for a weekend pass. They also got danger pay, going up to the Border, plus their stripe immediately. And being part of the PF crew, the pilot – who was always a captain – said, 'He's not standing guard for the weekend. He's on my team and I need him.' They never stood beat, those ous. They were treated so well. It must've been the best job in the air force.

I ended up as a staff sergeant. The first camp you did you became a sergeant. Then I did a Staff's Course in Kimberley. I did eight camps, but I didn't do townships, fortunately, as I was more in the South West Operational Area. I never had contact.

In 1984 I did a camp in the Caprivi at Katima Mulilo. I went to fight a war, got there, and found out that we played golf and went tiger fishing instead. They had a Katimo Mulilo country club. There was a big bar where all the air force guys used to hang out. I arrived there and checked these okes with their golf carts. 'Hey! What's going on here?' I asked.

'Nee wat, boet. Ons speel gholf, man!'

'Oh. I play golf.'

'What's your handicap?'

'Ag, about eleven.'

'Hey, kom saam.' One oke gave me a putter, another oke a wood and another oke an iron. I got a whole set of clubs. The course was diesel and sand. There were no greens – instead they were called 'browns'. Diesel killed the weeds and thickened the sand. You could tee up all along the fairway. The first ball I hit, I lost. If you chipped onto the brown, the ball stopped dead. There was also a putting strip, smoothed out with a piece of washing line. The hole was in the middle of the strip and, if you were closest, it was the best advantage because the back okes would putt and you'd check the groove in the sand, then just follow it and sink the ball. So the key was to be closest.

As a mortarist I was sent with thirty troops, including my lieuty, who had never done mortars. I had a platoon of seventeen drivers, ten chefs and *one* mortarist. He and I had two weeks to train them. If we'd shot the mortars that the readings had indicated we would've blown up the town. Our town. Because of my knowledge I also had to train okes at Mpacha and the navy base at Wenela for two weeks at a time. They had mortars in their bases but didn't have mortarists! I had to get the troops au fait with the weapons. You had the SA Marines up there because of the Zambezi River, which ran down to Lake Kariba. They had a big military barge, which transported people up and down.

In 1978, prior to us going there, one of the Katima bases was hit by those 122-mm Red Eyes. A bungalow was taken out by a direct hit. Ten ous killed, with about the same number injured. We saw photos of the place. There were bodies in trees. By the time we got there, in '84, nothing was going on. All we did was base protection and suntanning.

One time we had a situation where the Bren carrier was very upset that he was humping the thing around. It was quite heavy. His buddy had all the ammo. The Bren guy, a red-headed ou, was moaning, 'Hey, Corporal, this is a kak job. Why do I have to carry it and clean it?'

'Because when you need to use it, and you haven't cleaned it, you're going to have a big problem!' Within half an hour of him cleaning it, we heard, 'Kontak! Kontak! Wag. Uit.' Some okes had action a little further away from us. The oke stopped whingeing and always had the thing Brassoed after that. It shone!

We had a camper up on the Caprivi who shot a troep straight through the chest because the guy had no respect for the corporal. We'd just arrived at a new base. The camper came to me and said, 'Hey, Sergeant, I'm not going to cope here. I need to go on patrol or I'll go mad sitting in this place.' We went to the base OC and told him we had a problem. We explained that our main company was doing patrols in the Oshakati area and we wanted to send him over because he wasn't going to cope where we were. His response was, 'Ag, you's okes is in charge here. You make him cope.'

The thing was, this guy was about thirty years old, had already done his ten camps, and knew that he wasn't going to manage.

They were doing base protection at a little island somewhere down the river. The troepie became cheeky with one of the corporals. This camper pulled out his R1 and shot the troepie point-blank through the chest. He didn't die, fortunately, because he was shot from so close. It just went straight through. The R4 would've done more damage – would've made a big hole at the back. As National Servicemen we had R4s, of course, but in that area we were only issued R1s. He got off without charges because we'd previously warned those in command that he shouldn't be there.

Jeez, on a different subject, I can recall the times with Platoon 3. They were busy with National Service and not on camps. They were real rubbishes. All the bad okes were in this platoon. They were rebellious, those guys – even the lieuty – just all plain bad okes, and being on the Border didn't help. I had a couple of run-ins with them. One oke scaled Sosegon from my medic bag. As part of the morning parade I had to inspect the troops. I noticed an ampule missing, and I knew who it was. 'Where is it?' I asked.

'I don't know, Sergeant.'

'Well, then I'm going to have to charge you.' Then he told me what had happened. He and his mate had been sleeping 'buddy-buddy' – one oke kept chips while the other slept. When he woke his buddy up, the guy, still half-asleep, started pummelling him to pieces. He said he needed the medication to give to his buddy. That was his excuse. Crazy things like that happened.

Hah – Platoon 3! A starving cow once wandered into the TB and collapsed. My buddy and I tried to feed it some leaves. It got up and staggered over to Platoon 3. They began playing with it. Two of the really bad boys actually started shagging this cow! They'd already attempted to rape one of the local ladies, but she'd bolted. Guys took photos of them naaiing this half-dead cow. They must've been plaasjapies.

That night was silent; not a single noise could be heard. We were sitting around, having orders, and one officer asked the captain, 'Het jy gehoor wat vandag gebeur het?'

'Nee.'

'Twee ouens het 'n koei genaai.'

'WAT? GAAN KRY DIE DONNEEEERS!' They reckoned his shout echoed for kilometres. When they called for them, one was missing. The other oke was brought in. The captain asked, very slowly, 'Sê vir my, hoe *is* dit om 'n koei te naai?' The oke looked at the captain and, also very slowly, replied, 'Kaptein, 'n vark is beter.' That's when the captain cracked, and hit the ou with an ammo case.

These two were later sent back to the main base, given a dishonourable discharge and sent back to Middelburg. Got caned six of the best by the police. It became a civilian case and they were jailed for a year: attempted rape and bestiality. After their sentence they were called up for another two years – not that the army needed those okes.

Meanwhile, Platoon 3 disappeared from the TB and there was no radio contact from them. Vanished. We couldn't find them anywhere. They all said, 'Bugger this!' and left. Platoon 4 went out and, within the hour, it sounded as if a war was going on next to us. We heard gunshots and, over the radio, 'Kontak! Kontak! Wag! Uit!'

The captain heard two different contact calls over his radio and worked out that the two platoons were shooting at each other. 'STAAK VUUR! STAAK VUUR! JULLE SKIET FOKKEN DONNERSWIL OP ME-KAAR! STO-O-O-P!'

We didn't know it at the time, but it was Platoon 3 versus Platoon 4! Number 3 were sitting around, all vrot in a cuca, when they saw an armed black guy, who happened to be the tracker ahead of Platoon 4. When they checked him, they opened fire. He himself let rip – about 200 rounds – straight into this kraal, but not one oke was hit. After the dust had settled, Platoon 3's lieuty and corporal got into serious trouble and were eventually court-martialled.

On my first camp we guarded an ammo dump east of Pretoria. Then, on another camp, I went to Oshivelo. It was 1988, the year South Africa pulled out of Angola. We established a quartermaster base in the bush for all the provisions that were expected to come out. It was only after I left that the stuff came in, so what arrived there I can't really say. But I'm sure there was ammo returning as well, because there was a dump about 200 metres away.

On my last camp, right at the end, in '88, when we got beaten – because we did, we got messed up badly – I was in hospital with diabetes. I saw over sixty guys come in with 'malaria'. I said to the nurses, '*Malaria*? What are you talking about, malaria? I was up on the Border for almost two years and in that time only one guy, in a camp of thousands, had malaria! So now how come all these guys have malaria?' That was just their explanation; that's what they said, but in reality we got shot to pieces. MiG-23s donnered us. Their gunships, too. Our Ratels didn't stand a chance. But no one will talk about that. Our okes were way up in Angola in late '87 and early '88, during Ops Hooper and Ops Packer, during the battle of Cuito Cuanavale. Look, it may have been a political decision to withdraw, and the ANC and the Cubans have now turned it into a propaganda spiel about defeating the racist SADF. But we were still mashed.

On one camp, at Rundu, the RSM was an old Armoured guy. He saw us – in Armour too – and called me over. He said I was to lead the parade. I'd never done a parade in my life, in spite of my stripes, and tried explaining this to him, but he would have none of it. It was one of those massive flag-hoisting parades. I asked the others, quickly, what I had to do. In the end, I managed; I got it right. The guys on parade helped me out. They were all laughing.

The last camp I did was just as I started employment. Then that was it – I was finished.

Into Angola

In '83, during Ops Askari, we were based close to Calueque Dam and patrolled part of the Cunene River. Next to us was 32 Battalion. Then, one day, they literally ran past us – officers and men – with all their equipment. They just suddenly appeared in the middle of the bush. The whole battalion came by and we cheered them on, but I was like, 'Huh?' They were on their way up towards Ongiva, while others were coming down.

I was still a rifleman and became a major's batman. On one occasion, two platoons from Bravo Company got lost along the river, near the dam. They were part of our company in the Cape Town Highlanders. For some reason they didn't have any radio contact; like me they were campers, which might explain things. Unknown to me, a volunteer was needed to escort a sergeant major to locate them. This guy was a Portuguese bloke who lived in the area. The entire company lined up. I was still dazed and half asleep. Suddenly the whole company took three steps backwards, and I'm left standing there like a dodo. I was 'n bietjie dof and still hadn't figured out how the whole system worked. So he and I went out – me with radio pack, full kit and rat packs.

We found them, after a day and a half, along the river. They didn't know how to read their maps properly – not even their sergeant. A lot of guys didn't. It was crazy. I had fun, in a way, just me and this sergeant major.

Most of the time during my National Service, and on camps with the CTH, we got ourselves totally drugged on dope. I'm sorry, I don't like saying that, but I think even the officers got themselves doped up – perhaps because they weren't sure if they'd get a bullet from behind. They became all sweetie-pie when we got up to the Border. Their whole attitude changed. When we were on base they drilled us like crazy, but when we went up north it was a whole different ball game. We became their buddies. Sure, we respected them and followed commands, but up there the whole thing was completely different, such as being seconded to 32 Battalion. We handled this side of the Calueque River and 32 were on the other side, near the dam. They overlapped onto the areas that we didn't cover, going all over the vicinity. We'd assist with picking up arms caches – stacks of stuff.

As a musician, one thing CTH got me into was playing the bagpipes, but, if you want my opinion, I think they're bosbefok. Totally. I mean, who takes bagpipes over the Angolan border and says, 'Right! Play the "Reveille" and "Last Post".'

'You guys have got to be crazy!' I'd say.

'No! No! We *want* them to know we're here! Let them come! We've got a good team.' It was like saying 'Hello! Here we are! Pinpoint us! Come and shoot the hell out of us!' It was craziness! There's something really crazy about that. It was bossies – totally bossies – but they were certainly not afraid. When it came to action they won a lot of battle honours. So, there I stood, out in the bush, and played the bagpipes for the CTH. Played 'Cock o' the North', 'Barren Rocks', 'Reveille'. Woke the guys up: played at sunrise and sunset.

'Ah! There they are!' the enemy eventually said, and pinpointed us. They knew very well where we were. I remember seeing Katyushas coming in and everybody looking for cover, and then they hit us with mortars. I got absolutely pissed that day – finished a lot of whisky – and got alcohol poisoning.

On this camp, I was still with the mechanised infantry. It was heavy in those days. Food wasn't always freely available. Rat packs, which were supposed to last for one or two days, were sometimes stretched to a week. Also, a lot of our guys who went in didn't come back. Got blown to bits, obviously. You ask if I want to share this with you. Well, some of it's still deep down and I can't get it out. I had a friend covering me. I thought he was on the ground because it was fire and movement, and it was his turn to cover me. Then I went down, as it was his turn to get up and run again. I thought, 'Where the hell is he? He should get up.' Then I heard, 'Medic!' and I knew he'd gone. Somebody you shared a space with in the Ratel was gone. It wasn't a joke. Buddies – close buddies. It wasn't funny.

When I came back I didn't talk about things any more. I totally with-drew. Then I got religious and threw myself into it. That camp was to be my last. I refused to go back. I just said, 'No more. That's it.' Then the MPs came after me, but I wasn't around. They contacted my mother, who told them she'd informed the army chaplain that I wasn't coming back. I didn't go overseas, but hitched to the Transkei instead. In those days it was a homeland, and I went on the run from homeland to homeland until it was all clear. I just laid low because that's what I had to do. I had no choice.

I first went up to the Border during National Service in December 1978. Afterwards it was on to the University of the Orange Free State. I tried to get all my camps done before I finished varsity and started working. There were two-month camps over the varsity holidays, and you could do courses over June and July. I already had corporal's rank because of National Service experience. I did a Sergeant's Course, which counted as a one-month camp, at De Brug, in the bloody winter. I passed, and got my third stripe, even though I hadn't been an instructor before that.

Many times we left in Flossies on a direct flight from Bloemspruit Air Force Base, in Bloem, up to Grootfontein. Once, we flew to Pretoria and then to Ondangwa. I was on Ops Askari in December '83; it was a camp I'd volunteered for. We were sent up with the Free State University Commando to relieve the guys looking after the bases in south Angola. They didn't have enough experienced National Servicemen to do this, so we were ordered up.

I'd previously trained in all the driving courses for Ratels during my National Service days. I went on to gunnery, and then trained as crew commander as well. They wanted experienced guys. Take our crew: we had a captain as a gunner, a two-pip lieut as a driver and a sergeant, me, as a crew commander, so I could've given the captain orders. You chose what you wanted to do and what you enjoyed the most. It was all the guys who studied with you. You'd see them in class every day, so there was a relaxed atmosphere. Discipline wasn't lax, though, and we all knew what we had to do.

On Ops Askari I was a loader and alternated with the driver. We went to Cahama and buggered around there. Tried to attack it from all sides, but they wouldn't budge; we couldn't move them. The politicians told us to move out, so on Old Year's Eve we left. We thought we were going home but instead turned left and attacked Cuvelai, taking the town. We used Ratel 90s. There were about twenty armoured vehicles and about twenty specialised infantry vehicles, including rocket launchers, as well as the back-up vehicles with petrol, food and ammunition, and a company of infantry of about 140 troops. Usually we worked with mechanised infantry, but on this occasion we were supported by normal infantry from 1 SAI.

My crew commander was hit. He was also the squad leader and on the radio the whole time. He had a shitty job. He'd have to give targets to the gunner, tell me as the driver where to go *and* speak to the guys upstairs. I don't think he could handle it. The gunner was also trigger-happy and looking for targets to shoot. When the commander was hit, everyone was shooting. All you could hear was, 'We got him! We got him!' But the commander hadn't even given a target yet. Both he and the gunner had their hatches open. The gunner's hatch opened towards the back and the commander's towards the front, like a shield. These two popped their heads in and out, looking for targets, and there must have been a terr watching this. The third or fourth time it happened, he let loose with an AK. Two bullets hit the hatch and ricocheted into the Ratel. All I received were a few paint flecks on my face from the shrapnel. The gunner got hit, but not seriously. The crew commander was bleeding badly, though. We put all the bandages we could on him, but it was decided that it was best to take him away, and he was casevaced. Then I got into the turret and the second-in-command took over as troop commander.

We had to fight T-34s and T-55s. The T-34s weren't mobile, but dug into the ground. We were totally outclassed, but our training was better than theirs. We shot out one and the others just stopped. Their crews ran away – they were mainly FAPLA, but Cubans as well. They were normally the first guys to bugger off when the shit hit the fan; they just jumped into their vehicles and left. We could see that they'd left in a hurry. One left his wallet, with money and personal stuff in it. We shot out eighteen tanks and captured twenty-one, with not a mark on them. Some of the engines were still idling. We didn't have a single loss.

At Cuvelai we wandered onto a minefield. The vegetation was very overgrown and suddenly we found this big, open plain. We spread out and moved forward. The commander had known we were near this minefield. These were the days before GPS, so the exact location of the place wasn't certain. We didn't know that this was their killing field. Then, I think, two Ratels were hit and we were ordered to stop right where we were. We were out in the open and there was no cover. The infantry were ordered to dismount. Trenches were seen where the bushes began on the edge of the field, and small-arms fire was coming from there.

The next thing, the Infantry Ratel between mine and my friend's was hit on its side. The impact made a hole about a metre wide. We realised that there was a tank somewhere in the bushes, but we couldn't see the bloody thing. What saved us was his barrel knocking against a tree, so he had to move forward, which made huge plumes of smoke. Then we saw the tank. It was about 200 metres away, behind the trenches. Both my friend and I let fly with anti-tank projectiles. We hit it 'point-blank', as my buddy says, but it caught fire and drove away into the bushes.

My friend witnessed what happened to the Ratel. He remembers a bright light and seeing the hole with fire inside. A hatch opened and coloured smoke came out. It closed and opened again, but the inside was totally consumed by fire. The hatch dropped closed for the last time. All fourteen infantry troops were killed.

The other infantry, with their weapons on fully-automatic, eventually overran the terrs. They were identified as FAPLA. We found the tank a few days later. Two crew members were still inside. One guy's head was completely gone. The other's body was split in half. The third, who must've been the driver, was missing. My buddy kept the crew commander's cap and an AK-47 bayonet found inside.

I was chatting with an ex-PF member, a former captain in Military Intelligence who left the SADF in 1993. It's his firm belief that it wasn't really the first-time National Servicemen, or even the PFs, who bore the brunt of the war in Angola. It was the Citizen Force – the ou manne, the campers, the bos oupas. 'They were the real cannon fodder,' he said.

The Townships

Jussee! Did I do camps! Six in four years. Two times I got called up twice in one year. I hated camps. They were all in the townships because by then, the mid-eighties, the internal crap had started. Our okes were carrying on like cowboys – shooting and sjambokking and acting at will. The campers and National Servicemen performed like bloody savages. If they saw a group of guys walking together, then they were 'terrorists'. They got out and beat the bejesus out of them, for no reason at all. The corporal may have ordered it, or the lieut didn't mind. They'd come back and have a laugh at the pub. Even the commandant would go down to the pub and ask, 'Hoeveel kaffers het julle vandag gedonner?' Big laugh. It was crap; I really didn't like those camps at all. It was also disruptive. I was working, and on the later ones I'd just got married. I didn't want to be there but I had to go. We all had to. I didn't have a choice, really.

Nobody cared what was happening in the townships. People lived in crap conditions there. You could see it. We'd drive around, looking, and say, 'Jeez, this is not a nice place to live.' One of the camps was at Springs Command. We went into Daveyton, where those protesters were shot in 1961. Did Soweto and Alexandra, as well. Southern Transvaal Command was the unit where I did most of my camps. The HQ was just outside Gold Reef City, so all our camps were in the bloody townships! I much preferred being on the Border as an ops medic. No comparison.

Did camps, one a year, for years. Sixty-day camps, ninety-day camps. Twice I went back up to the Border, but most of the time I did townships – guarding bus stops and getting sworn at by commuters on the passing buses, every day, while you stood at the gates. Soweto, Doornkop, Diepkloof – lots of places. This was in the early days, 1986, '87.

We used to tie our R4s to our belts because they'd surround us, about twenty ous. They'd all chatter away and then a little laaitie would snatch and grab. They'd try to take our weapons, so what I used to do was take a piece of chalk, find a corner at the station, draw a wide circle around me and park off. I'd say, 'That's *my* space. You step in here and you're dead. You come that close to me, so that you're a threat to me, and you're dead. You want to ask me something? I don't know what you want, but stand outside the white line. Come inside and I'm going to shoot you.' End of story, and they knew it. I'd even tune big mamas who came too close.

We'd go out on patrols in those little Buffels. Once, one of the kids threw a tennis ball at us. We didn't know it was a tennis ball – all we saw was him throwing. Next thing, an ou skiemed, 'Grenade!' We all leapt out. Rondomverdediging. The driver tuned, 'Nooit, it's a flippin' tennis ball.' Then, the next time, another kid also threw something. While it was still in the air one of the okes shot him. Gone. The cops came and sorted out the situation. The kid had lobbed an avocado pear. He lost his life for that. How were we to know what it was?

That stuffed it up for us. It all changed after that. No more Buffels went into that location. Instead, they sent us in in something similar to tiny Datsun bakkies with box-like canopies and flaps. We'd sit on either side on plastic chairs, with our R5s, just waiting for someone to kill us – we were six easy targets inside. It was stupid. Ridiculous.

Did a bit of townships towards about the fourth camp. They didn't know where to allocate us. Things were starting to get bad. Then the townships took off, so they put us in Youngsfield in Cape Town. Any shit happened there and we'd shoot out to wherever needed. We had stones and bricks thrown at us, but we couldn't do anything about it. All our magazines had plastic on them, and if it got broken you were in deep kak. There you were, sitting in the vehicle and having to dodge stones. Hoped to God it wasn't a hand grenade or petrol bomb coming your way. But, ag, we handled it. Guys just gelled. Those were the days.

———————

On the first camp, at Heidelberg in the Transvaal, a lot of the old 'group' got together again. We were called up as a unit. The first night we got so drunk that they took away our rifles.

We were supposed to do anti-riots in the townships. Instead we drove into a white neighbourhood and harassed a bunch of Boere riding under the AWB flag. We stopped them and searched for illegal weapons. They were the only guys we liked to point our rifles at. This didn't go down too well at our Command, which took away our rifles again.

It's not that I didn't enjoy the camps – we were allowed two beers a day, and we accumulated ours. Also, the barman was our mate. One of us assisted him and got us as many beers as we wanted. We ended up having a royal time, basically spending the remainder of the two-month camp drinking in the bungalow every day and messing with the system, while being paid. They left us alone – they didn't appreciate our attitude.

They had us on the second camp for three days before sending us home. On the first day we didn't pitch up for parade. Then we 'lost' all our sleeping gear. Eventually they just let us go.

SO, IN THE END ...

If National Service wasn't compulsory I wouldn't have bothered. But it was compulsory, so I just did it. In 1990, the law was that we had to give over all our details when we turned sixteen. All the boys had to go to the school hall and were told to fill in some forms, which were then sent to the army. I didn't know what I was filling in. It was wrong to have done that to kids. Why not sign the papers when you were older and ready, and when you'd know what it was you were signing? Just before the end of matric you'd get your first call-ups.

January '93 was the last compulsory call-up. I was still in two minds about it the day before I left, and kept thinking, 'Should I do this or not?' But you didn't know what to do, really, or for how long it would be compulsory, so I felt that the safest thing to do was to go. People would still be put in DB if they didn't pitch. From the second you arrived, it was too late to change your mind and leave. Okes still AWOLed, and a lot of guys didn't even arrive. 'Cheers, see you later,' they said. Those guys took a fat chance.

Klaared in at Ysterplaat, then went up to Kimberley for three months' Basics and finished the rest of the year at Anti-Aircraft. It wasn't that empty. Must've been about three or four companies, almost 500 guys, that klaared into 10 Anti-Aircraft. The Infantry at Bloem was full, the Bats was full, Medics was full. I heard this from friends who went to Bloem. They said that they also had lots of people.

I was at Discobolos for Basics, which wasn't very big. It's a dull little town about twenty kays outside of Kimberley. Intelligence and Signals were there before we arrived. Basics was a walk in the park. I was already so super fit, with all the sports I'd done, that they couldn't make me breathe hard enough. My heart rate was sixty during exercises. The only disadvantage I had was that I was really small. When I arrived, all my army-issue clothes were too big. I struggled with heavy things like trommel PT. I didn't have the physical size to do it, but, endurance-wise, I could run for miles. At least you got to do that, rather than sitting around doing something arb. I grew about fifteen centimetres in the army.

After Basics it was on to Secondary. I did movements up in Lohatlha. The idea was to go in at the same time as the Bats, secure the area and send in further troops. Anti-Aircraft fell under Artillery. Anti-Aircraft were trained on the mobile 20-mm and 23-mm guns. There was also the 35-mm, which was stationary. Everything was already set up. It was longer range. A 20 was stationed on the Ystervark, which was mobile. You'd pop the flaps and there you go – up and running. The 23 was a bit trickier. You had to pull and drop everything so the wheels came off. Then it was stationary and you were ready to shoot. Took longer.

We did our Basics, then got trained in order to do whatever they needed us to do. Then we'd sit there every day doing nothing, cleaning cannons. Stripped the cannon, degreased it, oiled it, greased it up again and reassembled it. The next day we'd do the same thing. I joined HQ because this became so boring. There I could do whatever I felt like, really.

When we were halfway through, guys from the old MK unit started klaaring in over June. These guys joined in order to further their careers in our Defence Force. At that stage, we were told that the army wasn't compulsory any more. They said we had to finish the year, though. We weren't allowed to leave. If you did, it was still AWOL and DB.

I klaared out. When I finished they still wanted me to do camps. I said, 'Not a chance,' and tore up my papers when they came. I felt that there were people in the army who wanted to be there, so *they* should go and do camps. What was the point if you didn't want to be there? I needed to study and get on with my life. Things dissolved in April, 1994, so it was silly to think they could still be hard-arsed about it.

I feel fine about National Service but it was a bit of a rondfok, to put it bluntly. The Defence Force taught us various things, but I thought it was a bit of a waste of time because my dad was PF. I knew about being paraat. I didn't really need that year to make me a 'square, rounded person'.

APPENDIX I

The Development of National Service

THE SOUTH AFRICAN DEFENCE FORCE

The South African Defence Force (SADF) served as South Africa's armed forces from 1957 to 1994 and was organised into four branches, or arms, of service. The three combat branches – the army, the air force and the navy – were supported by the medical services division, which formed the fourth branch of the SADF from the late 1970s.

Each was commanded by a representative chief, who fell within the ambit of the national defence strategy laid down by the State President on the advice of the State Security Council. In any decision-making the chiefs of the SADF were assisted by several committees and councils: as a single unit, they decided on matters of strategy, management and financial allocation.

The SADF was essentially a Citizen Force. While Permanent Force members accounted for 10 per cent and National Servicemen for a further 10 per cent, members of the Citizen Force and Commandos accounted for the remaining 80 per cent.

The SADF was succeeded by the South African National Defence Force (SANDF) in 1994.

THE BALLOT SYSTEM

With only a small full-time, professional army, South Africa, like many of the Allied nations after World War II, realised how ill-prepared it had been for war. In 1951 the Union of South Africa introduced the ballot system, according to which one in every three able-bodied white male South African citizens was selected on a random basis for two to three months' compulsory military training. This was known as the Active Citizen Force (ACF). Before 1964 this three-month training period was changed first to six and then to nine months, whereafter it became ten months until 1968.

The Defence Force tried to place men in the roles to which they were best suited. Accountants would, for example, have been placed in an administrative capacity, while civil engineers typically would have managed bridge-building projects and mechanics would have supervised vehicle maintenance.

Below is an official 1956 letter to potential ballottees, reproduced here as it appears in its original form.

REGISTERING OFFICER AND OFFICER-IN-CHARGE OF
CITIZEN'S RECORDS,
UNION DEFENCE FORCES,
DEFENCE HEADQUARTERS,
PRETORIA.
3RD JANUARY, 1956.

PEACE TRAINING IN THE ACTIVE CITIZEN FORCE.

1. Please note that you, as a registered citizen, may be compelled to undergo peace training. A percentage only of the citizens who register themselves annually, can be posted for military training and to ensure fairness it is necessary to resort to a system of balloting.

2. You are informed that you are subject to balloting during 1956, and that, should your name be drawn and provided you are pronounced medically fit for training, you will be allotted to a unit with effect from January, 1957, in order to undergo your **FIRST YEAR'S training during 1957**.

3. The prescribed training at present consists of:-
   1st YEAR...................: A camp of three months' duration.
   2nd, 3rd and 4th YEARS..: Camps of 21 days' duration each year. (Dates are fixed later.) Where distances and circumstances permit, citizens may also be required to attend a number of parades each year.

4. **SHOULD A CITIZEN CONSIDER THAT HIS CIRCUMSTANCES ARE SUCH THAT HE CANNOT ATTEND MILITARY TRAINING AS FROM JANUARY, 1957**, he may apply for either DEFERMENT OF or EXEMPTION FROM the ballot by completing the detachable affidavit form (he must do so personally) before a Commissioner of Oaths or a Justice of the Peace.

   NOTE.—Affidavits must reach this office **before** 16 April, 1956. Affidavits received after this date are not considered in any circumstances. (AFFIDAVITS SUBMITTED FOR THIS PURPOSE ARE EXEMPT FROM STAMP DUTY.)

5. All applications for deferment of or exemption from the ballot that are RECEIVED TIMEOUSLY, will be considered by an Exemption Board whose decision is final and against which there is NO appeal. The Board meets for only 5 or 6 days and is then disbanded, hence the warning that affidavits must reach this office before 16 April, 1956.

6. Should the Board grant deferment of the ballot to a citizen, such deferment will hold good for only one year. If the citizen desires a further period of deferment, he must again apply therefor in the following year.

7. Citizens who contend that they have religious or conscientious objections cannot, on that ground, be considered for exemption from ballot but may apply to serve in non-combatant units.

8. If you are anxious to undergo training and desire to ensure that you do not miss it by not being drawn by ballot you may apply during January, 1956, (the date must be observed), to be accepted for training as a volunteer. (Volunteers have a choice of unit.) Your name will, if you are accepted, not be included in the ballot and you will be posted for training as from January, 1957.

9. It is compulsory that every change in your address be
   notified immediately to this office, and you must ensure
   that each notification is acknowledged. Your address must
   be that to which communications can be sent to you direct.

10. No citizen is exempt from his obligations, unless he is
    notified to that effect in writing.

J.S.J. VAN DER MERWE, Colonel,
Registering Officer and Officer-in-Charge of Citizens' Records

To request deferment, ballottees were required to supply the Defence Force with documentation verifying their enrolment for tertiary education. If granted, the Defence Headquarters in Pretoria would reply in writing, as follows.

                                        Defence Headquarters,
                                        PRETORIA.

Please note that your name was not drawn in the recent
ballot of citizens and that you are no longer required to
inform this office of any change in your address.

Commandant.

Officer-in-Charge of Citizens' Records.

NATIONAL SERVICE

In 1968 a new call-up system was introduced, according to which National Service became compulsory for all white males. It was the SADF's plan to mobilise 100 000 men for Citizen Force and Commando units over the following ten years, a figure that was to increase dramatically as the Border War intensified.

Within two months of their sixteenth birthdays, all white male citizens were registered with the Defence Force. Conscripts were expected to perform military service for a period of nine consecutive months – a period that was then extended to twelve successive months – followed by five annual camps of nineteen days each. Upon completion they were transferred to the military reserves and remained liable for service until the age of fifty-five.

From 1974, National Servicemen were no longer permitted to indicate service preference: they were dispatched strictly according to the needs of the SADF. From this time conscripts had the option of extending their service for a further six or twelve months. Many conscripts elected to serve either of these extended periods – largely as a result of the financial incentives attached – and were subsequently exempted from further duties entirely. Then, in 1977, those finishing their one year of service were obliged to serve a further twelve months, and Citizen Force duties increased to ten years. Conscripts could be called up for an annual thirty-day camp, or once every two years for a maximum of ninety days per camp.

About 27 000 intakes per year were recorded during the mid-1970s. Until then, most conscripts complied with their call-ups, but the political climate was shifting again. Insurgency from Angola into South West Africa intensified and, consequently, in January 1979 a full two years' National Service and annual camps for ten successive years became mandatory.

In 1983, the total time commitment required for camps was increased to 120 days every two years, but some found themselves serving that time annually for many consecutive years.

National Servicemen were called up in one of two annual intakes, in January or July. They were sent around the country to various bases and installations, and for the subsequent ten to thirteen weeks they were initiated into the Defence Force by way of Basic Training, a physically and mentally demanding course designed to promote physical fitness and discipline.

During this time, National Servicemen were educated in the essentials of drilling, theory and weapons training. The last period, known as bush phase, usually lasted for ten to fourteen days, although this varied considerably. The troops lived and slept in tents and were trained in fieldcraft exercises and theory. During Basic Training no alcohol was permitted or provided, except during bush phase, when a 'two beer per day' maximum was granted. After returning to base, the troops' Basic Training was complete.

Basic Training was followed by specialist training, referred to as Secondary Training or second phase according to the Servicemen's particular units, for a further six- to nine-month period. Upon completion, the conscripts were fully prepared for military service in an operational area. (This was not always the case, however. Some Servicemen were sent to an operational area almost immediately after Basic Training concluded.)

While on camps during the ten-year period following their two years' National Service, those absent from their civilian occupations were legally protected against discrimination by their employers and could not be dismissed or demoted. However, the employer was not obliged to pay a salary during the conscript's absence so, depending on the duration of the camp, the Citizen Force camper effectively lost an income during that time. Civil servants were usually given permanent deferment from camp duties.

With the withdrawal of both the SADF and the Cuban forces from Angola in 1988, the Border War came to an end. As a result, the two-year National Service period was altered to one and a half years in 1990, and to one year in 1991. The last official compulsory intake took place in January 1993. National Service was abolished in the same year.

Over 600 000 conscripts responded to their call-ups between 1951 and 1993. It has been estimated that 300 000 served on the South West African border from 1966 to 1989, during which time the SADF recorded a total of 1 772 casualties, both operational (contacts, landmines, etc.) and non-operational (training accidents, illness, etc.). Of these, the army accounted for 1 526, the air force for 207 and the navy for 39. The number of fatalities that occurred in the operational area totalled 715. All three SADF branches experienced their highest casualty rates in 1982.

Between 1989 and 1993 there were 230 casualties. The army accounted for 215, the air force for thirteen and the navy for two.

APPENDIX II

Deferment

A white South African male who did not wish to comply with National Service had several alternatives: he could leave the country; he could join the South African Police for four years; he could join the Prison Services for five years; he could engage in tertiary study; or he could be detained by the Military Police to serve a minimum of three years in Detention Barracks. Many men were conscientious objectors and refused to respond to their call-ups. Failure to report for National Service constituted 'Absent Without Leave' (AWOL), and the Military Police would seek out all offenders.

The prospects were therefore grim for those who would not carry out their military service on the basis of political, ethical or religious beliefs. In contrast, there were those who embraced the opportunity to serve their country, viewing National Service as an act of patriotism. Between the two extremes lay the majority, who resignedly accepted the consequences of a system that was, simply, the law. Indeed, the anti-communist rhetoric employed by the National Party's government during the Cold War silenced most doubts about the integrity of National Service.

POLICE DEFERMENT

A matriculant had the option of performing his military service in the police force. His intentions had to be made known to both the SADF and the police well in advance. If approved, he mustered in at the Police College in Pretoria, where Basic Training commenced for three months. The training was much the same as its Defence Force counterpart. Counterinsurgency training, which usually took place at Maleoskop Counterinsurgency Training Centre near Groblersdal in Mpumalanga, followed for a further six weeks. He could then be called up for Border duties or sent to any police station in the country.

After four years in the police force his National Service was deemed complete. Those who trained with the police very often remained permanently with the force; those who chose to leave were placed on a reserve list and were expected to carry out monthly camps once a year for eight years.

PRISON SERVICES DEFERMENT

A matriculant could join the Prison Services for five years, whereupon his National Service would be considered fulfilled. If he elected to leave the Prison Services after completion of that period, he was expected to attend one month-long camp per year for eight years. If he chose to stay on, the following thirteen years' service counted as a substitute for further military service and camps.

TERTIARY EDUCATION DEFERMENT

A matriculant could defer his call-up if he chose to study directly after school. The SADF made allowance for tertiary education at a college or university for the requisite length of time. Proof of enrolment was required by the SADF on a yearly basis; failure to provide such documentation would obligate the student to proceed with call-up instructions. On completion of tertiary education, conscription commenced either in January or July, depending on the specific call-up instructions. The number of tertiary education deferments increased in the eighties, and graduates often became officers. Trainee teachers in particular were encouraged by the SADF to graduate and then attend the School of Infantry.

DUAL CITIZENSHIP

Those with dual citizenship were free to leave South Africa to carry out military service in their respective countries. Upon returning, proof was required of completed service, which absolved them from responsibility to the SADF.

CONSCIENTIOUS OBJECTION

Conscientious objection was first raised in the mid-1970s by the South African Council of Churches, which sent a petition to the chaplain general of the SADF. It wanted the SADF to acknowledge the right of Christians to choose whether or not they participated in the escalating Border War. The movement failed to receive widespread support at the time.

In 1983, the End Conscription Campaign (ECC) was founded in protest against compulsory military service. The organisation supported those who refused their call-ups on the basis of religious, political or personal convictions, and provided information and education to the public on conscription as well as on possible alternatives to military service. The ECC attained momentum only towards the latter half of the 1980s, but was banned by the South African government in August 1988 under emergency regulations. Its popularity and support, however, continued to increase with the political uncertainty of the late eighties and early nineties.

APPENDIX III

The Angolan/South African Border War

The Angolan/South African Border War, commonly referred to as the 'Border War' or, more recently, the 'Border Campaign', took place from 1966 to 1989 in South West Africa (now Namibia) and Angola. South Africa and its allied forces fought in opposition to the Angolan government, the South West Africa People's Organisation (SWAPO) and their allies. In addition to the SADF, the following groups were involved in the conflict:

ANC: African National Congress. Formed in 1912 to defend the rights of the black South African population. Banned in 1960 by the National Party. Found sanctuary in Mozambique and Angola.

MK: Umkhonto we Sizwe (Spear of the Nation). The ANC's military unit, formed in 1961. Military opponent of the SADF.

MPLA: Movimento Popular de Libertação de Angola (People's Movement for the Liberation of Angola). Ruling political party in Angola since the country's independence in November 1975; recognised by the Organisation of African Unity (OAU) as the legitimate government of Angola in February 1976. Forced into exile in the 1960s. Re-emerged in Angola after Portugal's withdrawal. Armed by the Soviet Union and its allies: received Cuban-piloted MiG-19s and MiG-21s, tanks, armoured personnel carriers, rocket launchers, heavy artillery and anti-aircraft missiles. Strongly Cuban-backed, Marxist organisation. Military opponent of the SADF.

FAPLA: Forças Armadas Populares de Libertação de Angola (People's Armed Forces for the Liberation of Angola). The MPLA's armed wing from August

1974. Became Angola's official military unit when the MPLA took control of the government. Sent troops to the Soviet Union for training. Cuban military advisors assisted from 1975. Military opponent of the SADF.

SWAPO: South West Africa People's Organisation. Formed in Cape Town in 1958 and adopted the name in 1960. Sam Nujoma became president of SWAPO in 1959. Angola became safe haven for SWAPO after fall of Portuguese rule in 1975. Military opponent of the SADF.

PLAN: People's Liberation Army of Namibia. SWAPO's military unit from 1963. Trained by Cuban, East German and Russian military instructors. Military opponent of the SADF.

FNLA: Frente Nacional de Libertação de Angola (National Front for the Liberation of Angola). Nationalist militant group formed in 1962. Resisted Portuguese rule. Fought against and defeated by Cuban-assisted MPLA after Portugal's withdrawal from Angola. Most members became part of Bravo Group (initiated by South Africa and under the leadership of Commandant Jan Breytenbach), which later became 32 Battalion. Military ally of the SADF.

UNITA: União Nacional para a Independência Total de Angola (National Union for the Total Independence of Angola). Socialist organisation led by Jonas Savimbi. Formed in 1966. Rebelled against Portuguese rule. Assisted by and military ally of South Africa.

FALA: Forcas Armadas de Libertacão de Angola (Armed Forces of the Liberation of Angola). UNITA's military unit and ally of the SADF.

In the early seventies, skirmishes between SWAPO and the South African Police, which was empowered by the Suppression of Communism Act and the Terrorism Act to enforce control in South West Africa, were low-intensity but steadily increasing in scale and frequency.

From 1973, a gradual, somewhat clandestine South African military presence began to expand along the border, a 460-km stretch running from the Cunene River in the west to the Kavango River in the east. From April 1974 the SADF took over the role of defending the border and maintaining internal stability in South West Africa.

In 1974 a military coup in Portugal led to the country's withdrawal from all of its African colonies, including Angola, which was officially granted independence in November 1975. Attemps to get the three main political factions – the FNLA, the MPLA and UNITA – to form a coalition that would serve as a transitional government were ineffective. The three rival groups instead engaged in a bloody struggle for individual leadership of the country and a civil war broke out in Angola – a war that would last for 30 years.

The MPLA established a government in Luanda and received aid from the Soviet Union, which supplied weapons and funded Cuba to send in thousands of troops. In the meantime, the FNLA and UNITA had formed an alliance and were armed with the aid of some African and Western countries, as well as China, a traditional foe of Russia. The United States's Central Intelligence Agency also covertly provided aid in order to advance the FNLA's standing with foreign mercenaries. At the same time, SWAPO was given a secure haven inside Angola, an ideal country from which to organise the struggle for the independence of South West Africa due to its geographical location.

South Africa had been marginally involved in the Angolan situation since SWAPO had begun its incursions into South West Africa from the neighbouring Angola in the mid-sixties. With the struggle for political dominance consuming all of Angola, the SADF initiated a campaign in September 1975 that would effectively engage South Africa in a full-scale war against highly trained Cuban forces armed with some of the most sophisticated Russian weaponry available.

South African Prime Minister John Vorster gave the order for approximately 2 000 SADF troops to cross the border into Angola to assist the FNLA and UNITA. This operation became known as Operation Savannah. The South African Minister of Defence, PW Botha, cited security against an ever-increasing 'refugee problem' as the reason for the invasion. Western powers, opposed to the action, placed an arms embargo on South Africa.

By February 1976, over 4 000 SADF troops were based fifty kilometres inside of Angola, having successfully penetrated FAPLA-occupied regions and faced the full array of firepower available to the Russian-backed FAPLA. Operation Savannah was a partial success: the South African-led forces captured two-thirds of Angola, yet were recalled before any final intentions could be carried out. Foreign pressure on the South African government forced their withdrawal in early 1976, by which time 15 000 Cuban troops had arrived in Angola.

With the retraction of South African troops, the MPLA and its Cuban allies were free to expand. Despite the fierce efforts by the FNLA and UNITA to establish political supremacy, the MPLA was recognised by the OAU as the legitimate government of Angola in February 1976.

In 1977, PLAN constructed base camps in UNITA-controlled areas of southern Angola, and the Border War intensified. South Africa moved in more men, machines and weaponry to defend itself against the expected flood of armed insurgents, and an operational area that ran the entire length of South West Africa's northern border was zoned.

By 1981, a new security-force structure had been put in place, which included three operational sectors. These were Sector 1Ø (Kaokoland and Ovamboland; a length of 700 kilometres, Headquarters Oshakati), Sector 2Ø (Kavango and West Caprivi; a length of 250 kilometres, Headquarters Rundu) and Sector 7Ø (East Caprivi to the Zambesi River and covering the Zambian border; a length of 150 kilometres, Headquarters Katima Mulilo). Each sector controlled SADF and South West Africa Territorial Force (SWATF) battalions.

The operational area was now a line of military camps, watchtowers and border posts whose primary objective was to guard the border and react to all insurgent actions. The SAAF provided air support whenever needed, and the Border became a restricted area heavily monitored by the SADF.

The Border War continued until 1988, when representatives from Angola, Cuba and South Africa met to negotiate agreements that would bring peace to the region and initiate the implementation of United Nations Security Council Resolution 435. The complete withdrawal of all South African troops from Angola and South West Africa was agreed upon, as were the start of Cuban troop withdrawal and eventual independence for South West Africa.

On 1 September 1988 the last thousand troops withdrew from Angola in compliance with the tripartite agreement. Cuba also complied and moved its troops north to begin sending them home. In April the following year, Resolution 435 was implemented, in accordance with which SADF personnel began to leave South West Africa under the watchful eye of UNTAG peace-keeping forces.

Despite the transitional agreements and the conclusion of hostilities, on 1 April 1989 SWAPO made a final advance towards the South West African border. Having obtained permission from the United Nations, the SADF took action and, in the nine-day war that followed, killed over 300 of the approximately 1 600 SWAPO insurgents who had crossed the border into South West Africa. The SADF lost 26 men, emerging as the clear victors of this engagement, the last of the Border Campaign.

By November 1989 all remaining SADF personnel had completely withdrawn from South West Africa. The territory later gained independence on 21 March 1990 and was renamed Namibia, with SWAPO as its recognised government.

APPENDIX IV

Township Patrols and the State of Emergency

TOWNSHIP PATROLS

Towards the end of 1984, civil unrest spread across South Africa. The ANC rallied its supporters to render apartheid unworkable and South Africa ungovernable. This wave of unrest caught the National Party government off guard, which encouraged efforts to strengthen resistance. Township residents rebelled by destroying any government-connected institutions, structures and services, including schools, municipal offices, libraries, communication and electricity service depots, post offices, police stations, transport services and houses owned by municipal employees. Black government representatives and policemen, whether on or off duty, were targeted in particular: they were seen as traitors to their people and to 'the struggle' and, as a result, their houses were attacked and family members murdered. Between 1985 and 1993 almost 1 000 SAP personnel were killed during service, with almost the same number murdered while off duty.

To combat the increasing township violence and civil unrest, a state of emergency was declared in 1985 (see below). The police needed assistance, so the SADF was ordered into the townships, their primary function to quell the violence that was threatening to evolve into civil war. In 1986 the ANC, in alliance with the United Democratic Front (UDF), went to war against the Zulu-nationalist Inkatha Freedom Party (IFP). While the UDF challenged the government it was also ideologically opposed to black conservative movements, the most influential of which was the IFP. This led to widespread clashes between the ANC, which was strongly associated with the UDF, and the IFP – a rivalry that was covertly fuelled by the government.

By this stage, over 3 000 citizens had been killed or murdered, many by means of the infamous 'necklace'. The police were vastly outnumbered and called for further back-up from the SADF, which was then deployed in far greater numbers. In 1986 a black Special Constables unit was formed, whose main objective was to patrol the townships, frequently accompanied by a squad of SADF troops.

By the late 1980s, the belief among most of the ANC leadership, Umkhonto we Sizwe (MK) and the South African Communist Party (SACP) was that government control should be attained using revolutionary military methods. Yet, without the knowledge of such groups, negotiations between top ANC and NP leaders were under way.

In 1990, parts of the state of emergency were lifted by President FW de Klerk, who also unbanned the ANC, the SACP and other organisations that had once been illegal. Yet township violence continued. The ANC called for an end to armed action, a bitter blow for MK who, like many others, were left feeling angry and betrayed. They believed that the ceasefire had been instituted too early and were convinced that apartheid would have fallen by military means.

From February 1990, with the release of Nelson Mandela from Victor Verster Prison and the imminent democratic election, the political situation in the country gradually stabilised. SADF troops patrolled the townships until conscription fell away and the 'new' South Africa emerged.

STATE OF EMERGENCY
The following extract was published in August 1985 in *Paratus*, the former South African Defence Force magazine.

PARATUS

Uit die SAW vir Suid-Afrika sedert 1949.
AUGUSTUS 1985.

State of Emergency

For the benefit of our readers, we publish the text of the announcement by the State President, Mr PW Botha, on 20 July 1985, of the proclamation of a State of Emergency in various magisterial districts in the Republic of South Africa.

Every responsible South African has, with growing concern, taken note of conditions of violence and lawlessness which, in recent times, have increased and have become more severe and more cruel in certain parts of the country, especially in Black townships.

These acts of violence and thuggery are mainly directed at the property and person of law-abiding Black people, and take the form of incitement, intimidation, arson, inhuman forms of assault and even murder.

This state of affairs can no longer be tolerated.

Thus far, the Government has shown the utmost patience. However, I cannot ignore the insistence of all responsible South Africans, especially of the majority of the Black communities, who ask that conditions are normalised and that they are granted the full protection of the law to continue their normal way of life.

It is the duty of the Government to ensure that a normal community life is re-established and that community services are efficiently rendered. Children must be able to receive tuition. Bread-winners must be able to fulfil their daily task. The life and property of all people must be protected, and law and order must be maintained.

In view of the prevailing conditions it is essential that the situation be normalised in such a way that the climate for continued dialogue in the interest of all people in the constitutional, economic and social fields is ensured.

Against this background, the government has, in terms of the Public Security Act, Act 3 of 1953, decided to proclaim a state of emergency in the following Magisterial Districts:

Port Elizabeth, Albany, Uitenhage, Cradock, Kirkwood, Somerset-East, Adelaide, Fort Beaufort, Bedford, Alexandria, Hankey, Humansdorp,

Bathurst, Steytlerville, Jansenville, Graaff-Reinet, Pearston, Benoni, Delmas, Kempton Park, Brakpan, Boksburg, Alberton, Springs, Nigel, Heidelberg, Balfour, Germiston, Randburg, Johannesburg, Roodepoort, Randfontein, Weston-aria, Vanderbijlpark, Sasolburg and Vereeniging.

Article 2(1)

The State President may declare the existence of a state of emergency in any area. (1) If in the opinion of the State President it at any time appears that–

(a) any action or threatened action by any persons or body of persons in the Republic or any area within the Republic is of such a nature and of such an extent that the safety of the public, or the maintenance of public order is seriously threatened thereby; or

(b) circumstances have arisen in the Republic or any area within the Republic which seriously threaten the safety of the public, or the maintenance of public order; and

(c) the ordinary law of the land is inadequate to enable the Government to ensure the safety of the public, or to maintain public order, he may, by proclamation in the Gazette, declare that as from a date mentioned in the proclamation, which date may be a date not more than four days earlier than the date of the proclamation, a state of emergency exists within the Republic or within such area, as the case may be.

The proclamation authorising this measure was signed by me this morning.

I wish to give assurance that law-abiding people have nothing to fear. At the same time I wish to issue a warning that strict action will be taken against those persons and institutions that cause or propagate disruption.

I appeal to everybody for their co-operation so that conditions can return to normal. I wish to give the assurance that the state of emergency in an area will be terminated as soon as this is justified by local conditions.

In closing, I just want to say that South Africa has the ability to rise above pettiness and violence. I call upon all well-meaning and reasonable South Africans to take hands in these times and to stand together to restore order and peace, in order that we can work in the interest of peace and prosperity for all in the country.

APPENDIX V
National Service Medals

PRO PATRIA MEDAL

The Pro Patria Medal was instituted in November 1974 to reward service in the prevention or suppression of terrorism by all ranks of the SADF and armed forces affiliated with the SADF. Recipients of the award were required to have been involved in combat, or in a skirmish or combat situation; participated in a specific operation acknowledged by the Ministry of Defence; or served in a declared operational area for a continuous fifty-five-day period or for a cumulative period of at least ninety days.

The octagon-shaped medal is bronze with a gilt finish. On its front is a stylised, golden aloe on a dark-blue roundel, while on the reverse side the recipient number is inscribed. Original Pro Patria medals are two-piece constructions with the disc attached to the suspender by means of a small ring. The roundel is dark-blue enamel. Secondary versions are cast as a single piece, with some roundels displaying a blue resin surface that is lighter in colour.

The ribbon represents the previous South African flag's colours of orange, white and blue.

A clasp inscribed 'Cunene' was issued for Operation Savannah, which took place from 1975 to 1976 (See Appendix III).

SOUTHERN AFRICA MEDAL

Instituted in 1989, the Southern Africa Medal was awarded for participation in specific cross-border activities in Angola, Mozambique, Zimbabwe, Zambia and Tanzania in the defence of the Republic of South Africa.

An octagonal nickel-silver medal, the front depicts an acacia tree with a prowling leopard below it. The leopard represents the stealth and speed of the SADF. The reverse side shows an open laurel wreath embracing the old South

African coat of arms, beneath which appear the words 'SUIDER-AFRIKA/SOUTHERN AFRICA'.

The ribbon's central thin white stripe is flanked on either side by black, yellow and red stripes.

Initially named the 'Trans-Jati Medal' ('across the cut line'), the medals were to be made from the metal of a smelted, captured Russian tank. Although this metal proved unsuitable, a small amount was added to the nickel-silver.

The Southern Africa Medal is known by some as the 'hot pursuit' medal.

GENERAL SERVICE MEDAL

The General Service Medal was instituted in 1989 and was awarded to all SADF personnel for service within the Republic of South Africa after January 1983.

The front of this circular nickel-silver medal contains a laurel wreath enclosing the SADF emblem – the crossed swords, wings and anchor of the army, air force and navy within an outline of the Castle of Good Hope. On the medal's reverse side appears the old South African coat of arms and the words 'GENERAL SERVICE/ALGEMENE DIENS'.

The ribbon has a dark-blue central stripe edged on both sides with orange, white and blue stripes.

UNITAS MEDAL

The Unitas Medal was awarded to all who were active as members of a serving force (SADF personnel, members of the homeland armed forces, the MK and APLA, military wing of the Pan African Congress (PAC)) during South Africa's first democratic elections, between 27 April and 10 May 1994.

Made of lacquered brass, the medal is circular and shows a seven-pointed star enclosing the Greek letter *alpha*. The reverse side depicts the old South African coat of arms with the date '1994' below it. On the outer circumference appears the word 'unity' in all of South Africa's eleven official languages.

The ribbon of the Unitas Medal is light blue with a central green stripe flanked by white stripes.

In 1994 the armed wings of the ANC and the PAC (MK and APLA respectively) were integrated with the SADF. Eighteen new awards and medals were instituted in 1996 to honour the members of these former organisations for service prior to 27 April 1994.

APPENDIX VI
Basic Training Manual

The following are excerpts from the manual distributed to all troops during Basic Training. Although the various units had individualised training manuals, all handbooks displayed a similar political emphasis and technical focus. The manuals were produced in a mixture of Afrikaans and English.

THE ROLE OF A FREE PRESS IN A DEMOCRATIC COUNTRY
The free press is an instrument by which the people put across their ideas, satisfaction or dissatisfaction. A free press does not however mean that it can publish everything they want to. There may be restrictions when it comes to the security of the country being threatened, as well as when information is of a classified type.

WHAT IS A DEMOCRATIC SYSTEM
It is difficult to give a detailed definition of a democracy because it covers such a wide field of the general community life. Normally democracy is described as 'a government <u>from</u> the people, <u>for</u> the people, <u>by</u> the people'.

WHAT IS THE MEANING OF THE WORD:

'NATION'
'Nation' is a political concept and indicates a group of human beings to share the same political system that is, who live in and are subject of a single common state.

'POPULATION'
'Population' is a vague term indicating a number of human beings living in a certain area. The word say nothing about their language, culture or their political affiliations.

'POPULATION GROUP'

A 'Population Group' is a section of the population of a country which can be distinguished from other sections of the population by some or other characteristic. The distinction can be made for example for reasons of language, dialect, economic situation, colour and so on.

THE AIM OF THE SA DEFENCE FORCE

1. To defend the RSA and SWA.
2. To prevent or suppress terrorism.
3. To prevent or suppress internal disorder in the RSA and SWA.
4. To preserve life, health or property or the maintenance of essential services.
5. To execute such police duties as may be prescribed.

THE TASK/AIM OF THE SA ARMY

'The activity of the SA Army is aimed at maintaining and utilizing a balanced and prepared land force with which to discourage or repulse conventional, semi-conventional, or insurgency attacks against the RSA and SWA.'

KNOW YOUR ENEMY

WHO IS THE ENEMY

1. THE FOLLOWING COUNTRIES/ORGANISATIONS CAN BE REGARDED AS HOSTILE TOWARDS US EITHER BY DIRECT AGGRESSION OR BY HARBOURING HOSTILE FORCES:
    A. THE SOVIET UNION (MILITARY ADVISORS, PILOTS ETC AS WELL AS THE SUPPLY OF BILLIONS OF RANDS OF MILITARY EQUIPMENT).
    B. CUBA (FORCES IN ANGOLA AND MOZAMBIQUE).
    C. EAST GERMANY (MILITARY PERSONNEL IN ANGOLA).
    D. NORTH KOREA (MILITARY PERSONNEL IN ZIMBABWE).
    E. ALL WARSAW PACT COUNTRIES.
    F. ANGOLA (EXCLUDING UNITA).
    G. MOZAMBIQUE (HARBOURING ANC TERRORISTS).
    H. ZAMBIA (HARBOURING ANC TERRORISTS).
    I. ZIMBABWE (HARBOURING ANC TERRORISTS).
    J. ANC (AFRICAN NATIONAL CONGRESS).
    K. SWAPO (SOUTH WEST AFRICAN PEOPLES ORGANISATION).
    L. SACP (SOUTH AFRICAN COMMUNIST PARTY).
    M. PAC (PAN AFRICAN CONGRESS).
2. THE FORCES OF HOSTILE NEIGHBOURING COUNTRIES ARE ORGANISED AND TRAINED ACCORDING TO SOVIET/WARSAW PACT DOCTRINES AND PRINCIPLES.

THE ROLE OF SURROGATE FORCES IN HOSTILE COUNTRIES

THE QUESTION CAN BE ASKED WHY ARE THERE SURROGATE FORCES IN
HOSTILE NEIGHBOURING COUNTRIES?

THE ANSWER IS TWO FOLD.

FIRSTLY IT IS PART OF THE SOVIET UNION'S MASTER PLAN TO CONTROL
SOUTHERN AFRICA AND BY DOING SO CONTROLLING THE MINERAL RICHES OF
THE WORLD. SOUTH AFRICA HOLDS A VIRTUAL WORLD MONOPOLY OF MANGANESE
— CHROMIUM — VANADIUM, A POWERFUL COMBINATION OF MINERALS WITHOUT
WHICH STEEL MANUFACTURING COUNTRIES CANNOT GO WITHOUT.

SECONDLY. THE PRESENT GOVERNMENT'S OF THE HOSTILE NEIGHBOURING
COUNTRIES ARE UNABLE TO GOVERN THEIR COUNTRIES WITHOUT THE
MILITARY ASSISTANCE THEY RECEIVE FOR EXAMPLE: THE ANGOLAN MARXIST
GOVERNMENT (MPLA) WOULD LOSE ITS POWER TO THE UNITA MOVEMENT
IF THE 45 OOO CUBANS PRESENTLY THERE WERE TO LEAVE. THE SOVIETS
KNOW THIS AND TO ENSURE THAT THEIR PLAN TO CONTROL SOUTHERN
AFRICA WORKS THEY NEED THE CUBAN PRESENCE. MOZAMBIQUE HAS THE
SAME PROBLEM AS WELL AS ZIMBABWE. THESE SURROGATE FORCES ARE
A DESTABILISING FACTOR IN SOUTHERN AFRICA AND ARE A CONCERN
TO THE SAFETY OF SWA AND SOUTH AFRICA.

THE SURROGATE FORCES PRESENTLY INCLUDE THE FOLLOWING:

ANGOLA   :   +/-45000 CUBANS
                               +/-2500 EAST GERMANS
                               SEVERAL THOUSAND NORTH KOREANS

MOZAMBIQUE   :   10000 ZIMBABWEAN TROOPS
                               2000 CUBANS
                               1000 SOVIETS
                               500 EAST GERMANS

ZIMBABWE   :   NORTH KOREANS

WITH THE LARGE AMOUNT OF SURROGATE FORCES IN THESE COUNTRIES, THE
MOST COUNTRIES ARE FACED WITH ECONOMICAL RUIN. THE SOVIETS ARE
SUPPLYING BILLIONS OF RANDS WORTH OF MILITARY HARDWARE INTO THESE
COUNTRIES WHILE ECONOMICALLY NOTHING IS DONE.

The following are handwritten notes found in the manual from which the above excerpts were taken:

All military knowledge is classified.

Important not to disclose: training, morale, commanders, movements, personnel, military areas, number of intake.

Places enemy 'hangs out': pubs, bus stop, train station, movie theatre, dining car, hotels, hitch-hikers, telephone.

Key positions: plofstofbergplekke, ou depots, treine en stasies, lughawens, belangrike geboue, V.I.P., schools, training centres.

SOURCES

APPENDIX I

Heitman, Helmoed-Roëmer. *South African War Machine*. Johannesburg: Central News
    Agency, 1985
SA-Bushwar. 'The South African Bush War, 1966–1989'. www.geocities.com/sa_bushwar/
Steenkamp, Willem. *South Africa's Border War 1966–1989*. Gibraltar: Ashanti Publishing, 1989
Williams, David. *On the Border: The White South African Military Experience 1965–1990*.
    Cape Town: Tafelberg, 2008

APPENDIX III

Heitman, Helmoed-Roëmer. *South African War Machine*
Steenkamp, Willem. *South Africa's Border War 1966–1989*
Williams, David. *On the Border: The White South African Military Experience 1965–1990*

APPENDIX IV

King, A. Terence. *Gallantry Awards of the South African Police 1913–1994*. Rhino Research, 2000
PARATUS, Volume 36 (8), August 1985

APPENDIX V

Alexander, EGM, GKB Barron and AJ Bateman. *South African Orders, Decorations and Medals*.
    Cape Town: Human and Rousseau, 1986
Medal Yearbook 2002. Devon, United Kingdom: Token Publishing, 2002

Translation of
Afrikaans dialogue

p. 13   'As 'n vlieg in jou neus kruip en in jou longe kak, BEWEEG
         JY NOG STEEDS NIE!'
         'If a fly climbs into your nose and shits in your lungs, YOU
         STILL DON'T MOVE!'

p. 25   'Jammer, boetie. Byt vas of pis in jou broek.'
         'Sorry, bru. Endure or piss in your pants.'

pp. 26–7 'As julle rowe wil gaan, kan julle, maar julle sal vandag nog in
          die DB wees want van nou af noem ons dit AWOL! As enige
          van julle dwelms of alkohol het, verklaar dit nou terwyl jy die
          kans het, want die honde gaan julle uitruik! Niks sal met
          julle gebeur as julle dit nou verklaar en erken nie. Nou!'
          'If you recruits want to go, you can, but you'll end up in DB
          no later than today as from now on we call it AWOL! If any of
          you have drugs or alcohol, declare it now while you have the
          chance, because the dogs will sniff you out! Nothing will
          happen to you if you declare and admit it now. Now!'

p. 29   'Hey! Langmoer! Kom hier!… Hey! Soutpiel! Kom hier!'
         'Hey! Tall fuck! Come here!… Hey! Salty dick! Come here!'

p. 29   'Word wakker! Word wakker! Die dag word al hoe kakker!'
         'Wake up! Wake up! Today's shit won't stop!'

p. 32   'Kom, Willie, rus 'n bietjie, boet. Park off.'
              'Nee! Ons kan nie dit doen nie. Die korporaal sal ons
         vang. Ons sal in die moeilikheid beland. Ek kan nie.'

'Well, let's take turns. We'll keep a lookout for each other.'

'Nee, nee, ons moet staan.'

'Come, Willie, rest a mite, brother. Relax.'

'No! We can't do it. The corporal will catch us. We'll get into trouble. I can't.'

'Well, let's take turns. We'll keep a lookout for each other.'

'No, no, we have to stand.'

pp. 32–3   'Ja, boet, 'n pis sonder 'n poep is soos 'n plaas sonder 'n stoep!'

'Yes, bru, a piss without a fart is like a farm without a porch!'

p. 33   'Ek's nie jou meneer nie, roof, ek's jou korporaal! Het jy my?'

'Ja, meneer!'

'Wat? Is jy dom, roof?'

'Nosir! Yessir! Nee, meneer! Korporaal!'

'Ek is nie … jou … fokken … MENEER NIE! EK … IS … JOU … KORPORAAAAL! HOOR JY MY, TROEP?'

'Ja, Korporaal.'

'SÊ DIT WEER!'

'Ja, Korporaal!'

'SÊ! … DIT! … WEER!'

'JA, KORPORAAL!'

'SAL JY MY OOIT WEER MENEER NOEM, ROOF?'

'NEE, KORPORAAL! DANKIE, KORPORAAL!'

'I'm not your sir, *roof*, I'm your corporal! Have you got that?'

'Yes, sir!'

'What? Are you dumb, *roof*?'

'Nosir! Yessir! No, sir! Corporal!'

'I'm not … your … fucking SIR! I … AM … YOUR … COOOOORPORAL! DO YOU HEAR ME, TROEP?'

'Yes, Corporal.'

'SAY IT AGAIN!'

'Yes, Corporal!'

'SAY! … IT! … AGAIN!'

'YES, CORPORAL!'

'WILL YOU EVER CALL ME SIR AGAIN, *ROOF*?'
'NO, CORPORAL! THANK YOU, CORPORAL!'

p. 34   'Peloton … regs! Peloton … links!'
                'Platoon … right! Platoon … left!'

p. 35   'Moenie fokken huil nie! Jy's in die mag, jou bliksem!
                Moenie huil nie!'
                'Don't fucking cry! You're in the force, you bastard! Don't cry!'

p. 37   'Geen strawwe dril, LO, roetemarse, hardloop.'
                'No hard drilling, PT, route marches, running.'

p. 37   'Korporaal, rondfok asseblief.'
                'Corporal, fuck me around, please.'

p. 38   'Nee wat, vetseun Engelsman. Jy kan lekker hardloop …
                Lekker pret.'
                'No, fatboy Englishman. You can have a good run …
                Good fun.'

p. 40   'Kom! Kom! Kom! Roer jou!'
                'Come! Come! Come! Move!'

p. 42   'Troep, hoekom wil jy 'n Parabat wees?'
                'Troep, why do you want to become a Parabat?'

p. 42   'Drink jy?'
                'Nee, Sa'majoor!'
                'Twak, troep. Nou lieg jy vir ons! Natuurlik drink jy.'
                'Ja, Kaptein. I do have the occasional beer, Kaptein.'
                'En dwelms?'
             'Do you drink?'
                'No, Sergeant Major.'
                'Rubbish, troep. Now you're lying to us! Of course you
            drink.'

'Yes, Captain. I do have the occasional beer, Captain.'
'And drugs?'

p. 43   **'Ja, Kaptein.'**
     'Reg so, troep. Jy kan maar gaan.'
     'Dankie, Kommandant.'
'Yes, Captain.'
'All right, troep. You can go.'
'Thank you, Commandant.'

p. 43   **'Moenie jouself só wys nie, roof, jou bliksem!'**
'Don't make such a display of yourself, *roof,* you bastard!'

p. 44   **'Ja. Bakgat. Jy's oppie trok.'**
'Yes. Excellent. You're on the truck.'

p. 47   **'Jy's nou in die army! Die army's jou ma, en ek is jou pa, en ons is nie getroud nie, so weet jy wat maak ek jou? Ek maak jou 'n fokken hoerkind!'**
'You're in the army now! The army's your mother, and I'm your father, and we're not married, so you know what I'm making you? I'm making you a fucking whorechild!'

p. 48   **'Fok jou, roof.**
'Fuck you, *roof.*'

p. 50   **'Ek sal 'n draadkar van jou bril maak, rofie, as jy weer so skeef vir my kyk!'**
'I'll turn your spectacles into a wire car, *rofie*, if you look at me like that again!'

p. 51   **'Moenie vir my loer nie, jou fokken troep! Ek suig jou oog uit en spoeg hom uit sodat jy self kan sien hoe 'n groot poes jy is!**
'Don't peer at me like that, you fucking troep! I'll suck out your eye and spit it out so you can see for yourself what a big cunt you are!'

| p. 52 | 'Aah. Julle's bakgat. Julle kom reg.' |
| | 'Aah. You guys are doing well. You're getting there.' |

p. 53	'Draai hom! Draai hom!… Liter water! Liter water! Nou!…
	As ek die fluitjie blaas is jy af! As ek hom weer blaas is jy op!'
	'Turn him! Turn him!… Litre water! Litre water! Now!…
	When I blow the whistle, you go down! When I blow it again,
	you get up!'

| p. 54 | 'Haai! Moenie fokken hardloop nie, jou fokken vuil hondekak!' |
| | 'Hey! Don't fucking run, you fucking dirty piece of dogshit!' |

| p. 55 | 'Haal uit sigarette!… Monde toe!' |
| | 'Take out cigarettes!… Mouths closed!' |

p. 57	'Het jy al ooit bloed geskenk?'
	'Nee, ek het nie, but my girlfriend does it often.'
	'Moenie bekommerd wees nie. Dit sal all right wees …
	Hoe voel jy?… Is jy reg om te gaan?'
	'Have you ever donated blood?'
	'No, I haven't, but my girlfriend does it often.'
	'Don't worry. Everything will be all right … How do you
	feel?… Are you ready to go?'

| p. 58 | 'Hierdie fokken soutie wat hom so slim hou.' |
| | 'This fucking Englishman who thinks he's so clever.' |

| p. 58 | 'Ek sal jou piel uit jou pens ruk!' |
| | 'I'll pull your prick out your stomach!' |

p. 58	'Sien jy daardie boom?'
	'Ja, Korporaal!'
	'You see that tree?'
	'Yes, Corporal!'

| p. 60 | 'WIE'T MY GEVLOEK?' |
| | 'WHO SWORE AT ME?' |

| p. 64 | 'Is iemand hier?' |
| | 'Is there anybody here?' |

| p. 64 | 'Maak oop jou trommel … Lêhouding af!… Staan op! Doen dit weer!' |
| | 'Open your trommel … Lie down!… Get up! Do it again!' |

| p. 65 | 'Jy sien. Jy kan hom maak. En omdat jy dit aan my bewys het, kan jy dit weer doen.' |
| | 'You see. You can make it. And because you proved that to me, you can do it again.' |

| p. 65 | 'Roof, *nou* moet jy hierdie ding was.' |
| | '*Roof, now* you have to wash this thing.' |

| p. 69 | 'Die army's nie 'n plek vir moffies nie.' |
| | 'The army's no place for queers.' |

| p. 70 | 'Julle's almal hondekak!' |
| | 'You're all as bad as dogshit!' |

p. 70	'Alles lekker skoon, luigatte!'
	'Ja, Korporaal!'
	'Everything nice and clean, lazy arses!'
	'Yes, Corporal!'

| p. 72 | 'Kry 'n klip. Skeer!' |
| | 'Get a stone. Shave!' |

| p. 74 | 'Vat hom net, troep. Hulle's almal diesel'de, jong!' |
| | 'Just take it, troep. They're all the same, man!' |

| p. 78 | 'Klim in. Agtersitplek … Jy sal uitvind.' |
| | 'Get in. Back seat … You'll find out.' |

p. 84   'Sak!... Gee my nog vyftig!... Nog vyftig!'
'Down!... Give me another fifty!... Another fifty!'

p. 92   'Goed so. Nou praat ons. Nou verstaan ons mekaar.'
'Good. Now we're talking. Now we understand each other.'

p. 92   'Ja, oukei, haal hom uit. Maar dan moet jy hom nou klaar
rook. Onder 'n minuut.'
    'Dankie Sersant.'
'Yes, okay, take it out. But now you have to finish smoking it.
In less than a minute.'
    'Thank you, Sergeant.'

pp. 93   'Wat sien jy daar?'
    'Sersant, ek sien God, Sersant.'
    'Ja, jy het hom, reg oppie kop.'
'What do you see there?'
    'Sergeant, I see God, Sergeant.'
    'Yes, you've got it, spot on.'

p. 93–4 'Is jou sak oppie trok?'
    'Nee, Korporaal!'
    'Gee my jou pikstel ... Hulle's vuil! Hoekom is jou fokken
pikstel vuil, jou vuilgat?'
    'Korporaal, hulle is nie vuil nie, Korporaal! Ek wou net
die stof vir Korporaal afvee, Korporaal.'
'Is your kit on the truck?'
    'No, Corporal!'
    'Give me your pikstel ... It's dirty! Why is your fucking
pikstel dirty, you dirty arse?'
    'Corporal, it's not dirty, Corporal! I just wanted to wipe off
the dust for you, Corporal.'

p. 94   'Nee, Sersant!'
    'En hoekom is jy G3?... Op jou rug, roof. NOU! Sandsak
bo jou kop!'

'No, Sergeant!'
　　'And why are you G3?... On your back, *roof.* NOW!
Sandbag above your head!'

p. 94　　**Sersant was *die man*, jong!**
　　　　Sergeant was *the man*, dude!

p. 94　　'**Is hy swaar? Gee hom nog 'n sak.**'
　　　　　'**Ek kan nie, Sersant.**'
　　　　　'**Kom, jou fokken soutie!**'
　　　　　'**Sersant. Asseblief ... fok.**'
　　　　　'**Wat? Vloek jy my? Moenie vir my FOKKEN VLOEK
NIE, JOU FOKKEN HONDEKAK!...**
　　　　　'**Kyk. Soutie huil. Hy fokken huil!**'
　　　　'Is it heavy? Give him another bag.'
　　　　　'I can't, Sergeant.'
　　　　　'Come, you fucking soutie!'
　　　　　'Sergeant. Please ... fuck.'
　　　　　'What? Are you swearing at me? Don't FUCKING
SWEAR AT ME, JOU FUCKING DOGSHIT!...
　　　　　'Look at that. Soutie's crying. He's fucking crying!'

p. 96　　'**Seker. Kom volgende week weer.**' ... '**Vertel my nog 'n storie.**'
　　　　'Sure. Come again next week.' ... 'Tell me another one like that.'

p. 97　　'**Dankie, Korporaal.**'
　　　　'Thank you, Corporal.'

p. 103　　'**Wie die fok ... Watter fokken bliksem het my fokken Landy
gesteel?**'
　　　　'Who the fuck ... What fucking bastard stole my fucking
Landy?'

p. 106　　'**O fok! 'n Majoor!**'
　　　　'Oh fuck! A major!'

p. 122   'Ek doen die majoor se kopieë.' … 'Jammer, Luitenant, die masjien is gebreek.'
'I'm doing the major's copies.' … 'Sorry, Lieutenant, the machine's broken.'

p. 128   'Hey! Word wakker, jong!'
'Hey! Wake up, man!'

p. 128   'Kaserne! AANDAG!'
'Bungalow! ATTENTION!"

p. 135   'Kyk mooi, boet.'
'Look carefully, bru.'

p. 136   'Twee, op … Twee, af.'
'Two, up … Two, down.'

p. 136   Lekker paraat, ek sê.
Really paraat, I tell you.

p. 144   'Ag, baas … Ek't gedink daai goed gaan net vir wit mense af.'
'Oh, boss … I thought those things went off only for white people.'

p. 147   'Ouens, julle het pos.'
'Guys, you've got mail.'

p. 147   'Skiet daar! Skiet daar!'
'Shoot there! Shoot there!

p. 148   'Jy't gemis!'
'You missed!'

p. 148   'Kyk daar!'
'Look there!'

p. 148	'Nope. Sorry, manne, bly hierso. As julle beweeg is julle in die kak!'
	'Nope. Sorry, men, stay here. If you move, you're in shit!'

p. 158	'Hou jou bek!'
	'Shut your mouth!'

p. 162	They'd take the bikes out at night for runs, ommie vyand te wys ons is daar!
	They'd take the bikes out at night for runs, to show the enemy we were there!

p. 162	''n Hoender is fokkol!'
	'Engelsman! ENGELSMAN! Wil jy my opfok?'
	'A chicken is fuckall!'
	'Englishman! ENGLISHMAN! Do you want to fuck me up?'

p. 163	'Ons sal 'n plan maak.'
	'We'll make a plan.'

p. 164	'Julle moet wag staan vanaand!'
	'Ja, Luit'nant, *jy* gaan wag staan vanaand.'
	'You must stand guard tonight!'
	'Yes, Lieutenant, *you're* going to stand guard tonight.'

p. 165	'Swart kaffer.'
	'Black kaffir.'

p. 172	'Liewe dapper soldaat …'
	'Dear brave soldier …'

p. 199	'stand-twee … stand-drie'
	'status two … status three'

p. 204	'Waar is jy?'
	'Hierso!'

'Where are you?'
   'Here!'

p. 206   **'Fok! Hier's 'n groot fokop! Hier's groot kak hierso! Stuur versterkings in!'**
'Fuck! This is a big fuckup! There's major shit over here! Send reinforcements!'

p. 241–2   **'Nee wat, boet. Ons speel gholf, man!...**
      'Hey, kom saam.'
'No worries, bru. We're playing golf, man!...
      'Hey, come along.'

p. 242   **'Kontak! Kontak! Wag. Uit.'**
'Contact! Contact! Wait. Out.'

p. 244   **'Het jy gehoor wat vandag gebeur het?'**
      'Nee.'
      'Twee ouens het 'n koei genaai.'
      'WAT? GAAN KRY DIE DONNEEEERS!...
      'Sê vir my, hoe *is* dit om 'n koei te naai?'
      'Kaptein, 'n *vark* is beter.'
'Have you heard what happened today?'
      'No.'
      'Two guys fucked a cow.'
      'WHAT? GO GET THE BASTARDS!...
      'Tell me, what *is* it like fucking a cow?'
      'Captain, a *pig* is better.'

p. 244   **'STAAK VUUR! STAAK VUUR! JULLE SKIET FOKKEN DONNERSWIL OP MEKAAR! STO-O-O-P!'**
'CEASE FIRE! CEASE FIRE! YOU'RE FUCKING SHOOT-ING AT EACH OTHER! STO-O-OP!'

p. 252   **'Hoeveel kaffers het julle vandag gedonner?'**
'How many kaffirs did you beat up today?'

Glossary

1Ø: Sector one-zero

101: 101 Battalion. Based at Ondangwa and founded in 1974 as 1 Owambo Battalion

2IC: second in command

2Ø: Sector Two-Zero

20-mm cannon: mobile light anti-aircraft gun, see **Ystervark**

23-mm: SADF-captured Soviet twin 23-mm anti-aircraft gun

2,4: 'two comma four' (kilometres), a standard running length to measure fitness

25-pounder: World War II–vintage artillery field gun/howitzer (see **howitzer**)

.303: British-designed .303-calibre Lee Enfield bolt-action rifle

32: 32 Battalion. Pronounced 'three two'. Formed in 1975, it was originally named Bravo Company and was led by Colonel Jan Breytenbach from 1976 to 1977. It was incorporated into the SADF in March 1976 before disbanding in 1993

35-mm: stationary twin 35-mm automatic anti-aircraft gun

5.5: World War II–vintage 5.5-inch (140-mm shell) British-designed artillery medium field gun/ howitzer, Armscor-produced

61 Mech: mechanised infantry battalion

1 Mil: 1 Military Hospital, Pretoria

2 Mil: 2 Military Hospital, Cape Town

3 Mil: 3 Military Hospital, Bloemfontein

1 SAI: Bloemfontein, Orange Free State, founded 1951 at Oudtshoorn, 1973 transferred to Bloemfontein

2 SAI: Walvis Bay (former South West Africa), founded 1962

3 SAI: Potchefstroom (former Transvaal), founded 1962 at Johannesburg, 1968 transferred to Potchefstroom

4 SAI: Middelburg (former Transvaal), founded 1962

5 SAI: Ladysmith (former Natal), founded 1962

6 SAI: Grahamstown (former Cape Province), founded 1962

7 SAI: Phalaborwa (former Transvaal), founded 1973

8 SAI: Upington (former Cape Province), founded 1973

aandag: attention

aantree: fall in, get in formation

aanvulling: replenishment, restocking

ACF: Active Citizen Force, consisting of ballottees

ADK: Adminastratief Diens Korps (Administrative Services Corps)

afdak: shed

afkak: severe physical exercise or exertion; literally 'shit off'

aggro: aggressive

AK-47: Avtomat Kalashnikova Obrazets, Russian-designed 7.62-mm assault rifle, based on German-designed World War II Stg 44 – first assault rifle to fire shortened (7.62-mm) cartridge and capable of single shot or automatic fire (Stg 44: Sturmgewehr – assault rifle)

AKM: modified version of AK-47

alkie: alcoholic

Alou/Alouette: French-designed, single-engined light transport helicopter, received by the SAAF in 1969, see **gunship**

AP: armour-piercing

APLA: Azanian People's Liberation Army, military wing of Pan Africanist Congress, a black political organisation

Armscor: Armaments Corporation of South Africa Ltd, government-owned industry responsible for building and obtaining armaments, founded in 1976

ATC: air traffic controller

Atlas: Atlas Aircraft Corporation, founded in 1965. Worked in association with Armscor for SAAF requirements

avgas: high-octane aviation fuel

AWB: Afrikaner Weerstandsbeweging (Afrikaner Resistance Movement), extreme right-wing organisation founded in 1973

AWOL: absent without leave

Baja Bug: modified Volkswagen Beetle intended for off-road use

bak: trough of a truck, see **platbak**

bakkie: pick-up truck

balkie: small rectangular corps badge worn on a beret, issued after completion of Basic Training

ballas bak: being lazy; literally 'testicle baking'

balsak: tubular canvas or nylon army kitbag; literally 'ball bag'

bandiet: prisoner

bang: afraid

bankie: plastic bank bag filled with cannabis

Basics/Basic Training: the first three months of a conscript's military training

battalion: three to four companies, including headquarter company, see **brigade**

battery: artillery unit of guns, men and vehicles

battle jacket: lightweight nylon webbing used to carry ammunition and provisions

BCR: Bronze Cross of Rhodesia

Bedford: British-designed three-ton general purpose truck, usually troop or cargo carrier

befok: crazy, mad

belemmering van 'n operasie: obstruction of an operation

berede: horse-mounted infantry, 'mounties'

beskadiging van staatseiendom: damage to state property

beskerming: protection

bivouac, bivvy: groundsheet or temporary encampment without tents

Black Sash: South African anti-apartheid women's organisation, founded in 1955

bliksem: beat up, scoundrel

blind: unfair, unfortunate

blitsbreker: muzzle-flash suppressor

bloekombos: blue gum bush, also called *blougomboom* (blue gum tree)

Blue Peter: saltpetre (potassium nitrate), supposedly used to lace food and drink to keep troops temporarily non-erectile

boep: paunch

boere: farmers or police

boerie: traditional South African sausage, known as boerewors

boet: literally 'brother'; an affectionate term of address meaning 'brother' or 'buddy'

boetie: little brother

Bofors: Swedish designed 40-mm anti-aircraft gun

bogs: toilets

bokkie: girlfriend, boyfriend; literally 'small buck'

bokkop: Infantry beret badge or infantryman

boma: small open-aired area encircled by thorny bushes, or an outside thatched leisure area

boom: cannabis; literally 'tree'

Border, the: South West Africa's northern border with Angola and Zambia

bos/bosbefok/bossies: aggressive, angry, mentally deranged: bush mad

boshoed: bush hat

bos-op: bush 'oppie', see **oppie**

bos oupa: National Serviceman having completed two Border duties; literally 'bush grandfather'

braai: cook meat over a fire, barbecue

brass: officers

Bren: Czech-designed British-developed 7.62-mm NATO magazine-fed light machine gun, see **FN MAG**

brigade: three to four battalions

Browning .50: 50-inch (calibre) vehicle-mounted infantry-support and anti-aircraft heavy machine gun, see **MG-4**

bucks: money

Buffel: Armscor-produced mine-protected armoured personnel carrier (APC, 4×4), introduced in 1978; literally 'buffalo'

bundu-bash: driving through dense bush

Bungalow Bill: a designated representative who liaised with officers and NCOs on behalf of the National Servicemen in a bungalow as well as calling troops to attention

bust: caught out, to tell on a person

C-130: American-designed four-engined heavy transport aircraft known as a 'Flossie'

Cactus/Crotale: mobile low-level surface-to-air missile (SAM) operated by the SAAF for airfield defence, French-developed to South African requirements

casevac: casualty evacuation

Casspir: mine-protected counterinsurgency infantry combat vehicle (ICV, 4×4), acronym of CSIR and SAP. Armscor-developed, introduced in 1979, used mainly by Koevoet and 101 Battalion

checking: looking

Cheetah: South African–designed multi-role fighter jet

cherry: girlfriend, women

china: friend, buddy; affectionate or friendly term of address

chips, keep: keep a look out, watch out

chookie: jail

chorbs: pimples

chow: to eat; food

ciggie: cigarette

civvy: civilian

civvy street: civilian life

CO: commanding officer

COIN: counterinsurgency

comms: radio communications

company: three to four platoons, including headquarter element, see **battalion**

crunchie: derogatory term for an Afrikaner

CSIR: Council for Scientific and Industrial Research

CTH: Cape Town Highlanders, consisting of Citizen Force personnel

cuca: small makeshift commodities shop within the operational area

named after local Portuguese–
Angolan brewed beer

cut line: area cleared of bush in a
straight line demarcating the
Angolan/SWA border

daar: there

dagga: cannabis

daggadronk: stoned on cannabis;
literally 'cannabis drunk'

Dak, Dakota: American-designed
twin-engined transport aircraft

dassie: a small plump guinea-pig-like
animal officially called a
rock hyrax, also known as a
rock rabbit

DB: Detention Barracks

deurgangs kamp: transit camp

dik: bulky, stocky

dixie: two rectangular aluminium
containers fitting into one
another, used for cooking
and/or eating

doggies: guard-dog handlers

dominee: minister

donner: to hit powerfully; bastard,
swine

doodsakker: killing ground

doos: derogatory term for female
genitalia; dumb person;
literally 'box'

dop: booze, drink

dop-en-chop: booze-and-meat

doppie: empty bullet casing

dos: sleep

double-cheeser: two landmines, one
placed directly above another

dowwerd: dud, unexploded
ordnance, 'dummy'

drill: march formation practice

drol: turd

druk: press; pressure, stress

Dutchman: derogatory term for
an Afrikaner

ECC: End Conscription Campaign

EDs: extra duties

Eland: Armscor-produced armoured
car with a crew of three, also
known as a Noddy Car

engeltjie: little angel, sweetheart

Esbit: paraffin-saturated firelighter

Fanny Adams: nothing, fuck all

FAPLA: Forças Armadas Populares
de Libertação de Angola (People's
Armed Forces for the Liberation
of Angola)

floppy: derogatory term for a black
African; an insurgent's corpse

Flossie: see C-130, C-160

FNLA: Frente Nacional de
Libertação de Angola (National
Front for the Liberation of
Angola)

FN MAG: Belgian-designed
7.62-mm NATO belt-fed
General Purpose Machine Gun
(GPMG), see **Bren**

fok: fuck

fokkol: fuck all

fokken: fucking

foofie slide: tensioned wire slide with seat and/or handgrip

G1K1: medical term declaring a soldier fit for active military service (Gesondheid 1, Kondisie 1 ('Health 1, Condition 1'))

G3K3: medical term declaring a soldier fit for military service, yet excluding him from excessive exercise or drill

G3: German-designed Heckler and Koch 7.62-mm assault rifle manufactured under licence in Portugal

G5: discharge on medical grounds; British-designed Armscor-developed 155-mm gun/howitzer introduced in 1979

ganja: cannabis

gatvol: at the end of one's patience, fed up

gee gas: go for it, literally 'give it gas'

geelsug: jaundice, yellow fever

gelukkig: lucky

genie: engineer

gesuip: drunk

gippo guts: diarrhoea

gooi: throw

gooi duim: hitchhike

gramadoelas: middle of nowhere

grootsak: backpack

GSM: General Service Medal

gunship: Alouette III helicopter with floor-mounted 20-mm machine guns

gwaai: cigarette, inhale

gyppo: cheat, beat the system

gyppo-nate: cheat-seams

haak-en-steek: type of thorn bush; literally 'hook-and-prick'

hairyback: derogatory term for Afrikaner

hanteering: management

hardegat: hard-arse

HE: high explosive

HEAT: high-explosive anti-tank

helde: heroes

hondekak: dog shit

Honoris Crux: highest SADF decoration awarded for bravery

howitzer: a high-angle gun that fires shells at high elevations

HQ: headquarters

HSI: Head of Staff Intelligence, Hoof Staf Intelligensie

Impala: Italian-designed light jet ground-attack aircraft, received in 1966

Inkatha: Inkatha Freedom Party, Zulu political organisation

ja: yes

jaai: hey

jaag: chase

jati: area cleared of bush in straight

line running one kilometre south of, and parallel to, cut line; firing line

Jerries: Second World War slang for German soldiers

Jirra: from the Afrikaans *Here*, God, the Almighty

JL/JLs: junior leader/junior leaders; Junior Leadership Course

jol: have fun; a good time, a party

joller box: large portable radio

jong: friendly term for younger person

kaalgat: naked; literally 'bare-arsed'

kaffir: extremely insulting word for a black South African

kak: shit

kakhuis: long-drop; literally 'shit house'

kakhuisdiens: toilet duty; literally 'shit-house duty'

kaplyn: cut line; the area cleared of bush demarcating the Angolan/ SWA border

kaptein: captain

kas: cupboard

kasern: bungalow

kasern-korporaal: bungalow corporal

Katyusha: 122-mm mobile rocket launcher, see **Stalin Organ**

kays: kilometres

keuring: efficiency selection

kiff: nice

klaaring in: reporting for service

klaarstaan: stand down

klaed aan: charged for contravening the military's disciplinary code

klap: slap, hit

klicks: kilometres

Klim in. Agter sitplek: Get in. Back seat.

Klippies: Klipdrift, a cheap brand of South African brandy

klonk: use up

KM store toe: to the quartermaster stores

knol: insult; rude hand gesture with thumb between fore- and middle fingers

Koevoet: South African Police COIN unit, established in 1979. Units based in Oshakati (HQ), Opuwa and Rundu. Literally means 'crowbar', as in 'prying loose' of SWAPO insurgents from thick bush

kok: cook

kommandant: commandant, lieutenant colonel

konstabel: constable

kop: head

koppie: hill

korporaal: corporal

kotch: vomit

kousrek: elastic sock band

kraal: rural village with round huts made from branches and woven grass enclosed by either a log or a thorn-bush palisade

kragwaardigheid: staunch
  stubbornness
Kriek: modified off-road motorbike;
  literally 'cricket'
Kwêvoël: Samil 100 mine-protected
  general purpose cargo dropside
  truck, see **Samil**; literally
  'Go-away bird' (referring to the
  Grey Loerie)

laaitie: child, young person
lag: laugh
lam-siek-en-dooies: lame-sick-and-
  dead, derogatory term for
  G3K3 squad
lance jack: lance corporal, corporal
  with one stripe
langarm: traditional Afrikaans dance,
  see **sokkie-sokkie**
langmoer: tall fucker
larney: upper-class white male
lekker: nice, good
lieut/lieuty: lieutenant
LMG: light machine gun
location: small township
LSD: hallucinogenic drug (lysergic
  acid diethylamide)
LSD squad: lame-sick-and-dead
  squad, lam-siek-en-dooies squad
ligte vrugte: literally 'light fruits';
  derogatory term for
  G3K3 squad
luigat: lazy arse
luitenant: lieutenant
lus: inclined

MAG: 7.62-mm belt-fed automatic
  light machine-gun, see
  FN MAG
magsnommer: force number, the
  number allocated to all members
  of the SADF
majoor: major
makhulu: large
mal: mad
malpitte: hallucinogenic plant that
  induces temporary insanity;
  literally 'mad seeds'
manne: men; important men,
  tough guys
Marnet system: signal-hopping radio
  communications
matric: final year of high school
meneer: sir
mevrou: married woman, Mrs
MiG-23: Mikoyan-Gurevich
  Russian-designed fighter-bomber
  and interceptor jet aircraft
min dae: few days (left)
Mirage: French-designed Atlas
  Aircraft Corporation–enhanced
  fighter jet or fighter-bomber,
  received in 1963
MK: Umkhonto we Sizwe
  (Spear of the Nation)
moer: anger; beat up, hit
moerse: very; large
moffie: homosexual
mohangu: grain sorghum beer
MOTH: Memorable Order of the
  Tin Hats, South African war

veteran's association founded
in 1927

mozzie: mosquito

MP: Military Police

MPLA: Movimento Popular de
Libertação de Angola (People's
Movement for the Liberation
of Angola)

naai: fuck

nag: literally 'night'; death, lights out

Nasrec: National Recreation Centre

nate: seams

NATO: North Atlantic Treaty
Organisation

'n bietjie dof: a little stupid

NCO: non-commissioned officer,
from lance corporal to regimental
sergeant major

NGK: Dutch Reformed Church
(Nederduitse Gereformeerde
Kerk)

Noddy Car: see **Eland**

nodule: slang for brain

noointjie: girlfriend

nooit: never, no ways

number one (haircut): hair shaved to
short bristle

nutria: brown colour, esp. with
reference to uniforms, or 'browns'

OC: officer commanding

OHMS: On His Majesty's Service

oke: man, guy

Olifant: British-designed Armscor-
produced main battle tank with a
crew of four, introduced in 1981;
literally 'elephant'

one-liner: lance corporal

one-pip: first lieutenant

Oom Willie se Pad: Uncle Willie's
road

OP: observation post

opfok, oppie: fuck up, severe
physical exercise used as form
of punishment

ops: operations

ops medic: a medic trained to treat
combat injuries

opskepper: server, one who dishes up

opstaan: stand up

ordentlik: decent

Oryx: upgraded South African
version of the Puma helicopter

ou/ous: man/men

ouens: guys, men

ou man: National Servicemen in final
year of service; literally 'old men'

Ovambo: largest ethnic group
in SWA, constituting over
50 per cent of the population

pakhuis: warehouse

panga: machete

pap: deflated, tired

paraat: prepared, top form; slang for
someone who is eager

paraatheid: preparedness

Parabat: a Parachute Battalion
member; paratrooper

PB: plaaslike bevolking (local population)

PF: Permanent Force

PFP: Progressive Federal Party, a liberal political organisation

pikstel: fork, knife and spoon combination

plaas: farm

plaasjapie: country bumpkin

PLAN: People's Liberation Army of Namibia

plank: derogatory term for an Afrikaner

platbak: flat interior of a truck's trough

platoon: three to four sections, including small headquarter element, see **company**

pluk: adrenalin rush

poephol: idiot, arsehole

poes: derogatory term for female genitalia; used as an insulting name

poppie: girlfriend

Porra: Portuguese

POW: prisoner of war

PPSh: Russian-designed 7.62-mm Shpagin sub-machine gun, with drum magazine

ProNutro: Pro Patria Medal, so-called because many were 'dished out' like the cereal after which it is named

Puma: French-designed twin-engined standard transport helicopter, received by the SAAF in 1969

puttees: plastic ankle sheath, worn with cravat and stable belts

R1: 7.62-mm NATO assault rifle based on Belgian 1964 pattern FN-FAL (manufactured by Fabrique Nationale: Fusil Automatique Legere – Light Automatic Rifle), Armscor-produced

R4: 5.56-mm assault rifle based on Israeli Galil, replaced R1 from 1978 onwards, Armscor-produced and modified

R5: as above, with shortened barrel

rag: tease

Ratel: armoured standard infantry combat vehicle (ICV, 6×6) introduced in 1976 and Armscor-designed. Named after the African honey badger, which is known for its viciousness

Ratel 20: as above, with 1 × 20-mm semi-automatic cannon ICV, three crew plus nine troops

Ratel 60: with 1 × 60-mm breech-loading mortar ICV, introduced in 1981, three crew plus seven troops

Ratel 81: with 1 × 81-mm mortar ICV, introduced in 1981, crew of five (including mortarists)

Ratel 90: with 1 × 90-mm low-pressure gun fire-support vehicle (FSV), introduced in 1981, crew of three plus six troops

rat pack: ration pack

Recce: a member of the Reconnaissance Unit

Red Eye: mobile rocket launcher, see **Stalin Organ**

rockspider: derogatory term for Afrikaner

rofie: see **roof**

Romeo Mike: phonetic name for Reaksie Mag (Reaction Force) units consisting of four to five Casspir ICVs and 101 Battalion personnel

rondfok: literally 'fuck around'; to mess a troop around

rondom verdediging: perimeter defence

roof(s), rofie(s): new intake(s), new recruit(s)

rooikop: redhead

rooikrans: species of wood

rooinek: derogatory term for English-speaking South African; literally 'redneck'

rook: smoke

RP: Regimental Police

RPD: Russian-designed 7.62-mm light machine gun (Ruchnoi Pulemet Degtyarev)

RPG: Russian-designed recoilless shoulder-mounted rocket-propelled grenade launcher used as anti-tank weapon

RSA: Republic of South Africa

RSM: regimental sergeant major

RTU: return to unit

SAAF: South African Air Force

SACC: South African Cape Corps

SADF: South African Defence Force (pre-1994)

SADFI/SAWI: South African Defence Force Institute / Suid-Afrikaanse Weermaginstituut

Safair: civilian airline used by SADF for logistic trooping

SAI: South African Infantry (Battalion)

sak: lie flat, get ready for push-ups

sa'majoor: sergeant major

Samil: SAMIL (SA Military) Armscor-designed truck

Samil 50: general purpose truck, troop/cargo carrier (4×4)

Samil 100: see **Kwêvoël**

san: sanatorium

sandsak: sandbag

SAP: South African Police (pre-1994)

sarge: sergeant

SAWI: see **SADFI/SAWI**

scaled: stole

schnoz: nose

section: basic unit of ten to twelve troops, see **platoon**

sersant: sergeant

shebeen: illegal township pub without liquor licence

shona: large ground indentation that fills with water in the rainy season

siekeboeg: sickbay

siff: disgusting

Sit, lê, staan, run: Sit, lie down, stand, run

sjambokking: being beaten with a long leather or plastic whip with a lead-based tip

sjoe: phew

skaam: embarrassment, shame

skedonk: old car

skeef: give a bad look; skew or crooked

skelm: devious, no-good person

skep op: serve up

skiem/skiemed: think/thought

skietbalkie: marksmanship proficiency badge awarded in bronze, silver and gold class, worn above right breast pocket

skottelbraai: gas barbeque

skrik: scare

slangvel: Parabat jump smock; literally 'snakeskin'

slapgat: untidy; slack arse

smaak: enjoy

snotneus: 40-mm six-shot grenade launcher; literally 'snot nose'

sokkie-sokkie: a style of Afrikaans dancing or music, see **langarm**; a social dance or party

sommer: just; for no reason

Sosegon: painkiller, similar in effect to that of morphine, injected in single-dose vials

Southern Cross Fund/ Suiderkruisfonds: patriotic civilian women's organisation focused primarily on supporting National Servicemen

soutie/soutpiel: derogatory term for English-speaking South African, who has one foot in South Africa and the other in England with his penis dangling in the ocean; literally 'salty penis'

space-mannetjie: spaceman

SSB: Special Services Battalion

stadig: slow

staaldak: steel helmet, literally 'steel roof'

staalkas: steel cupboard

stable belt: cumber belt in Corps colours with buckle usually displaying unit badge

Staff: staff sergeant

Stalin Organ/Orrel: Russian-designed 122-mm mobile multiple rocket launcher

States, the: South Africa

steekbos: thorny bush

steeked: fanatical, obstinate, overzealous

stelling: system

stompie: cigarette butt

stooring: blockage, weapon-jam

stoppe: finger-sized packages of cannabis rolled in newspaper

stormbaan: obstacle course

streepie: NCO's rank chevron; literally 'little stripe'

strek: come to attention extending arms straight to one's side if standing, to the knees if sitting

stripped his moer: lost his temper

stukkie: girlfriend; literally 'little piece'

suip: booze, to drink

SWAPO: South West African People's Organisation

SWATF: South West African Territorial Force

T-34: World War II Russian battle tank

T-55: post-1954 standard Russian battle tank

TA: Technical Assistant

takkies: running shoes, sneakers

tandeborsel: toothbrush

Tassies: Tassenberg, a cheap brand of South African red wine

TB: temporary base

TDK: Tegniese Dienskorps, Technical Services Corps

tee en koek: tea and cake

terr: terrorist

theodolite: instrument with spirit-level, compass and small telescope to measure horizontal and vertical angles

three-oh-three: derogatory term for a captain; three pips on either epaulette with zero inside his head

tiffies: Technical Services Corps personnel

Tigercat: mobile surface-to-air missile system (SAM)

top brass: senior ranks

trapping: walking

tree aan: fall in, assemble

troep: troop

troepie-doepie: degrading term for troop

trommel: metal container, trunk

trots: proud

TSC: Technical Services Corps

tune: inform, tell

Tupperware flashes: flexible unit insignia fastened through epaulettes

two-liner: corporal

two-pip: second lieutenant

two-striper: corporal

UDF: Union (of South Africa) Defence Force; United Democratic Front (political organisation)

uitkak: reprimand; literally 'shit out'

uitklaar: finishing National Service or clearing out of a unit

uitpak: unpack

uitreik: hand out, issue

uittreeparade: falling-out parade

Unimog/Mog: Mercedes-Benz two-ton general purpose vehicle (4×4), later adapted to Buffel

Unisa: University of South Africa

UNITA: União Nacional para a Independência Total de Angola (National Union for the Total Independence of Angola)

UNTAG: United Nations Transition Assistance Group

Valkiri: Russian-designed mobile multiple rocket launcher (24×127-mm, MRL) based on Stalin Organ, Armscor-developed, introduced in 1980

varkpan: zinc eating tray; literally 'pig pan'

vas: secure, tight

vasbyt: persist; literally 'bite fast'

veld: field, grassland

veldkombuis: field kitchen

verandah: patio

verklaring: declaration

verkramp: conservative

vetkoek: type of deep-fried dough filled with mince; literally 'fat cake'

vetseun Engelsman: fatboy Englishman

vloek: curse, swear

Voëlvry: late eighties/early nineties Afrikaans anti-establishment movement; literally means 'free as a bird'

voertsek: go away, bugger off

Volk en Vaderland: 'People and Fatherland', a patriotic term that parallels the British 'King and Country'

vrot: drunk; rotten

VTH: Voortrekkerhoogte, major military base outside Pretoria

vuilgat: slovenly person; literally 'dirty arse'

waterkop: name for members of a Maintenance unit, who wore blue berets; literally 'water head'

webbing: canvas or nylon body kit

welsyn offisier: welfare officer

wikkel: sprint

windgat: loudmouth; literally 'wind hole'

woes: furious

Wolf: mine-protected infantry combat vehicle (ICV, 4×4), used mainly by Koevoet

wys: obstinate; smart-arse

Ystervark: self-propelled anti-aircraft vehicle usually armed with 20-mm cannon; literally 'porcupine'

zik: steal

zol: cannabis

Bibliography

Alexander, EGM, GKB Barron and AJ Bateman. *South African Orders, Decorations and Medals.* Cape Town: Human and Rousseau, 1986

Baker, Mark. *Nam: The Vietnam War in the Words of the Men and Women Who Fought There.* London: Abacus, 1982

Heitman, Helmoed-Roëmer. *South African Arms and Armour.* Cape Town: Struik Publishers, 1988

———. *South African War Machine.* Johannesburg: Central News Agency, 1985

King, A. Terence. *Gallantry Awards of the South African Police 1913–1994.* Rhino Research, 2000

Medal Yearbook 2002. Devon, United Kingdom: Token Publishing, 2002

Nortje, Piet. *32 Battalion: The Inside Story of South Africa's Elite Fighting Unit.* Cape Town: Zebra Press, 2003

PARATUS, Volume 36 (8), August 1985

SA-Bushwar. 'The South African Bush War, 1966–1989' www.geocities.com/sa_bushwar/

Smith, WHB. *Small Arms of the World.* Pennsylvania: Stackpole Books, 1960

Steenkamp, Willem. *South Africa's Border War 1966–1989.* Gibraltar: Ashanti Publishing, 1989

Thompson, JH. *An Unpopular War: From afkak to bosbefok.* Cape Town: Zebra Press, 2006

Williams, David. *On the Border: The White South African Military Experience 1965–1990.* Cape Town: Tafelberg, 2008

ALSO PUBLISHED BY ZEBRA PRESS

An Unpopular War, by JH Thompson

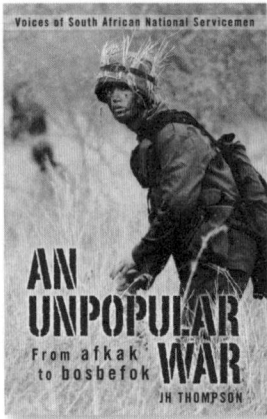

Voices of South African National Servicemen

AN UNPOPULAR WAR
From afkak to bosbefok
JH THOMPSON

In the 1970s, 1980s and early 1990s, hundreds of thousands of young men were called up for military service, most of them going through extreme physical training and many being sent to fight the war in northern Namibia and Angola. This book is a collection of reflections and memories of that time, collected by JH Thompson, who interviewed numerous former National Servicemen.

Over 50 000 copies sold in English and Afrikaans

Contributors include ordinary soldiers and Special Forces members, chefs, medics and helicopter pilots. They provide varying perspectives on klaaring in, training, inspection, gyppoing, Border patrols, covert operations and open combat, and readjusting to life in civvy street.

This book is a compelling read that captures the spirit and atmosphere, the daily routine, the boredom, fear, camaraderie and other intense experiences of an SADF soldier. For everyone who did military service, as well as their family and friends, this book is a must.

Also available in Afrikaans as *Dit was oorlog*

At Thy Call We Did Not Falter, by Clive Holt

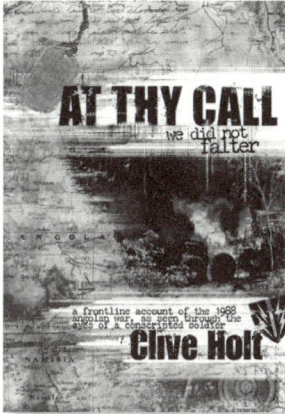

At Thy Call We Did Not Falter is a gripping frontline account of the Angolan war, as seen through the eyes of a 19-year-old conscript soldier. It tells the story of so many young white South Africans who, like him, were sent into battle against overwhelming forces straight after finishing school.

Clive Holt was at the Battle of Cuito Cuanavale, where the South African Defence Force supported the rebel movement Unita after a massive build-up of Cuban and Angolan troops. It was the bloodiest and most significant battle fought by South African troops since World War II.

With diary extracts, previously unpublished photographs and a riveting narrative, this book transports the reader into the firing line and the dark realms of war. *At Thy Call We Did Not Falter* is a classic account of war, as well as a window into the world of post-traumatic stress disorder. It is a chilling account of how a government took schoolboys and turned them into killing machines.